THE WIRED PROFESSOR

THE WIRED PROFESSOR

A GUIDE TO INCORPORATING THE WORLD WIDE WEB IN COLLEGE INSTRUCTION

ANNE B. KEATING WITH JOSEPH HARGITAI

NEW YORK UNIVERSITY PRESS
New York and London

NEW YORK UNIVERSITY PRESS
New York and London

Keating, Anne B.
    The wired professor : a guide to incorporating the World Wide Web
in college instruction / Anne B. Keating with Joseph Hargitai.
        p. cm.
    Includes bibliographical references and index.
    ISBN 0-8147-4724-8 (alk. paper). — ISBN 0-8147-4725-6 (pbk. : alk. paper)
    1. College teaching. 2. Computer-assisted instruction. 3. Web sites—Design.
4. World Wide Web (Information retrieval system)
I. Hargitai, Joseph, 1959–   . II. Title.
LB2331.K35 1999
378.1'7344678—dc21   98-40918
                                                      CIP

New York University Press books are printed on acid-free paper,
and their binding materials are chosen for strength and durability.

Manufactured in the United States of America

10 9 8 7 6 5 4 3 2

Presumably man's spirit should be elevated if he can better review his shady past and analyze more completely and objectively his present problems. He has built a civilization so complex that he needs to mechanize his record more fully if he is to push his experiment to its logical conclusion and not merely become bogged down part way there by overtaxing his limited memory. His excursion may be more enjoyable if he can reacquire the privilege of forgetting the manifold things he does not need to have immediately at hand, with some assurance that he can find them again if they prove important.

—VANNEVAR BUSH, "As We May Think" (1945)

Contents

THIS is a book about the World Wide Web and specifically about incorporating Web-based course materials into college curriculums and instruction. Written for professors with limited experience on the Internet, *The Wired Professor* is a collegial, hands-on guide to building and managing instruction-based Web pages and sites. This book also explores a variety of topics, from the history of networks, publishing and computers to such hotly debated subjects as the pedagogical challenges posed by computer-aided instruction and distance learning. As with the hands-on sections of this book, these discussions are geared to the non-computer-savvy reader and written with an eye to extracting the intellectual patterns and drawing comparisons to noncomputer media. These concepts are critical in order to comprehend fully the power and potential of the Internet: as a creative medium, unparalleled research resource, community-building medium and vehicle for the delivery of content-rich materials. This book provides a timely and solid foundation for using this technology thoughtfully and effectively. *The Wired Professor* has a companion Web site at *http://www.nyupress.nyu.edu/professor.html.* At this site are updates, additional information and dynamic examples of the techniques described in the hands-on chapters of this book.

The rationale for using the World Wide Web to deliver course material, as well as to promote classroom interaction, rests in the potential that this technology has for providing twenty-four-hour access to information from any computer connected to the Internet. The Internet is rapidly becoming a necessary and natural part of the way we access information. However, while students are increasingly Internet literate, many professors have found themselves lacking either the necessary skills or the intellectual framework for effectively working with and understanding this new tool and medium. This has been further compounded by a lack of time to learn new skills and the lack of critical resources such as computers and Internet connections.

By the time you read these words, the Web and related online technologies will have been further enriched by capabilities that we can only guess at now. This is the challenge of the Internet—the moment you take it on you become a participant in its development. Writing for the Web is not a static enterprise. As you incorporate the Web into your classroom teaching or departmental agendas, you will be contributing to a growing base of knowledge among educators about how to use this medium effectively. Although there is no one "correct" way to use the Web in teaching, we hope that we can provide a series of critical steppingstones and some practical advice on how to get on the Web quickly and how to design effective class Web pages.

This book is a hybrid: part hands-on guide, part history, part design manual and part discussion of the implications of using the Web in college instruction. In chapter 1, we provide an analytical but uncomplicated framework for thinking about networks, publishing and computers that will serve as a conceptual foundation for the later chapters on Web design. We also offer an informal history of computing that situates the Web in the history of academic uses of technology in research and teaching. We include this analysis and history because, all too often, the Web is treated as a brand-new technological innovation. However, although in many ways it is truly innovative, the Web—and more generally, networks and computers—emerged out of other great innovations of history.

Chapter 2 continues to trace this history with the development of ARPANET ("Advanced Research Projects Agency Network"), the precursor to the Internet and the Web. This chapter includes descriptions of the technologies and online innovations in communication technology that make up the Internet as a whole. Chapter 3 begins with a discussion of online research. This is followed by a discussion of how academic computing centers on college campuses adjusted their mission as a new community of academic computer users emerged from fields outside of computer science and the physical sciences. This narrative highlights the conceptual issues and challenges faced by college technical support staff and the faculty who pioneered the use of the Web as an instructional medium. The chapter concludes with a series of vignettes about faculty members' first experiences with integrating the Web into their classroom practice.

In chapter 4, the first of our hands-on chapters, we present the tools a college teacher will need to learn in order to construct a Web site. In this chapter, we cover design issues and the basics of Web page construction. Chapter 5 continues this hands-on approach by covering advanced Web design and looking at administrative issues. Chapter 6 examines the future of this technology and the pedagogical and design challenges of distance learning. People come to computers and the Internet by way of many different paths and life experiences, which in turn influence the way they approach the medium. We thought it might be useful to offer some of our own experiences here.

Anne B. Keating | My students are often surprised to learn that I have no computer degree and have in fact never taken a single class on computers. I was an English major in college and if I could have looked almost twenty years into the future and seen how much computers would become a part of my life as an adult, it would have been as strange to me as if someone had said there were little green men on Mars. Then, I had no interest in computers and in fact did not see one until my senior year, when I remember watching a friend of mine typing away at a small dark keyboard-and-box contraption that he had hooked into his black-and-white television set. All I could see on his television set were cryptic bands of computer code. I was singularly unimpressed.

In the mid-1980s, on a whim, I bought a broken Tandy 64k color computer in a swap shop for ten dollars and soldered a loose part back onto the board. I was not into computers but I did like tinkering with clocks and other small machines, so I thought it would be fun to have a look at the insides of a computer. While I do not recommend this kind of cavalier treatment of computers, fixing the Tandy was a critical first step for me to get over my fear of these cryptic machines. The fact that my repair worked inspired me to buy a few simple programs for the computer down at the local Radio Shack and some parts that I needed to connect it to my television. A friend who had the same computer supplied the support and taught me how to run the programs. I still keep the small switching device that hooked the computer and the television together as a memento next to my present computer.

I did not do much more with the Tandy than write papers, and frankly, I am not sure even now if it was capable of being more than a souped-up typewriter. (In any event, I certainly was not thinking of using a computer as more than a glorified typewriter.) In the late 1980s, while I was working on my Ph.D., I hit a critical watershed when using a computer became an essential part of how I did my work. Mary Corbin-Sies, a graduate professor of mine at the University of Maryland, had the good common sense to insist that knowledge of both computers and computer-aided research was critical for Ph.D. candidates. She instilled in us the need to be proficient and knowledgeable about computers and how they could be used in research in our field of American Studies. She told us we did not have the luxury of ignoring computers any longer, and she was right.

I began writing my dissertation on the IBM PC that replaced the Tandy, and in 1991 I began to explore the Internet. I was fortunate to have a close friend at the time who ran his own Bulletin Board Service (BBS) out of his spare bedroom. I spent much of the time when I was not writing watching Jamie working on his BBS. He set me up with my first Prodigy account and I started to get hooked, but I was still intimidated by the complexity and number of commands that one needed to know to get around on the Internet.

The next real watershed came the night that Jamie downloaded the first version of the Mosaic browser from the Internet. By this point I was more than familiar with an Internet that could only be navigated if one knew exactly how to invoke cryptic UNIX commands. However, there on his computer screen was the home page of the National Center for Supercomputing Applications (NCSA) at the University of Illinois at Urbana, the first Web page with colors and images and links (no more UNIX) that I had ever seen (and in fact that just about anyone had ever seen, as Mosaic was the first graphical Web browser.)

I received my Ph.D. just before Christmas in 1995. Friends warned me that I might go into a temporary slump for a month or so afterwards as I dealt with the sudden end of the dissertation project. They had visions of me spending hours watching old movies on television. I got hooked on the Web instead. This book, in fact, grew out of a partnership that began that January when I walked into the Innovation Center, a faculty computer lab at New York University, and sat down with Joseph Hargitai, a member of the center's technical support staff. Over the space of two hours, I watched him take my ideas for putting course information online and transform them into a Web page. I remember initially being completely mystified at the process. However, at the end of the session, I also remember asking Joseph if he thought I could ever write HTML (HyperText Markup Language—the principle programming language of the Web).

I walked out of the Innovation Center, the proud possessor of a Web page that was already "live" on the Internet. Joseph also provided me with the necessary accounts to access, update and add to the online material for my course. I remember being simultaneously impressed and overwhelmed. Would I ever be able to use the accounts Joseph had given me or would I need to go to the Innovation Center every time I wanted to add to my Web site? How was I going to deal with the fact that as a teacher I would no longer be a couple of steps ahead of my students, but learning right alongside them about this technology and no doubt making some very public errors along the way (nothing like having all your colleagues and your school, not to mention the world, as your potential audience).

For the last two years, I have continued to learn from Joseph. The Web pages I created for my students as an adjunct assistant professor in the Adult Degree Studies Division of the School of Continuing Education drew the attention of Cynthia L. Ward, director of the Liberal Arts Program, who believed in my work and encouraged me by giving me opportunities to share with my colleagues what I was learning. My workshops drew the attention of Gerald A. Heeger, dean of the School of Continuing Education, who shared with me his interest in the intelligent integration of technology into higher education and the implications of distance learning. He wholeheartedly encouraged my work and gave me the time necessary to explore and learn more about this technology. I received additional support from William F. Cipolla, who became the new associate dean of the Adult Degree Studies Division during this period. He encouraged me to build educationally oriented Web pages and to explore the pedagogical implications of using the Web to deliver course materials.

I believe that this medium, combined as it has been with a series of critical partnerships, demonstrates the best of what is possible with computers in any setting, but certainly in the academy. Computers are more than glorified typewriters or adding machines. In our time, they are creating physical connections to the familiar ideals of community, collegiality and the sharing of knowledge that constitute "the university" in the sense that includes but also goes well beyond the bricks-and-mortar reality of our campuses.

John L. Caughey, my dissertation advisor and graduate school mentor, knowing that I wanted to become a college teacher, encouraged me not to limit my reading and contemplation solely to my field, but also to think about the idea of the university. In one of the books he recommended, *Zen and the Art of Motorcycle Maintenance*, I underlined the following passage:

> The real University is a state of mind. It is that great heritage of rational thought that has been brought down to us through the centuries and which does not exist at any specific location. It's a state of mind which is regenerated throughout the centuries by a body of people who traditionally carry the title of professor, but even that title is not part of the real University. The real University is nothing less than the continuing body of reason itself.[1]

Though I did not realize it then, this passage describes some of what the Internet offers the academic community—an ever-expanding collection of ideas available beyond the borders of time, the limitations of space and the formal structure of academic authority.

Thus, although my younger undergraduate self might have scoffed at the notion of anyone being actually "interested in computers," I believe that I am not so different now. Rather, I am deeply enriched by what I have learned, by those who have been my teachers and by the prospect that there is still so much to learn. I started teaching college in an era of typewriters and mimeograph machines. It is exciting that today we have a new and malleable creative tool to work with. Certainly, students stand to benefit from our knowledge of these tools. However, I believe that it is actually their professors—those of us who feel the most behind on the "new technology"—who stand to be the most enriched by this exciting and creative time in the history of the university.

Joseph Hargitai As a child, I had a learning problem. It was not that I could not digest what was on my plate; rather, I never thought I had enough to learn. Education was linear; I wanted more information, and I wanted it faster—preferably everything at the same time. Like many others, I was destined to multitask. When I look at my nine-year-old son, I am a little bit relieved. He is on his computer playing a game in one window, drawing a picture in another and writing mail in a third, all this while watching TV and talking to me. Now and then, he jots down a few lines on a piece of paper: he is also writing a maze game for me. We have arrived. Information is everywhere, and so are the mechanics of delivery.

When people ask me what the Internet is, I do not know what to tell them. I find that when I believe I have arrived at a point of understanding, somehow there is always a little bit more to add. Working on this book forced me to search for a good metaphor for the larger human and cultural endeavor that the Internet represents. In the process, I discovered that my ideas of the Internet are linked to a curiosity and zest for learning shaped by growing up in Hungary that I carried with me to America and then to the Internet.

Pushkin, the great Russian poet, was once asked to name the greatest musical talent who ever lived. The poet, who was always deeply concerned about the abject poverty of his people, replied, unfortunately we shall never know her. My grade school Russian teacher, who was always full of good anecdotes, told this one many times as a token of assurance that in our socialist world such underdevelopment of talent would never be possible. The paradox of this statement struck me only later as a young man.

I first came across underground literature at Kossuth Lajos University, when a book arrived in class during a marathon lecture on Roman civilization. Those loosely bound pages—a poor and hardly legible copy—possessed an incredible power. When I held this book in my hands, I was excited but also thoroughly petrified—not because of what I read in the book, but because my sense of justice rebelled. This was not a way for information to see the light of day.

However, my awareness of this injustice came earlier. In 1979, after years of rejecting the idea, our dean agreed to install a small bulletin board on the otherwise bare walls of the university. The articles needed a stamp of approval but could be submitted anonymously. To my surprise the board was not accepted as quickly as one would imagine. For a while, students just hurried by. A few of the braver ones pretended to stumble so they could at least get a glance at the headlines. This nervous dance lasted for months in front of our little "window of truth."

This sensibility may have come even earlier. I wrote my first computer code on a typewriter. We were like composers drafting sheet music not knowing if we would ever hear an orchestra play our compositions. I remember this typewriter well. It was an apple-green Olympia. It had my memory, white onionskin paper for storage, and it was the only writing instrument I ever owned that used my native alphabet. Sticky-keyed, loud and hard to come by—it was a most powerful publishing machine. For a long time our high school did not have a computer, only the notion that computing would one day be very important to us. Our first computer arrived some time later, literally with a bang. It came on trucks and replaced our French classroom. We were somewhat sad to see the heavy oak benches and blackboard go, but also excited to be part of something new.

As I look more deeply I realize that I can trace this awareness all the way back to my earliest childhood. My uncle, who had the good fortune to study at the Sorbonne, used to say that the only way to pursue a well-rounded intellectual life was through the understanding and appreciation of other cultures. When we grew older, he took my cousins and me to the library of the famous Reformatus Kollegium, where he hoped we would someday study, and showed us how to find and check out books. Founded in 1538, it was a grand old school, but in order to avoid future political complications my parents elected to send me to a high-profile state school instead.

In a wonderful statement about the permanence of great old institutions, while doing research for this book I came across the Reformatus Kollegium on the Internet. The familiar text that had adorned the entrance of the school now greeted me on their new home page: "Orando et laborando." So much had changed since my childhood, yet not before many of my generation had left Hungary for the West.

I left Hungary in 1980 during the Moscow Olympics, which were boycotted by many Western countries. Strangely, my first Western experience was of looking at the "truncated" Olympic broadcast through the windows of Kaufhalle and other West German megastores. For many refugees, this came as a bitter contradiction; we had lifelong dreams of living in a free society and valued the Olympic spirit. The Olympic movement was, or so we thought, beyond war and politics. It was much more than an international meeting place and competition among nations—it was a tradition, a concept and a way of life.

These ideas stayed with me and became intuitively entwined with the way I understood the Internet. Today my "window of truth" is a computer monitor. Through this window, I have seen the fall of the Berlin Wall and the emergence of democracy across Eastern and Central Europe. I have received thousands of e-mail messages and spent hours reading news posted by people all over the world. Some moments are unforgettable. I remember e-mail from a professor in Dubrovnik sent while the first Serbian warplanes descended on his city. On this monitor, I observed the political career of a friend who had been the first to post something on the university bulletin board. I watched as he rose to a high position in the new Hungarian civic government and, through the same window, read the sad news of his untimely demise.

How much has changed is demonstrated by the fact that today I am on the editorial board of one of Hungary's leading online magazines. I can write, edit and post my articles via their Web page without leaving my chair here in New York. Today, the ideal of a global citizenship brings my uncle's cosmopolitan ideas into even sharper focus. Just like him, I too believe that the foundation of a meaningful life lies in learning more about our larger community.

I have been privileged to spend these exciting years at the Innovation Center at New York University. I have been continuously amazed at the speed with which this new medium has taken hold, and at the camaraderie that has formed around it. It has been exciting to be a member of a team of pioneers, who have taken on the latest developments in technology and worked closely to fit them with educational ideas and needs.

The most exciting part of this work, no doubt, was the arrival of the first wave of instructors around 1995. Brimming with ideas and carrying rich material to be translated, these instructors had seen the educational potential of the Web from its inception.

What surprised me most was the wide range of disciplines they represented: from art history to performance studies and statistics. This was a major departure from the scientific predisposition of the Web—turning molecules around and viewing protein chains three-dimensionally seemed simple compared to giving a class on social anthropology a proper treatment. Luckily, these teachers were never short of ideas. Through lengthy exchanges new metaphors and working methods were developed. Once past the initiation phase, these pioneers quickly found their online voice, and within a short time their projects had grown into elaborate Web presentations.

I met Anne Keating in 1996 when she walked into the Innovation Center just before the beginning of the spring term. She was teaching a writing course at the time and wanted to use the Web in her class. Possessed by a keen admiration for machines and code, she wondered if she could ever learn HTML. Two hours later the question was answered and the frame of her course page was already on the Web. However, that was simply the technology. We both understood that the important part of translating part or all of a course to the Web is not the underlying code but the vision that a teacher has for this medium. This is where Anne, like many of our clients, excelled. She had a natural ability for exploring new ways of looking at ideas and showing these to her students. A year into watching the evolution of her work, I looked at her online discussion boards and was simply amazed at the level and quality of activity. The merging of her ideas with the Web as her medium has been a complete success.

Since our first meeting, Anne has written many HTML pages and taught many Web-enhanced courses. She has gone on to develop departmental pages and, more recently, to explore the possibilities of distance learning, while actually building four distance learning courses from scratch. Her gift with this medium has meant that our discussions over time have gradually shifted from technical issues and solving Web page problems to exploring ideas about the rational use of the medium.

We both hope that the era of a purely machine-oriented vision of computing has come to a close, and a realignment to a new human-centered computing paradigm is in our future. Computers as complex machines and programming puzzles may evolve into a nearly transparent interface that will both facilitate and revitalize human networks, communication and learning. The most important thing I have learned as a technologist is that the Internet is made up of the people, not the machines, that are connected to this global network.

March 1998
New York City

Acknowledgments

WE are grateful to the many people who provided support and encouragement throughout the research and writing of this book. We are very grateful for the support, dedication and sheer hard work of our editor, Suzanne S. Kemperman. We thank Despina Papazoglou Gimbel, the managing editor at NYU Press, for taking this book from manuscript to finished book. Her care with the details makes the book you hold now as much hers as ours. Special thanks go to Janet Tingey, our book designer. We are grateful to Nancy Lin, electronic publishing manager at NYU Press, for her work on the project and especially the companion Web site. For his advice and sound direction, we would like to thank Ed Friedman. For their unshakable faith in this project and their patience, support and willingness to read numerous drafts, we owe the deepest gratitude to our partners. Emily Hacker, an instructional technology coordinator with the Literacy Assistance Center, New York, lent to this project both the support of a loving partner and the weight of her experience working with teachers. Nancy Vesley, an interactive media designer with Prodigy Services Inc., lent both the support of a loving wife and also critical editorial skills and insight on the technical chapters of this book.

We are very grateful for the overall support and encouragement of our colleagues and friends in the School of Continuing Education (which became the School of Continuing and Professional Studies in September 1998), especially in the Adult Degree Studies Division (which became the Paul McGhee Division—Undergraduate Degree Program for Adults in September 1998); and in the Academic Computing Facility, especially the Innovation Center. In the School of Continuing and Professional Studies, we would like to thank Gerald A. Heeger, Frances Gottfried, Frank Miata, Dorothy Durkin, William F. Cipolla and Cynthia L. Ward. Special thanks go to Kate Millett, for her support of this project and for her encouragement and guidance over the years. Special thanks go as well to Kristine M. Rogers for many wonderful conversations on the history of ideas. At the Academic Computing Facility, we would like to thank George Sadowsky, Vincent Doogan, Eleanor Kolchin, Frances Bauer, Michael Puskar, Jill Hochberg, Carlo

Cernivani, Lisa Barnett and Melissa Whitney. In the Innovation Center, we would like to thank Jeffery Bary, Bill Horn, Adel Hana, Jeffrey Lane, Suprotim Bose, Johannes Lang, Shelly Smith and Phil Galanter. Additional thanks go to Tim O'Connor for his invaluable contribution to our understanding of computer networks as well as his patience in reading early drafts of the historical chapters of this book. We are grateful as well to Bill Burns for his generous gift of reading and editing our corrections to the final draft.

We are grateful to the educators and programmers who contributed material and consented to be interviewed and included in this project. Special thanks go to Michelle Adelman, Jon McKenzie, Julia Keefer, Caroline Persell, Barbara Kirshenblatt-Gimblett, Robin Nagle, Francine Shaw Shuchat, Turi Laszlo, Vajda Eva, Lanczi Eva, Jonathan J. Vafai, Paul J. Gans, David Garcia, Millard Clements, Brian Murfin, Christina Engelbart, David G. Stork and Selena Sol.

Finally, we can never repay the kindness of our own teachers. In particular this book owes much to the early influence of Sister Mary Berchmans Hannan, Sue Foreman, Claire McCaffery Griffin, and Marian Canney of Georgetown Visitation Preparatory School and is dedicated to them as a gift on the two hundredth birthday of that school.

THE WIRED PROFESSOR

| # A History of Information Highways and Byways

THIEL de la Sola Pool, MIT professor and computer visionary, argued in the early 1980s that computer communications would profoundly alter history. (At this point, the personal computer was still unheard of and the early Internet was the exclusive domain of engineers, computer scientists and scientists.) In a prophetic statement, he wrote:

> One could argue that computer communication is one of the perhaps four most fundamental changes in the history of communications technology. Any such list is, of course, judgmental, but the case can be made that writing 5,000 years ago, printing 500 years ago, telegraphy 150 years ago, and now computer communication were the four truly revolutionary changes, and that most of the thousands of other changes in communication technology have been but perfecting adaptations of these four.[1]

In the process of writing this book, we kept reaching back into the history of networks, publishing, computers and the development of the Internet for metaphors and descriptions of the cognitive and design issues raised by this new technology. We initially envisioned this book as a straightforward guide, similar to the many guides to using the Internet that were in print in 1997. However, as we began to write the book, we felt like the blind men trying to describe the elephant when we talked about the Internet with newly "wired" professors. We also realized that the guides on the market assumed either a level of technical proficiency with computers or only a basic level of immediate and practical application.

Our research into the historical background provided both fascinating anecdotal details that rounded out our own understanding of the Internet and the necessary framework for imparting this understanding to others. We offer this departure from the current trend in guides on the subject because your students may ask you about the origins of the Internet. More importantly, we feel that a solid grounding on the nature of the Internet is critical to even out the disparity that still exists between technology "insiders" who have worked on the Internet for the last fifteen to twenty years and the rest of us who only in the last few years have used e-mail with any regularity.

The Social Role of Communication Networks

To understand the Internet, we first need to understand the social role human networks have played historically. It is easy to think of networks solely as a computer concept—as in "local area network"—and to forget the fact that computer networks, including the Internet, were designed to enhance communication and timely sharing of information. In fact, one of the earliest sustained and widely read discussion groups on the Internet's precursor, ARPANET, was a mailing list called Human-Nets.[2] Posters to Human-Nets discussed computer-aided human-to-human communications but tended to focus less on issues of computer hardware and programming and reflected instead on their preoccupation with how people would actually use the new network, which in a prophetic moment they referred to as "WorldNet."[3] A regular poster to Human-Nets recalls, "It was a very interesting mailing list and possible only due to the ability of the network itself to permit those interested in this obscure topic to communicate."[4]

ANCIENT NETWORKS

The concept of networking to communicate and share information is neither new nor limited to computers. The earliest incentive to develop networks was the need to bridge distances and communicate beyond the line of sight. The need for a network system was primarily a military one. A well-known example is that of the Romans, who built some the earliest networks, with a road system that facilitated not only the rapid movement of troops but also the rapid exchange of information by messengers. In short, the words *networks* and *information* are nearly synonymous and emphasize the value of the timely acquisition of information. One has only to look at the terms "network of spies," "network of informers," and "networking" to see this relationship. It is also implied in military terms such as "gathering intelligence" and "reconnaissance." The architecture of these early networks—literally the roads that were constructed and the relay systems that were developed—is an evolutionary blueprint for the Internet and World Wide Web.

The earliest information networks predate the Roman *cursus publicus* road network by hundreds of years. In Greece between 1300 and 1100 B.C. signal fires were used to flash signals from mountain peak to mountain peak.[5] Homer described this system in the *Iliad*:

> Thus, from some far-away beleaguered island, where all day long the men have fought a desperate battle from their city walls, the smoke goes up to heaven; but no sooner has the sun gone down than the light from the line of beacons blazes up and shoots into the sky to warn the neighboring islanders and bring them to the rescue in their ships.[6]

Fire beacons are also mentioned by Aeschylus (525–456 B.C.), whose play *Agamemnon* opens with the lines: "And now I am watching for the signal of the beacon, the blaze of fire that brings a voice from Troy, and tidings of its capture."[7] Fire was not the only signaling system used to create a messenger network. King Darius of Persia (522–486 B.C.) devised a signaling system so that news could be sent from the capital to the provinces of the Persian Empire by means of a line of shouting men positioned on heights, who could relay messages across distances equivalent to a thirty-day journey. According to Julius Caesar, the Gauls used a similar method and could call all their warriors to arms in just three days.

As early as the second millennium B.C. in Egypt and the first millennium B.C. in China, courier relay systems were developed using messengers on horseback and relay stations situated on major roads.[8] References to messenger systems can be found that date back almost 4,000 years to the reign of Sesostris I (1971–1928 B.C.) of Egypt. Between 1792 and 1750 B.C., Hammurabi's messengers, by riding both day and night, were able to cover the 125 miles from Larsa to Babylon in two days. The Book of Jeremiah contains a reference to this relay system that shows it still operating in the time of King Nebuchadnezzar II (605–562 B.C.): "One post shall run to meet another, and one messenger to meet another, to show the king of Babylon that his city is taken."[9]

In Persia, King Cyrus the Great (599–530 B.C.) was credited with improvements to the courier system. Xenophon in *Cryopaedia*, his biography of Cyrus written more than a century later, described Cyrus's efforts:

> He experimented to find out how great a distance a horse could cover in a day when ridden hard, but so as not to break down, and then he erected post-stations at just such

distances and equipped them with horses, and men to take care of them; at each one of the stations he had the proper official appointed to receive the letters that were delivered and to forward them on, to take in the exhausted horses and riders and send on fresh ones. They say, moreover, that sometimes this express does not stop all night, but the night-messengers succeed the day-messengers in relays.[10]

The Persians used this highly developed system for fast and dependable communication between the capital and the distant regions of the Persian Empire, which stretched from modern-day Iran to Egypt. In his *History,* Herodotus expressed his admiration for how the relay system worked during Xerxes' rule (486–465 B.C.), in words that are still with us today:

> There is nothing on earth faster than these couriers. . . . Men and horses are stationed a day's travel apart, a man and a horse for each of the days needed to cover such a journey. These men neither snow nor heat nor gloom of night stay from the swiftest possible completion of their appointed stage.[11]

In Egypt, using the relay system, the Ptolemies were able to set up the ancient world's nearest equivalent to a modern postal system. Egyptian post stations, set at six-hour intervals (by horseback) or roughly thirty miles apart, handled at least four deliveries daily, two each from north and south.[12] Herodotus was amazed with the efficiency of the Egyptian system.

The Roman mail was another matter, and people often relied on travelers to take their mail to its destination. While on his way to Italy, Cicero wrote to his servant in Patras: "Have Acastus go down to the waterfront daily, because there will be lots of people to whom you can entrust letters and who will be glad to bring them to me. At my end I won't overlook a soul who is headed toward Patras."[13] Over short distances the mail moved quickly; however, long distances could be a different matter. A letter that Cicero wrote from Rome to his son in Athens took seven weeks to reach its destination, while another from Rome to Athens took only three.[14] (In the first instance, the courier ended up having to wait for the next available ship. In the second, the courier was lucky enough to find a ship waiting for him.)[15] However, sometimes the postal system was remarkable. In 54 B.C., Julius Caesar's letter from Britain reached Cicero in Rome in twenty-nine days. In 1834, Robert Peel, hurrying to get back to Britain, took thirty days to travel from

Figure 1.1. *The Tabula Peutingeriana* (c. a.d. 393), showing the network of Roman roads. Rome is represented by the seated figure wearing a crown. Image courtesy of Perry-Casteñeda Library Map Collection at *http://www.lib.utexas.edu/Libs/PCL/Map_co llection/.*

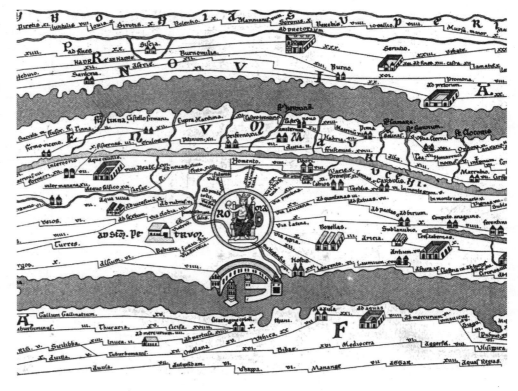

Rome to London.[16] (As I write this, my e-mail program has just chimed in with its "you have mail!" message. Checking my e-mail, I see that I have a message from a librarian at Oxford's Bodleain Library in response to a message I sent just half an hour ago. Both ways these two messages have covered a distance inconceivable to the Romans and at a speed that would have amazed Peel.—ABK)

The roads built by the Romans beginning in 312 B.C. form the most famous of these ancient networks.[17] The Roman Empire had 51,000 miles of paved highways and a network of secondary roads, which fanned out to link Rome with the distant areas of the empire. Aerial views of this system show the clear-sightedness of the Romans' long-distance network, which was not to be matched until the introduction of railroads in the nineteenth century. Many of these roads lasted for a thousand years without needing repair, and today many modern European roads run on top of the original Roman roads. Using this network of roads, it was possible to cover long distances with surprising efficiency. On one journey, Caesar was able to travel eight hundred miles in eight days. Messengers bringing the news of Nero's death covered 332 miles in thirty-six hours. The Roman postal system (despite Cicero's complaints) transported messages at an average of a hundred miles a day.[18]

The prosperity of the Roman Empire was largely built on quick military reaction: the ability to move troops efficiently over long distances and to transmit up-to-date information. The Roman Empire was knit together by its network of roads and outposts; its messengers, sailors, and horsemen; and Latin, its common language. Both the roads and Latin would continue to act as a network uniting the European continent long after the fall of the Roman Empire.

Across the Atlantic, the Incas in the fifteenth and sixteenth centuries A.D. (the period that saw the development and widespread use of the printing press in Europe) created a network system that has striking parallels to both the Roman system and modern computer networks. Like the Romans, the Incas had a highly evolved administrative system. Although they had no system for writing, they developed a unique method of record keeping and an efficient information network. The *quipucamayoc,* the Incan "accountants," developed a system to record births, deaths, crop yields and new laws on knotted, multicolored cords called *quipus.*[19] The Incas constructed thousands of miles of roads along a 2,000-mile stretch of the Andes and the western South American coast. Along these roads, *chasquis,* specially trained runners, ran in relays between carefully spaced *tambos,* or way stations. They carried *quipus* and relayed the memorized news and the orders of the empire.

Sixty years before Columbus landed in the West Indies, the Incas began their imperial expansion. They called their empire Tabuantinsuyu, "the land of the four quarters." The four quarters (Antisuyu to the east; Chinchaysuyu to the north; Cuntisuyu along the coast; and Collasuyu to the south) were in turn subdivided into more than eighty provinces. At the center of Tabuantinsuyu was Cuzco, the Incan capital. *Cuzco* in the Incan language means "the navel"—or, in a manner of speaking, the center of the universe—and Cuzco, like Rome, was the hub for the vast network of highways that linked all parts of the Incan Empire. Along these thoroughfares moved mobile army units, accompanied by pack trains of llamas and by the *chasquis* who formed the Incan communications network. These were young relay runners who had been trained since childhood for the task of carrying messages from *tambo* to *tambo*. These runners would shout "chasquis" ("receive the message") as they approached a *tambo*. Arriving at a *tambo*, a runner would pass off his satchel to a waiting chasqui who would continue running to the next *tambo*.

If an army general in a remote province needed to send a message to Cuzco he would give the oral message to a *chasqui*, who would start running from his *tambo* to another *chasqui*, waiting outside another *tambo*. The message would be relayed for hundreds of miles by hundreds of runners, until the last runner reached Cuzco and told the message, exact to the original word, because a severe punishment awaited the transmission of an inaccurate message. The *chasqui* relay system was so fast that runners could carry fish from the coast to Cuzco in the high Andes and it would still be fresh when it arrived. These messengers formed a communications system that could guarantee one-day delivery for every 150 miles of road. The trek from present-day Lima to Cuzco took *chasquis* just three days, although 430 miles of very bad roads separated the two. (Two hundred years after the Incas, Spanish mail carried by horseback took twelve or thirteen days to cover the same distance.)

Like the Egyptian and Persian networks, the Incan network was a two-way system— information could flow in both directions between the receiver and the sender.[20] On the Internet today, a group of latter-day Incas have adopted this communications system as the metaphor for "QuipuNet," their network. They explain that "QuipuNet will be using a 'chasqui' type of system to relay information from all parts of the world back to Peru, passing through 'electronic tambos' in order to reach not the Inca, but rather his descendants."[21] However, the system that the Incas developed has ties with the Internet that go well beyond the metaphorical reference at QuipuNet.

MODERN NETWORKS Of what relevance are these ancient networks to our modern computer networks? From the fire signals to the Incan *chasqui* network, these ancient systems foreshadowed the way computer networks and the Internet would work. To illustrate this, here is a brief layperson's description of the creation of the computer network at New York University (NYU). (Although each campus faced different networking challenges, this example should illustrate the kind of work and thought that went into the network at your school.)

NYU is located in the heart of Greenwich Village in an urban campus that loosely surrounds Washington Square Park and includes buildings scattered across New York City. In the early 1980s, the challenge was essentially to link these buildings together. Among the different solutions that were proposed was using Ethernet. However, while Ethernet worked well over short distances—such as within a building's local area network—it had strict limitations over distances greater than three hundred feet. As Tim O'Connor of the Academic Computing Center recalls:

> Ethernet . . . can support a cable of 300 feet long with no more than 30 devices attached; to do more of either, you need to add a repeater, which is like an amplifier; it would again allow for another 300 feet and another 30 devices. Then you hit another limit: the specification stated your limits are only two repeaters with three pieces of [Ethernet] on any segment of cable; for anything beyond that, you need a bridge, which then starts the count all over again. . . . In other words, Ethernet was perfect in a lab . . . or you could run a spine of Ethernet up the length of a building, and attach each floor to it. . . . [However] it was not realistic to cover Washington Square and beyond![22]

Like Cyrus of Persia's careful experiments with the exact placement of rest stops in the courier relay system, the laying of the network infrastructure at NYU faced the physical limitations of just how much distance a signal could travel through a wire before it degraded. The only feasible solution lay in using coaxial cable (broadband), the kind that carries cable television signals. Broadband offered a number of advantages over Ethernet, including the fact that it could carry signals over a greater distance. It was also inexpensive. A simple network system, broadband operated in a linear fashion. The network originated at the "head-end" and was expandable in sections, resembling a segmented snake in which "everything emanated from the 'head-end'—the hardware that kept the signal on the network alive."[23] Ethernet is simply cable that sits there whether in use or not. Broadband, on the other hand, had the added advantage of being able to be expanded as the need arose. In fact, by the end of the 1980s, as the electronic card catalog was being installed in NYU's Bobst Library, the network had become multilayered, with newer network technology sharing resources with older Ethernet and broadband network lines.

Without being aware of the underlying mechanics, people in Bobst were travelling across our Thinnet [Ethernet] which traversed each floor horizontally, along the traditional thick Ethernet, which ran up the spine of the building, through a bridge to NYU's broadband network, and into a series of devices in [NYU's main computing building], which allowed access to NYU's academic systems and to systems beyond NYU.[24]

However, broadband was limited; if a section of it **went down, all** information traveling through the network would stop at that point. Network services for the remainder of the broadband network would be suspended as well. With the introduction of fiber-optic cable, NYU's system was upgraded. In a description that echoes the topography of the Roman and Incan road networks, NYU's new network was "logically (and almost literally) a double ring encircling the campus. The idea [is] that even if one piece of fiber-optic was damaged, the network could work around it."[25] The double-ring loosely circles Washington Square Park, while hubs on the ring connect the outlying NYU buildings around Manhattan via fiber-optic cable leased from the telephone company.

While the ancient signal and courier relays laid out the topography for modern networks, it was the invention of the telegraph in 1792 that revolutionized signal networks. Crude telegraph schemes existed before this period, a testament to the tenacity of our ancestors to work with the technology at hand. However, while signal fires and couriers were effective, Herodotus noted that they were crude and insecure means of communication. He observed that the subtleties of "citizens having changed sides or having been guilty of treachery . . . cannot all be foreseen—and it is chiefly unexpected occurrences which require instant consideration and help."[26] Anyone who struggled with early clunky word processing packages like WordStar or braved UNIX-based e-mail programs will appreciate the efforts of Polybius in the second century B.C. to create a more efficient system using the existing fire beacon "technology." Polybius devised a code using the twenty-four characters of the Greek alphabet and a telegraph that consisted of two large screens that hid five torches each. Depending on the letter, the signaler raised different numbers of torches behind the two screens. However, this line-of-sight communication was limited until the invention of the telescope in the seventeenth century renewed interest in building communications systems.[27]

It should be noted that there are line-of-sight network solutions operating today. Wireless network technology has made it possible to cross otherwise impossible dis-

Figure 1.2. The Chappe telegraph.
Illustration by Anne B. Keating.

tances. Presently, a variation of line-of-sight using wireless networking technology is being used at the Villa La Pietra, a fifteenth-century estate in northern Florence that was given as a gift to NYU in the mid-1990s. Due to the building's status as a historical landmark, tunneling and laying cable as well as stringing wires were out of the question. The alternative solution was wireless technology. Wireless technology, similar to that used in 900 mHz cordless telephones, can carry a signal that can travel throughout a building and is not dependent on direct line-of-sight. Infrared, another common wireless technology, can be employed outside over short distances. However, it is heavily dependent on line-of-sight and can be thrown off by inclement weather, including fog. At the Villa La Pietra, establishing the wireless connection between other buildings on the estate relied on line-of-sight for obtaining the best possible signal from the network inside La Pietra. Connecting the villa with a smaller building used to house NYU students called for the installation of wireless antennas on the roofs of both buildings. These had to be manually adjusted to obtain the best possible line-of-sight over the five hundred yards separating the two buildings.

Claude Chappe (1763–1805) invented the "optical telegraph," a visual telegraph with signals based on the different positions produced by a system of cross-arms and pulleys. The telegraph resembled a windmill, with two lateral arms that rotated freely around a center. The signaling method was similar to that later used on the railroads. The different positions of the arms could transmit nearly 8,500 words from a general vocabulary of ninety-two pages, each containing ninety-two words. Only two signals were required for a single word—the page of the vocabulary and the number of the word. Telegraph towers were set at ten kilometer intervals—within range of telescopes and field glasses.

In March 1792, Chappe showed his invention to the French Legislative Assembly, which adopted it officially. The first connections were made between Lille and Paris, and a line of fifteen stations were operational by August 1794. The first telegram sent with this telegraph announced the victory of the French over the Austrians at Condé-sur-Escaut on November 30, 1794. At this time, the political situation in France was unstable and security was weak. These conditions required a communications system that could operate rapidly, efficiently and secretly. Messengers or couriers on horseback could not meet these criteria. Thus, when Chappe unveiled the Optical Telegraph, the French Assembly was in a particularly receptive frame of mind.[28] The network rapidly grew over the next decades into a system that covered approximately three thousand miles, included 556 stations and connected twenty-nine French cities. Many other European states also installed the Chappe telegraph system in their territories.[29]

Though supplanted in public memory by the electric telegraph, the Chappe telegraph was used extensively in both Europe and the United States. In the United States optical telegraph lines ran from Boston to Martha's Vineyard and connected Staten Island to Manhattan. One line ran from Philadelphia to New York so that the stockbroker who ran it could get word immediately of fluctuations in stock prices. Another optical telegraph operated in San Francisco from 1849 to 1853. Telegraph Hill in San Francisco was one of three optical telegraph stations in that city.[30]

However, the optical telegraph was slow (a short message could take up to fifteen minutes) and could not be used at night or during periods of poor visibility. Sending messages over long distances required a series of towers, each of which had to receive and then retransmit the message, increasing the chance of errors being introduced that could distort the original message. Also, though cryptic, the telegraph messages were viewable by anyone on the ground and thus were not secure—in some cases people living in the vicinity of a telegraph tower were actually able to learn the signals over time.

However, other developments in the nineteenth century would render the optical telegraph obsolete and have an impact on the development of computer networks. One of the earliest experiments with electrical telegraphs took place in the early nineteenth century. In 1795, Francisco Salva decided to build an electrical telegraph between Barcelona and Mataro. He planned to send his messages by illuminating letters of tinfoil with an electrical spark.[31] Alessandro Volta's invention of the battery in 1800 furnished a new source of electricity, better adapted for the telegraph, and Salva was apparently the first to recognize this. In 1804, he successfully developed a battery-powered electric telegraph system by which he could transmit messages over one kilometer, with each letter being carried on a separate wire.[32] In 1816, Francis Ronalds, also fascinated by electricity, developed an electric telegraph (using static high-voltage electricity) and succeeded in sending messages through eight miles of iron wire suspended above his garden in London. However, it was Samuel Morse who refined the electric telegraph.

In 1831, Morse, a painter, was forced to cut a trip to Italy short when a revolution broke out in the papal states. On the return trip to the United States he conceived of the idea of a "telegraph" based on electromagnetism. He spent the next six years in his studio at NYU working on his telegraph. In 1837, Morse demonstrated the electric telegraph by sending a signal over 1,700 feet of wire in a room at NYU. This was followed by

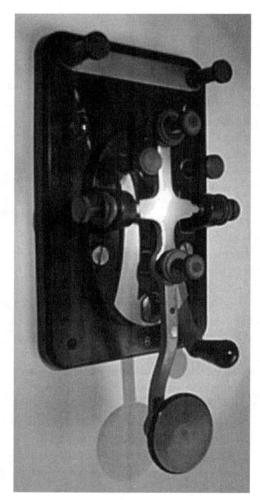

Figure 1.3. Telegraph key used to transmit messages. Collection of Anne B. Keating.

the development of Morse Code in 1838. On May 24, 1844, Morse sent his first telegraph—containing the words "What hath God wrought!"—from the U.S. Capitol Building in Washington, D.C., to the B & O Railroad Depot in Baltimore, Maryland. Of this invention American author Nathaniel Hawthorne would write: "Is it a fact—or have I dreamt it—that, by means of electricity, the world of matter has become a great nerve, vibrating thousands of miles in a breathless point of time? Rather, the round globe is a vast head, a brain, instinct with intelligence!"[33]

However, this new discovery was also met with a degree of skepticism. When Morse demonstrated the telegraph before members of Congress in 1842, one senator recalled: "I watched his countenance closely, to see if he was not deranged . . . and I was assured by other Senators after we left the room that they had no confidence in it."[34] In 1845, Cave Johnson, the Postmaster General, declared in his annual report that the "telegraph business will never be profitable."[35] However, others saw the electric telegraph with an entrepreneurial eye. For example, in 1886 Richard Sears, a telegraph operator and railroad station manager, started experimenting with mail order by selling watches via telegraph—an experiment that eventually led to the formation of Sears and Roebuck. The Associated Press got its start as an alliance of Morse telegraph services and operators dedicated to transmitting news dispatches. The American Civil War was one of the first full-scale demonstrations of the efficiency of this system for transmitting troop deployments and military intelligence.[36] By 1851, an international telegraph network was launched with the laying of a cable across the English Channel.[37] In 1866, just twenty-two years after the completion of the first telegraph line, the laying of a transatlantic cable connecting the United States with Europe marked the beginning of a new era in telecommunications. In the early years of this international telegraph network, eight words took a full minute to transmit at the cost of one hundred dollars.[38]

The nineteenth-century revolution in communications technology reached full fruition with the invention of the telephone in 1876 by Alexander Graham Bell. By the next year, the Bell Telephone Company had grown to a network consisting of a thousand phones. By 1880, there were fifty thousand telephone lines in the United States. By 1930, the telephone network had outgrown the telegraph network. (Ninety-three years after Bell's invention, the ARPANET sprang to life in the space occupied by telephone traffic traveling along the wires that first made telegraph possible.)

The development of telegraphs and networks is significant for understanding the Internet because it demonstrates the relentless push toward more speed, more capacity, more raw volume, more "consumers." Each of these inventions was designed for a single purpose but mutated over time to fill other needs. For example, Bell first envisioned that the telephone would be used to pipe music to homes. However, the telegraph and, eventually, the telephone developed into point-to-point communications. Even television, a broadcast medium, has followed this trajectory of diverging from its original uses and modes of delivery. While most television is broadcast in specific wavelengths, cable television literally strings together buildings and neighborhoods. Ironically, we are beginning to come full circle as some cable companies are fighting to provide both voice and data service on their physical networks.

The Social Role of Writing and Publishing

To understand the evolution of the Internet, we also need to understand the social role that communication, in the form of writing and publishing, has played historically. Although a thorough analysis of writing and publishing is beyond the scope of this chapter, we hope the following historical vignettes help to provide a sense of the antecedents to Web publishing and the use of the Internet to store and disseminate information.

Our use of communications technology is an extension of the development of speech, reading and writing. Over time we have developed sophisticated tools for enhancing the basic communications acts implicit in these three related skills. The use of computers and the Internet is simply our latest aid to enhanced human communication. Although computers are used widely, many people still think of them as having emerged solely from the realm of engineers and computer programmers—and thus as machines that exert a disembodied and faintly bureaucratic influence on our daily lives. This anxiety comes primarily from the misconception that the machinery in some mysterious way has a life and mind of its own.

This fact was not lost on Norbert Weiner, one of the earliest "computer designers" who, in the 1940s, suggested that the computer could be used for more than calculating mathematical figures. In *Cybernetics* (1948), he likened the anxiety about technology to the moral of Goethe's story "The Sorcerer's Apprentice," where magic is seen as a literal-minded force that can only be controlled by a skilled operator—in this case the magician. In *Cybernetics*, Weiner argued:

> The idea of non-human devices of great power and great ability to carry through a policy, and of their dangers, is nothing new. All that is new is that we now possess effective devices of this kind. In the past, similar possibilities were postulated for the

techniques of magic which forms the theme for so many legends and folk tales. . . . In all these stories the point is that the agencies of magic are literal-minded; and that if we ask for a boon from them, we must ask for what we really want . . . and not for what we think we want.[39]

Many of us who do not have engineering or computer science backgrounds, and who work primarily with word processors, tend to see the power of computers but not their literal-mindedness—except perhaps when we lose a file, and even then we tend to blame the mysterious workings of the computer. When this anxiety is focused on the Internet and magnified by media reports of the dangers that lurk there in the form of stalkers and pornographers, or that anathema to scholars everywhere—inaccurate information—this sense that the machine is more powerful than its operators is magnified.

However, we can see echoes of the same anxiety over social change at other moments in the history of writing and publishing. The changes brought about by new and different media for writing and publishing, as well as the anxiety over the passing of familiar tools and methods, is comparable to what many of us experience when integrating computers and the Internet into the way we work with information. The nature of the Internet "revolution" is not so much that the traditional rules of how we work with information have changed, but that the ideas we have about the nature of information are changing. It is easier to explain changes in history when the social backdrop or foundational ideas remain the same. However, when these change, everyone is thrown into the search for definitions.

A good place to begin exploring the antecedents of the Internet in writing and publishing is to situate our discussion within the cultural myth of the search for perfect language and the breakdown of universal literacy. In many ways, writing and publishing are attempts to transcend the limitations of only being able to communicate with one's immediate group, in "real time," and in one language. The power of this idea can be seen in the biblical story of the Tower of Babel. In the story, after the flood, Noah's descendants went east and eventually settled on a plain in the land of Shinar. These people shared a common language. They decided to build a city and a tower that would reach up to heaven. God, concerned that these people would become too arrogant, destroyed the tower, scattered the people and, by miraculous intervention, introduced different languages among them, generally creating great confusion. The place where

Figure 1.4. Detail from *The Tower of Babel* by Pieter Bruegel the Elder, 1563. Used by permission of Kunsthistorisches Museum, Vienna.

the tower stood was then called "Babel," "because the Lord did there confound the language of all the earth."[40] Paradoxically, while *babel* is popularly thought of as chaotic, nonsense speech—as in a "baby's babble"—etymologically, the word means "gate of God."[41]

As historical fact, the Tower of Babel is hard to verify, though scholars believe that it was a Babylonian ziggurat, possibly started by Hammurabi and located in the southern part of the city of Babylon. As a myth, however, the story is fascinating for its descriptions both of technological innovation and of the loss of universal literacy implied by a common language. The story is remarkable for the juxtaposition of technology and the age-old problem of multiple languages. The Tower of Babel has remained an important cultural metaphor throughout history. Umberto Eco, in *The Search for the Perfect Language* (1995), explores this idea and its impact on European thought and culture. Eco points to the crossroads between the search for a perfect language and the emergence of a European identity in the eleventh century. In this period, he explains, the awareness of the sheer number of vernacular idioms and dialects stimulated interest in developing a perfect language. Eco also cites a change in the contemporary depictions of the Tower of Babel as an indication of this awareness.[42] Up until this period, there had been few pictorial representations of the Tower. After the eleventh century, however, there emerged a wealth of new images. Eco theorizes that the stimulus for this outpouring was a change in public perception about the story that coincided with the cultural and social upheaval in Europe. Eco argues that in this period the story came to be seen not just as an example of divine intervention, but also as an account of a historical event. Large-scale cultural change, appearing to mirror the biblical catastrophe, swept Europe and brought with it a multitude of languages that constituted the beginning of modern European languages.

Jacques Vallee, in *The Network Revolution* (1982), argues that one of the earliest modern attempts to create a group communication medium took place during the Berlin airlift of 1948, when telex machines from different countries were wired together. The experiment broke down precisely because everyone tried to communicate at the same time in different languages.[43] In the age of the Internet, the Tower of Babel myth continues to exert an influence. In his introduction to a Russian-to-English translation program that he has named "The Tower of Babel Project," Stephen Braich, a computer science major at Portland State University, asks:

Can we rebuild the Tower of Babel? With the internet, we are no longer scattered all over the face of the earth. We can communicate with each other and share information much faster than ever imagined. The only barrier still left is language. . . . Imagine what we could accomplish if everyone in the whole world really understood one another.[44]

Writing in many ways has partially solved the problem of the search for the perfect language. Writing begins to transcend the limitations of time and space and, with translation, even some of the limits of multiple languages. It is remarkable, for example, that we can read today the observation an Assyrian king made over 2,500 years ago, who in turn was reading the observations of an earlier culture. Writing in about 700 B.C., Ashurbanipal, king of the Assyrian empire and an avid reader with an extensive library, reflected: "I read the beautiful clay tablets from Sumer and the obscure Akkadian writing which is hard to master. I had my joy in the reading of inscriptions in stone from the time before the flood."[45]

While not a technological development, the emergence of speech and language approximately 250,000 years ago created a medium by which ideas could be transmitted and shared. Although speech and language are learned, the development of writing was a technological breakthrough.[46] Approximately 40,000 years ago, symbolic visual images appeared on cave walls and began to extend and enhance the range of communication. In ancient Mesopotamia, writing was invented in response to the need to keep accounts and make lists. In Sumer, writing first appeared around 3300 B.C. as a response to the complexity of managing the "movements of personnel, salaries and incoming and outgoing goods and flocks of animals. Since the capacity of the human memory is limited, it became necessary to find a new and unified system of reference enabling oral information to be preserved and recovered later on in spoken form."[47]

The invention of writing led to the formation of a scribal class. The degree to which this class assumed a critical role in ancient societies can be seen in Egypt. Egyptian scribes held high positions in Egyptian society and had their own god, Thoth. In Egyptian mythology, Thoth is credited with inventing writing. He served as scribe to the other deities—notably as the scribe responsible for writing down the disposition of human souls in the Egyptian Book of the Dead. Thoth was also a measurer of time and seeker of truth. Thoth's great power in Egyptian mythology reflected the new influence ascribed to writing.

Figure 1.5. Thoth: the god of the scribes. Illustration by Anne B. Keating.

Furthermore, to borrow an idea from computers, writing became the first dependable storage device for ideas. Starting out as a simple memory aid—a way to keep track of business transactions—writing soon opened the way for histories that extended memory beyond account books. While the first histories were in fact exercises in record keeping and consisted of lists of rulers, law codes, and ritual manuals, historical epics also began to appear, including *Gilgamesh* (c. 2000 B.C.), the *Ramayana* (c. 250 B.C.) and the *Mahabharata* (c. 200 B.C.–A.D. 200).

In the Western tradition, the writing of history is popularly attributed to Herodotus, the Greek historian who wrote of the clash between Europe and Asia that led to the Persian War between 430 and 450 B.C. (It is from his history and that of other early historians such as Xenophon that we have the descriptions of the fire beacons and courier systems discussed previously.) The significance of using writing for preserving history and even as historical artifact was not lost on ancient peoples.

The invention of printing further extended the range of writing and married human production to machines in the process. The earliest known printed text is the *Diamond Sutra*, a Buddhist text, from A.D. 868. This was followed by a 130-volume edition of the *Nine Classics* printed in China between A.D. 953 and 923 by Feng Tao. These early volumes were produced using woodblock printing. Movable type was introduced in China between 1041 and 1049.[48]

Printing developed later in the West, and the creation of books and libraries took an interesting turn that, as we will see, parallels the development of the Internet. The medieval library and the production of hand-copied texts are especially relevant models for a contemporary understanding of the Internet. The Internet, and especially the World Wide Web, mirrors the joint medieval absorption with the careful preservation and copying of the world's knowledge as well as the exclusivity of a class of cognoscenti. To be literate in the medieval period meant being able to read and write Latin. Only the clerical class could do this: "the association of *clerici* with *litterati* and *laicus* with *illitteratus,* was a medieval creation."[49] This lasted until universities began educating laypersons in the thirteenth century. Then, being literate was reduced "from meaning a person of erudition to meaning a person with a minimal ability to read, albeit in Latin. A *clericus* was still a *litteratus,* but he was now neither a churchman nor a scholar: he was anyone who was literate in this minimal sense."[50]

The World Wide Web mirrors as well the medieval absorption with design and the blending of text and illustration. There is also a parallel between the medieval monasteries' housing of both library and scriptorium (the room where manuscripts were written, copied and illuminated) and the fact that the Internet incorporates both the electronic scriptorium and the library. A closer look at the history of books, libraries and manuscripts from the sixth century to approximately the end of the thirteenth century illustrates these points.

The book trade in the West collapsed with the fall of the Roman Empire. In the sixth century, church bishops in the West began taking control of all church property, including manuscript collections in libraries, which thereafter assumed the status of communal possessions that could be copied and distributed fairly freely. Not only did this process create a means by which texts could be made available in copies to those who wished to read them, but on a more profound level the Catholic Church took critical steps "in adapting to its use the power of the written word. It was not that Latin Christians were beginning to write, but they were now using the written word with sophistication to organize and control their world."[51] For the next eight hundred years, books and other texts were copied and disseminated among monasteries by a system dependent on hundreds of monks who acted as scribes.

By the middle of the sixth century, Benedictine monks were required to read daily. This practice of reading contributed to the perception that libraries constituted a natural part of monastic life. This perception was to continue through to the end of the fifteenth century. For example, in 1345, Richard de Bury, the Bishop of Durham, wrote:

> The venerable devotion of the religious orders is wont to be solicitous in the care of books and to delight in their society, as if they were the only riches. For some used to write them with their own hands between the hours of prayer, and gave to the making of books such intervals as they could secure and the times appointed for the recreation of the body. By whose labours there are resplendent today in most monasteries these sacred treasuries full of cherubic letters. . . . Wherefore the memory of those fathers should be immortal, who delighted only in the treasures of wisdom, who most laboriously provided shining lamps against future darkness.[52]

When missionary monks traveled to remote parts of Europe, Britain and Ireland, they took manuscripts with them. When these monks set up monasteries, space for libraries and scriptoriums was also part of the design. Monks traveled to Rome from far-flung

Figure 1.6. "Hugo pictor": self-portrait of a scribe and illuminator, placed as a colophon at the end of a manuscript of St. Jerome's *Commentary on Isaiah*, from the Benedictine Abbey of Jumieges, Normandy, late eleventh century (Bodleian Library, MS. Bodl. 717, fol. 287v, detail). Used by permission of Bodleian Library.

monasteries for the express purpose of bringing books back to their monastery libraries.

The manuscript books of this period were inaccessible to all except the clergy and a handful of wealthy laypersons. The books were kept locked in monastery libraries and thus, before 1100, only the clerics were literate. By contemporary standards, monastery libraries were small. Before 1200, most monasteries housed less than a hundred volumes and only a few libraries had collections that exceeded three hundred volumes. This was due in large part to the fact that forty monks, the average number of scribes at work in each monastery, were only able to copy two manuscripts per year. Given the amount of time, energy and financial resources that went into their production, books were too valuable to make available to the general public. Even the Bible was rare outside of monasteries—it took a year to copy one and a parish priest's salary for the year to buy one. The Church did not oppose Bible reading on the part of nonmonastic readers, but neither did it encourage Bible reading for fear of popular interpretations of the scriptures.[53] Nevertheless, copying and the creation of these libraries spread Latin high culture from Rome to monasteries located largely in rural Europe—an echo of the Roman network earlier in this chapter.

These themes would be mirrored in the Internet. For almost twenty years the Internet remained the exclusive province a class of technical "monks," who in addition to programming also worked to create a database of literature on the Internet (Project Gutenberg is a key example of this effort). However, these digital "monks," like their medieval counterparts, were only producing for other digitally literate readers. Most of us in the early years of digital literature were completely unaware of these libraries and would have been unable to access them. The fact that medieval manuscripts were expensive and thus inaccessible to the general public was also echoed in the fact that the Internet was originally limited to those who were given access to work on the government-sponsored ARPANET. Only gradually was access extended to universities. However, the issue of "access" was not limited to just being able to log on to the Internet. Here the image of the medieval "public" libraries (as opposed to monastic libraries) is even more appropriate. Just as medieval academics sometimes stood in groups using books chained to library desks, today we vie for limited "public" computer resources at terminals on campus. The notion of expensive and limited resources remains with us in the expense of purchasing a computer, the critical device that allows us to read the material available online. For many of us in the university, this has translated into a desperate

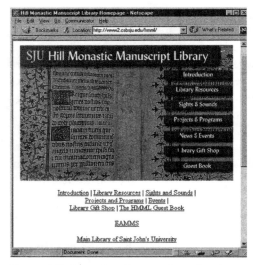

Figure 1.7. A modern library of medieval manuscripts: the Hill Monastic Manuscript Library Web Site at *http://www.csbsju.edu:80/hmml/*. Screenshot permission of Hill Monastic Manuscript Library, Saint John's University, Collegeville, Minnesota.

effort to get antiquated office computers upgraded to be Internet capable—or, outside the university, into setting up and paying for Internet access.

The copying of manuscripts, as we have seen in Richard de Bury's loving description, was more than an act of simple industry. Thus, while individual monks in the scriptorium might bury small notes in the margins of illustrations complaining of the tedium, the production of these texts was viewed as an act of worship. Today, we think of book illustrations as being distinct from the text. As medieval hand-copied manuscripts became increasingly elaborate, however, illustrations and text blended together in a way that redefined the nature of the book, making it an object of devotion. However, copying out manuscripts also demanded accuracy on the part of the copier. To certify the accuracy of the copy, monks followed an admonition that contained a warning similar to the one St. Irenaeus used with his monks, that on Judgement Day, Christ would judge the living and the dead and the hand-copied manuscripts for accuracy: "You who will transcribe this book, I charge you . . . Jesus Christ . . . will . . . compare what you have copied against the original and correct it carefully."[54]

In 1345, Petrarch discovered a manuscript containing Cicero's letters *Ad Atticum* (from which we have the description of the postal system discussed previously) in Verona. Shortly thereafter, Boccaccio discovered Tacitus's works in the monastery of Monte Casino. Their successes stimulated others to search medieval libraries for manuscripts containing additional Greek and Roman texts. Booksellers were also looking for books for wealthy book collectors but encountered difficulty finding the right ones because most of the world's books were in monasteries, which only provided limited access and even more limited cataloging. In most monasteries, books were shelved without anyone knowing or marking where. Libraries responded to these limitations by increasing the size and scope of their collections.

The Sorbonne, established in 1253, reflected many of these changes. By 1289 it had a library catalog of a thousand volumes. It also instituted a set of rules and regulations for library use and chained about 20 percent of its collection so that several patrons at a time could consult a manuscript. However, the majority of such libraries were not as large. For example, in 1424, Cambridge had only 122 volumes in its library.[55] A private library at the end of the fifteenth century might contain as many as twenty volumes. Whereas a hand-copied religious manuscript cost a priest's yearly salary, a bound manuscript cost as much money as an average court official received in a month. A scholar or student who was not exceptionally wealthy could acquire books by copying them by hand. In fact, by the thirteenth century, the typical manuscript was not the gorgeous illuminated manuscript produced in the monastery, but a simple hand-written copy made for personal use.

Two new institutions grew up around the universities to provide for the demand for books: stationers and book copiers. Stationers provided paper and kept libraries of textbooks that had been carefully studied and compared to other books for accuracy. They made these books available for copying by students. When a student needed a textbook for a class, he had to go down to the stationers and copy it out for himself by hand or pay a book copier to do it.[56] However, while a student might be able to get copies of the books he needed for a particular class, it was harder and sometimes impossible to get copies of other texts that might be required for independent research. Additionally, copying could not always keep pace with the demand for books. As copies were made, the copiers—who were not working under the admonition that they would be judged for their work on Judgement Day—made mistakes that were reproduced as books were made from copies of copies.

When Johannes Gutenberg introduced movable type to the West in 1455, European libraries changed significantly. Printing spread so rapidly throughout western Europe that by 1600 new presses had issued thirty thousand separate titles totaling twenty million volumes. For a time libraries—like their patrons—continued to favor hand-copied Latin manuscripts, but between 1450 and 1600 Europe experienced a series of social and cultural shifts that greatly influenced the dissemination of printed materials.

A highly literate and growing middle class emerged along with the capitalist economies in Europe. This new class demanded access to information. It is not uncommon these days to hear someone say that the Internet is as significant a development as Gutenberg's movable type. This parallel is striking on many points. The significance of Gutenberg's invention is that the printed word was no longer the strict domain of those who could afford the price of a hand-copied book.

Not only was the publishing process speeded up, but also multiple editions were possible. Gutenberg's invention created a revolution in publishing. The relationship of technology, machines and book production was not lost on Gutenberg, who included the following note in a book he printed in 1460: "this noble book *Catholicon* . . . without the help of reed, stylus or pen, but by the wondrous agreement, proportion and harmony of punches and types has been printed and brought to an end."[57]

The mechanical innovation of printing not only widened the audience for books, but also changed the act of reading. In the early sixteenth century, being able to memorize passages from essential texts was a critical part of education and an indispensable aide in argument and comparison. The invention of printing and the modern book, the proliferation of private libraries and increased access to books meant that sixteenth century readers could begin to rely on the book's "memory" rather than their own. Gadgets were built around this idea of books as "reference tools." Agostino Ramelli, an engineer, invented a "rotary reading desk" in 1588, which permitted a reader to have access to ten different books at once, each open to the required chapter or verse.[58]

While Gutenberg's invention revolutionized publishing and reading, it was not without its critics. In *De Laude Scriptorum* (1492)—literally, "In Praise of Scribes"—John Trithemius argued that "printed books will never be the equivalent of handwritten codices . . . the simple reason is that copying by hand involves more diligence and industry."[59] Trithemius noted—correctly—that the hand-copied books would last longer than those printed on paper. He also noted that scribes were more careful than printers were. However, these points aside, Trithemius was not a Luddite; in other documents it is clear that he used printed books. Rather, *De Laude Scriptorum* documents his sorrow at the passing of a way of life embodied by the monastic scriptorium. Trithemius, like Richard de Bury, viewed copying manuscripts as a spiritual labor:

> In no other business of the active life does the monk come closer to perfection than when caritas drives him to keep watch in the night copying the divine scriptures. . . . The devout monk enjoys four particular benefits from writing: the time that is precious is profitably spent; his understanding is enlightened as he writes; his heart within is kindled to devotion; and after this life he is rewarded with a unique prize.[60]

To illustrate his point, Trithemius tells the story of a monk who was such a passionate copyist that many years after they buried him, it was discovered that his three writing fingers had been miraculously preserved.[61]

Trithemius was not alone in his resistance to print. Some of the resistance was due to the quality of the hand-copied manuscript compared to the cheapness of the printed book. Thus, for example, in the late fifteenth century, Vespasiano da Bisticci, in his memoir of Duke Federigo of Urbino, observed that in the duke's library "all books were superlatively good and written with the pen; had there been one printed book, it would have been ashamed in such company."[62]

This resistance to printing presses illustrates an important theme: the perceived purity of an old technology over a new one. This has been a recurring theme in computer folklore as well. Some computer programmers speak of "neat" programming and "transparent" programming, or the idea of using tools that are "closest" to the machine's soul—for example, the Vi, Emacs and Pico text editors (used to create and edit files in UNIX). This often speaks of a sentimentality that is not limited to a need for fast and efficient ways to use computers. While many of us do not share this sentimentality because we have exclusively used programs like WordPerfect that place many layers of "user-friendly" interface between us and the machine, we also can be sentimental about the first word processing programs we used, like "WordStar." For programmers, the real divide is between people who use "high-level" means of speaking to a computer and those who work in "machine language." Thus, by analogy, Microsoft Word is looked upon as a printing press, whereas UNIX-based text and file editing programs are seen as handwriting.

Just as Trithemius and other scriptors mourned the passing of an era, so have contemporary computer nerds. Internet newsgroups like *Classic Macs* are heavy with sentimentalism for now obsolete computers. At no other time in history has there been such a fast recycle rate of goods, with the absurd result that we observe a mourning process every six months.

Then as now, there were arguments for employing both the old and new technologies. "Pico" is still on our top-ten list of usable programs; hand-copying, for reasons that went beyond luxury and style, was practiced after the adoption of the printing press. For example, Julius II, best remembered as Michelangelo's patron, while still a cardinal had a printed book hand-copied. The book in question was Appian's *Civil Wars* and the cardinal had a copy made in 1479 from an edition printed in 1472. The reasons for this apparent aberration, and for others like it during this period, are twofold. First, some people preferred the luxury of the handmade object over the utility of the mass-produced one. Second, and more important, hand-copying allowed one to get books that were not in print, and also to have specific texts that reflected one's particular needs assembled in one volume.[63] Our modern photocopied course packets reflect the same need for a specific and individualized collection of texts. The power of the Internet in this regard is its ability through hyperlinks to endlessly assemble "electronic codexes" for us. James J. O'Donnell, in his study of the transition from hand-copied to printed texts in the medieval period, extends this idea further by arguing that "we now praise electronic texts for their malleability in this way, forgetting sometimes that the relative stasis, not to say intransigence, of the printed book is the anomaly in the history of the written word, and that user-made anthologies are the norm."[64]

It is no coincidence that the surge of interest in books also spawned resistance. The earliest known call for press censorship was from Niccolo Perotti, a classical scholar who was upset with shoddy classical editions that were being printed in Rome. In 1471, Perotti wrote a letter to the pope asking for a system of prepublication censorship to be established to ensure that future editions were carefully edited. The first official Church censorship came in 1559 with the publication of the *Index Auctorum et Librorum Prohibitorum* ("Index of Forbidden Authors and Books"). The purpose of this index was to guide censors in their decisions on which publications to authorize and which to disallow. (Although printers no longer worked exclusively in monasteries, they were not free to publish books without official permission.)[65] This censorship is particularly interesting because it reflected an anxiety that went beyond ferreting out heresy or lewdness. It came about because the sudden surge in the sheer numbers of books and the ease by which they could be produced (compared to hand production) profoundly challenged existing methods of reading. This mistrust was not new; there is evidence of such mistrust with hand-copied texts as well. For example, Nicholas of Lyre, in his second prologue to the literal commentary on the Bible, was mistrustful of the limited hypertexting of the glossed manuscript page and complained: "They have chopped up the text into so many small parts, and brought forth so many concordant passages to suit their own purpose that to some degree they confuse both the mind and memory of the reader and distract it from understanding the literal meaning of the text."[66] Texts produced by other cultures—for example, the ancient cultures of Central America—were burned. Diego de Landa, bishop of Yucatan in the sixteenth century, justified the burning of books there by explaining that despite the fact that the books were beautiful, they were filled with superstitions and "falsehoods of the Devil." However, it is relatively easy to see how the multiplicity of texts reproduced quickly on printing presses created a crisis over interpretation. Walter Ong explains:

> Print situates words in space more relentlessly than writing ever did. . . . By and large, printed texts are far easier to read than manuscript texts. The effects of the greater legibility of print are massive. The greater legibility makes for rapid, silent

reading. Such reading in turn makes for a different relationship between the reader and the authorial voice in the text and calls for different styles of writing. . . . Manuscript culture is producer-oriented. . . . Print is consumer-oriented.[67]

The Church responded to the threat of increasing numbers of interpretations that could be applied to any given body of doctrine by preventing the publication of these conflicting interpretations.

O'Donnell has noted the relevance of this resistance to our current predicament with the Internet. If one looks "for the history of resistance to the new technology in that period, we can gain some advantage of perspective on controversies in our own time, when it is far from clear to many people that the revolution that is upon us will be a benign one."[68]

Before moving from the history of publishing to the development of computers, it is important to look at another resistance movement—that of the underground press—for how it has contributed to the publishing culture of the Internet. One of the more striking examples of the underground press are the revolutionary broadsides and pamphlets published during the eighteenth century in the American colonies. The British government suppressed many of the seminal works of the American Revolution, such as Thomas Paine's *Common Sense*, and systematically broke colonial presses and revoked printers' licenses. Despite this suppression, we can find examples of the power of technology and human inventiveness from this period. British presses were licensed until 1815, but licensing proved impossible to enforce when the printing technology changed from wooden presses to iron ones. Hundreds of wooden presses were literally dumped, found their way onto the market and were bought by so-called "radical" organizations. The wooden presses had a distinct advantage over their iron counterparts—they could be dismantled and moved quickly. Marc Demarest notes that the power of the underground press in Britain was indisputable by 1819. While a reputable upper-middle-class journal like *Blackwood's* might sell four thousand copies per issue, a radical and illegal working-class journal like *Black Dwarf* could sell roughly twelve thousand copies per issue.[69]

Samizdat, Russian for "self-publishing," refers to the more contemporary practice of distributing materials by way of underground channels. It originally referred to the underground distribution of banned books in the Soviet Union and was coined by dissidents after the old Russian revolutionary practice, from the days of the czarist censorship, of circulating uncensored material privately, usually in manuscript form.[70] *Samizdat* has been described as "not only the 'whispered grapevine,' but also a kind of human association and a service between friends."[71] By the early 1980s, within the Soviet Union and Soviet-bloc countries, *samizdat* was an underground institution represented by an extended network of literary groups and small workshops that produced their own editions. For many authors *samizdat* editions were literally the only way they could get their work published. In Hungary, when sociologist Miklós Haraszti's study of the state of the Hungarian working class was banned, *samizdat* editions were circulated. In Czechoslovakia, Josef Kroutvor recalls this network:

> In this way all sorts of people wrote at least something or copied the texts of their friends and colleagues on typewriters. Writing was a kind of cultural mania, in some cases leading to an almost uncontrollable urge to write. . . . The period of samizdat was not only one of writing and copying, but also of reading, the adventure of reading. In this way the whole of my generation harmed its eyesight a little, reading badly carbon-copied manuscripts and illicit photocopies.[72]

Another self-publishing venture that is worthy of note is the "'zine." These popular and often self-obsessed limited editions are descendents of the fan magazines or "fanzines" of the 1940s. However, Fred Wright argues that "in spirit they also hearken back to other, older self-publishing ventures of independent spirit and vitality such as American broadsides from Revolutionary days, Russian Samizdat material, Dada and other avant garde art and social movements' magazines."[73]

In the mid-1980s thousands of limited-edition photocopied 'zines were produced, often by bored temporary workers using company computers and photocopy machines. 'Zines were tracked by *Factsheet Five*, a 'zine that covered the 'zine scene. By 1995, *Factsheet Five*'s editor estimated that there were between twenty thousand and fifty thousand different 'zines. While many of these were in-your-face publications with titles like *Asian Girls Are Rad* and *Fat Girl*, others focused on personal obsessions, such as *Balloon Animals* and *European Trash Cinema*. With the advent of the Internet, many of the 'zines gravitated to the Web. One description of the 'zines reads as follows: "They were harbingers of the highly personalized culture that now thrives on the Internet; and the ease of creating and distributing World Wide Web home pages may eventually render the zine medium a nostalgic remnant of print culture."[74]

Development of Modern Computers

Howard Rheingold observed that "every desktop computer connected to the Internet is a printing press, broadcasting station, place of assembly, with world wide reach."[75] This suggests that the Internet and the Web, far from being solely the product of engineers and computer scientists, are deeply rooted in the history of publishing. One could argue that the Web in particular is a direct descendent of the printing press. However, in order to complete this historical sketch of the intellectual and cultural sources for the Internet, we must look at the development of computers and the way these machines shaped the Web.

Jay David Bolter explains that "the computer rewrites the history of writing by sending us back to reconsider nearly every aspect of earlier technologies."[76] Modern computers started out as machines created to solve complex mathematical problems. While the sixteenth century witnessed the revolution in printing, other developments were taking place that would advance the progress of technology in this period. In the first half of the fourteenth century, large mechanical clocks were placed in the towers of several large European cities. Determining time accurately is not only the antecedent to modern computers, it is also fundamental how society operates.[77] Early European clocks, like the one installed in the clock tower of Strasbourg Cathedral in the mid-fourteenth century, could be heard for miles and contributed to productivity and work.[78] However, the European clocks did more than "remember" time; they tracked it and measured it in new ways that had a dramatic impact on people's lives. The clocks did work that humans had done. This mechanization of timekeeping, coupled with the concept of time, created a revolution in concepts of space and the self. From this point forward, as machines were developed to do the work previously done by people, they often outstripped the simple expectations of their inventors.

These machines also spawned metaphors that described existing human activities. Thus, a clock came to be seen as a metaphor for the cycle of the day, as well as for the action of the heart or the span of a human life. However, machines also defined new kinds of human activities. The typewriter, invented in the nineteenth century, is a prime example of this. Mark Twain was the first American author to use a typewriter. In 1905, he recalled his initial experience working with the new machine: "Dictating autobiography to a typewriter is a new experience for me, but it goes very well, and is going to save time. . . . At the beginning . . . a type-machine was a curiosity. The person who owned one was a curiosity, too. But now it is the other way about: the person who doesn't own one is a curiosity."[79] What is interesting here is not just the novelty and then the assimilation of the typewriter, but also Twain's description of the typewriter not as a machine at which he is working, but rather as one to which he is "dictating." In the nineteenth century, "typewriter" referred to both the machine and the operator. (As we will see, "computer" also referred to a human calculator before it referred to the machines that took over this work.)

Richard Polt, scholar and avid collector of antique typewriters, argues that "there is a certain truth in this usage: when you type, your body becomes a typewriter. More precisely, you reinforce certain bodily habits that act symbiotically with the machine in order to carry out the activity of typing. A new activity thus opens up new, unpredictable possibilities for the human body."[80] This argument has also been put forth by David Stork, who works in the field of artificial intelligence, in an interesting parallel to computers. Stork argues that "before you have tools, the only device you have for getting things done is your own body. But with tools, you can go beyond that. Still, once you've built a tool, you're stuck with that particular tool. The idea of a universal computer is that you make a *universal* tool—a general purpose object—that you can program to do absolutely anything."[81]

In the hands of the people they were invented for, clocks and typewriters, along with many other mechanical inventions, became not only agents of social change, but also critical metaphors describing the workings of daily life. This assigning of machine metaphors to human life and interactions is described succinctly by Stork:

> The problems addressed by [Artificial Intelligence] are some of the most profound in all of science: How do we know the world? . . . How do we remember the past? How do we create new ideas? For centuries, mankind had noticed hearts in slaughtered animals; nevertheless, the heart's true function was a mystery until one could liken it to an artifact and conclude: a heart is like a pump. (Similarly, an eye is like a camera obscura, a nerve is like an electric wire. . . .) In the same way, we have known for centuries the brain that is responsible for thoughts and feelings, but we'll only truly understand the brain when our psychological and neurological knowledge is complemented by an artifact—a computer that behaves like a brain.[82]

The computer has always been a thinking man's machine, or put another way, a machine in the service of human thought. The first computers, in fact, were simple devices that served as aids in solving mathematical problems. The earliest computer was probably the slide rule. Counting devices such as the abacus could be cited as early computers, but the slide rule, developed in 1621 by William Oughtred, was the first analog computer (an analog computer produces an approximate or "analogous result.")[83] In 1642, Blaise Pascal (1623–1662) built a computer to help his father, a tax collector, with his computations. Pascal's machine, called a "pascaline," was essentially an adding machine.[84] In 1673, Baron Gottfried Wilhelm von Leibniz created the "Leibniz stepped wheel," the first mechanical multiplier.[85] Although mathematicians invented mechanical aids to speed up addition and multiplication, the direct ancestor of the computer program came out of the carpet industry. The first "program" was the Jacquard "punch card," invented in 1804 to control the warp threads on a carpet loom. The "punch card" had holes in it and could be mounted on a carpet loom, which would "read" the simple program to produce a particular weave.

These inventions were separate and as-yet-unrelated developments in the history of computers. This changed by the mid-nineteenth century—a period that marked the "true beginning of modern technology, when men embraced the machine as the heart of economic expansion."[86] By 1820, science and mathematics were quite complex and relied on long tables of calculations, produced by hand by people called "computers."[87]

The real beginnings of modern computers lie with the inventions of the British mathematician Charles Babbage and his partner, Ada Lovelace. Babbage was intrigued by the problem of finding a mechanical replacement for human "computers." He was frustrated by the many errors these "computers" produced and declared: "I wish to God these calculations had been performed by steam!"[88] Babbage proposed building a "Difference Engine" to mechanically figure out solutions to mathematical problems. His idea was for a machine that not only figured out the solutions to mathematical problems, but also printed out the results, thus eliminating most human error.[89]

He explained that his machine would work almost as fast as a manual computer, but would be more accurate and have far more endurance than any human. There was no limit to the number of differences the machine could handle; the bigger the task, the more it would outstrip the human computers. The significance of Babbage's proposed Difference Machine was that "it substituted a machine for the human brain in performing an intellectual process, which [was] one of the most revolutionary schemes ever to be devised by any human being."[90]

Babbage had an unlikely intellectual partner in Ada Lovelace, the daughter of the English poet Lord Byron. Lovelace met Babbage in 1833 and became a critical partner in the development of the "Analytical Engine," his next invention.[91] The Analytical Engine in design profoundly foreshadowed the modern computer—there was memory, a central processing unit (CPU) and punch cards for transmitting data back and forth. Lovelace, a gifted mathematician, was fascinated by the potential of Babbage's machine, and in 1843 she published her notes explaining the Analytical Engine. She understood the potential of Babbage's invention, declaring: "No one knows what power lies yet undeveloped in that wiry system of mine."[92] Her understanding of the machine made it possible for her to create instruction routines—or "programs"—that could be fed into the Analytical Engine. So significant was her work that Babbage in one letter called her the "Enchantress of Numbers." She is remembered as the first computer programmer, and in the 1980s, the U.S. Defense Department named a programming language ADA in her honor.[93]

The limitations on Babbage's design had more to do with the lack of technology to produce the machine than whether the machine would work. What Babbage designed outstripped both the materials and machining possible in the early nineteenth century. However, by the late nineteenth century, modern materials and new machining processes set the stage for the first working computers, which were developed as data processors.

By 1870, calculating the figures for the U.S. census had become a cumbersome task and the need for a solution to the problem of tabulating large columns of figures had become a critical one. In 1884, Herman Hollerith, working with Charles W. Seaton, the chief clerk of the census, developed the punch card tabulator by reinventing Jacquard's punch card as a way to simplify the census process.[94] By 1899, Hollerith's invention was used to process the U.S. census. This was the first time "a largely statistical problem was handled by machines."[95] In 1896, Hollerith formed the Tabulating Machine Company, the world's first computer company.[96] After a brief period as the Computing-Tabulating-Recording Company (CTR), in 1924 Hollerith's company became International Business Machines (IBM).[97]

Hollerith's machine and others like it became mainstays in companies where data was tabulated, and for a time it looked as if the function of computers would always be limited to calculating numbers. Until World War II, the only significant advance in computing was a serious attempt in 1930, by Vannevar Bush, to design a computer called a "differential analyzer." The differential analyzer would provide the foundation for wartime developments in computing.

The development of the modern computer was greatly spurred by World War II. The concentration of the research community and the huge resources of capital and manpower during the war formed the foundation of the postwar effort, which continued to receive governmental support. With this support, programming languages were developed, as was fundamental software that paved the way for the transformation of the computer from an electronic difference engine and giant calculator to a general-purpose analytical tool. However, the first digital computers built during the war were barely more than electric difference engines. Their purpose was primarily to perform huge calculations rapidly and accurately. The invention of the transistor in 1947 and the creation of the integrated circuit caused a major reorganization and redesign of the nascent industry. With transistors, the new computer became smaller, faster and more reliable and had much simpler requirements for power.

Babbage's design for the Analytical Engine did not incorporate the fundamental idea employed by modern computers—that programs, data and the internal workings of the machines should be carried out by the same form of data. Thus, for example, Babbage's machine was designed to work with programs that were stored on punch cards, while the actual calculations were "performed" by the mechanical wheels and cogs of the machine. Fundamental to Babbage's design was the "the rigid separation of instructions and data. . . . A hundred years later, . . . no-one had advanced on Babbage's principle. Builders of large calculators might put the program on a roll of punched paper rather than cards, but the idea was the same: machinery to do arithmetic, and instructions coded in some other form."[98]

To understand just how different this is from the way modern computers work, we need only understand that all software, our e-mail messages and Web pages are to the computer fundamentally no different from any other kind of data. Each is carried on a "data-stream" made up of a sequence of electronic on-or-off states. This is the fundamental idea behind the computer byte. A byte (as in "megabyte" or "2 gigabyte hardrive") is the smallest unit of computer information, made up of a sequence of eight "bits" represented by either a zero or a one. This eight-bit sequence is fundamental to most modern computer programs and functions. To get a sense of proportions involved here: a *megabyte*—as in the storage space on a floppy disk—is equal to literally 1,024,000 of

Figure 1.8. The ENIAC, "U.S. Army Photo." Courtesy of Mike Muuss at *http://ftp.arl.mil:80/~mike/comphist/*.

Figure 1.9. Two women wiring the right side of the ENIAC with a new program, "U.S. Army Photo." Courtesy of Mike Muuss at *http://ftp.arl.mil:80/~mike/comphist/*.

these bytes. This paragraph as a chunk of computer data saved in plain text (that is, with none of the extra coding that my word-processing package inserts) is made up of 950 bytes.

The scientists and engineers who built big electromechanical calculators in the 1930s and 1940s did not think of anything like this. Even when they turned to electronics, they still thought of programs as something quite different from numbers. In the United States, scientists built the first working differential analyzer that solved complex mathematical equations and provided critical solutions for ballistic firing tables. The ENIAC (Electronic Numerical Integrator and Computer), the world's first general-purpose electronic computer, was built at the Moore School at the University of Pennsylvania in 1943. It was an enormous machine that cost $486,804.22 to build and "took up 1800 square feet, was 100 feet long, 10 feet high, and 3 feet deep, and weighed 30 tons."[99] The ENIAC prompted one observer to declare that: "computers in the future may . . . weigh only 1½ tons."[100]

Designed to calculate the firing tables used to aim long-range guns, the ENIAC sped up the process that had previously been done by hand. Kay McNulty, one of a number of "computers" who did this work prior to the ENIAC, later recalled:

> We did have desk calculators at that time . . . that could do simple arithmetic. You'd do a multiplication and when the answer appeared, you had to write it down to reenter it into the machine to do the next calculation. We were preparing a firing table for each gun, with maybe 1,800 simple trajectories. To hand-compute just one of these trajectories took 30 or 40 hours of sitting at a desk with paper and a calculator. . . . My title working for the ballistics project was "computer." The idea was that I not only did arithmetic but also made the decision on what to do next.[101]

Many of the women who had done the figures by hand went to work "programming" the figures into the ENIAC.

Meanwhile, at Bletchley Park in Britain the development of modern computers took a different turn. While the ENIAC in the United States was designed to serve as a giant calculator, the Colossus, its British counterpart, was designed to break German secret codes. What spurred the development of Colossus in 1943 was the need (like that in the United States) for a machine that could work faster than its human operators. Alan Turing, a British mathematician who worked at Bletchley Park on the development of the code-

Figure 1.10. Alan Turing on a tape from the Turing Machine superimposed with a computer byte. Collage by Anne B. Keating.

breaking machines, became fascinated by the speed and reliability of machines in solving complex problems.

Turing, who is considered the father of modern computers, came to Bletchley Park with a foundation of ideas that made his interest in the code-breaking machines even more compelling. In the early 1930s, Turing began working on the theoretical problem of whether there was one principle by which all mathematical problems could be solved. He argued that in fact such a principle existed. The work at Bletchley Park supplied the machines on which this theory could be tested. For Turing, this theory could also be applied to the workings of the human brain. Turing argued that it was possible, if one assumed that the brain was capable "of finite number of possible states of mind," that a machine could be built to embody these states of mind. In fact, he spoke of "building a brain."[102]

In 1936, Turing had theorized that it was possible to build a machine that would work something like a typewriter, but would have the additional ability of reading symbols and being able to erase them as well. He theorized that a long tape could be fed into this machine that the machine would then "read." The tape would be divided into squares, with each square carrying a single symbol. The machine would "read" the tape one square at a time and perform a function based on what the tape "sent" in the way of instructions. (In effect, Turing had a vision of a computer program and the computer byte.)[103]

In 1945, Turing argued that computer programs should be stored in the same way as the data was. Turing had seen a proliferation of specialized machines doing different tasks. He believed that a universal machine could be designed that could switch from program to program and task to task—regardless of whether the task was solving a mathematical problem, playing a game or processing data. In the United States, by contrast, the ENIAC engineers also arrived at the idea of stored programs, but still only thought that computers were limited to performing massive mathematical calculations.

An American mathematician helped to pave the way for the development of the first programming languages. Grace Hopper—or "Amazing Grace," as she was often called—joined the Naval Reserve in 1943 and was assigned to work on the Navy's Mark I computer, designed like the ENIAC to do gunnery calculations. Hopper relished working on the Mark I: "I always loved a good gadget. When I met Mark I, it was the biggest fanciest gadget I'd ever seen. . . . It was 51 feet long, eight feet high, eight feet deep, and could perform three additions per second. . . . I had to find out how it worked."[104] After the war, she continued to work with computers. In the late 1940s, she went to work on the UNIVAC project, which led to the development of the UNIVAC I (Universal Auto Computer), the first commercial computer in the United States. By this time, Hopper had begun to believe that the major obstacle to computers in nonscientific and business applications was the scarcity of programmers for these far-from-user-friendly new machines. The key to opening up new worlds to computing, she knew, was the development and refinement of programming languages that could be understood and used by people who were neither mathematicians nor computer experts.

It took several years for her to demonstrate that this idea was feasible. Pursuing her belief that computer programs could be written in English, Hopper moved forward with the development a compiler for the UNIVAC computer that was built in 1950.[105] Using this compiler, Hopper and her staff were able to make the computer "understand" twenty statements in English and then recognize keywords in French and German. However, when she recommended that an entire programming language be developed using English words, she "was told very quickly that [she] couldn't do this because computers didn't understand English." It was three years before her idea was finally accepted.[106]

Turing's idea for a universal machine and Hopper's development of a programming language helped pave the way for the next significant development in computers, time-shared computers, which in turn led to the development of the Internet. These developments are covered in the next chapter. It is important to point out that in the period from roughly 1945 to the early 1960s computers were located in isolated computer centers and worked on by small groups of experts. Computers were so unusual and removed from mainstream culture that George Orwell in 1984 (1948) was able to write an effective futuristic scenario in which computers acted as watchers in the service of a totalitarian state. (The image of machinery controlling individuals predates computers and was used effectively by Fritz Lang in *Metropolis* [1926], with its dominant theme of people enslaved by machinery. In postwar science fiction films, computers played leading roles as dehumanizing machines in films from Jean-Luc Godard's *Alphaville* (1965) to Terry Gilliam's *Brazil* (1985), as well as in numerous low-budget B-grade films.) There was little sense in the postwar period that the evolutionary path of computers would deviate from the development of large, expensive and specialized mainframe computers. However, one man at the war's end envisioned a device that would link computers together as a means to disseminating information. In 1945, an essay titled "As We May Think" was published in the *Atlantic Monthly*. Written by Vannevar Bush, Harry S Truman's science advisor, this essay served as a conceptual blueprint for a small group of men who became the architects of the Internet. Their story and the computer network they built are the subject of the next chapter.

Research Links for Chapter 1

A cursory look at the endnotes reveals that many of our sources are available online. During the course of our research, we came across other sites that we want to bring to your attention. Even if your area of specialization or interest is not the ancient Middle East or antique machines, these sites are worth a look because they reveal both the depth and the creativity of online sources.

1. *The Perseus Project: An Evolving Digital Library on Ancient Greece* at *http://www.perseus.tufts.edu/* is a growing database that contains a vast array of information, including texts, lexicons, images and maps on ancient Greece.

2. *HyperHistory On-line* at *http://www.hyperhistory.com/online_n2/History_n2/a.html* presents three thousand years of world history with a combination of colorful graphics, lifelines, timelines and maps.

3. *WWW History of Telecommunications* at *http://www-stall.rz.fht-esslingen.de/telehistory/* offers a comprehensive summary of the history of telecommunications created by a team of communications engineering students at Fachhochschule für Technik Esslingen, Germany.

4. *The Early History of Data Networks* at *http://tmpwww.electrum.kth.se/docs/early_net/* is the Web version of a book about the optical telegraph by Gerard J. Holzmann and Björn Pehrson.

5. *The Telegraph Office—for Telegraph Key Collectors and Historians* at *http://fohnix.metronet.com/~nmcewen/ref.html* is a comprehensive site for collectors and telegraph historians. It contains annotated lists of many telegraph resources from Web sites to print resources.

6. *The Labyrinth: A World Wide Web Server for Medieval Studies* at *http://www.georgetown.edu/labyrinth/labyrinth-home.html* is widely considered the standard starting point for medieval studies on the Internet.

7. *The Library of Congress Vatican Exhibit* at *http://sunsite.unc.edu/expo/vatican.exhibit/exhibit/Main_Hall.html* presents approximately two hundred of the Vatican Library's manuscripts, books and maps, "many of which played a key role in the humanist recovery of the classical heritage of Greece and Rome. The exhibition presents the untold story of the Vatican Library as the intellectual driving force behind the emergence of Rome as a political and scholarly superpower during the Renaissance."[107]

8. *A Hundred Highlights from the Koninklijke Bibliotheek (The National Library of the Netherlands)* at *http://www.konbib.nl/100hoogte/hh-en.html* is the Web site that accompanies *A Hundred Highlights from the Koninklijke Bibliotheek,* published in 1994. It is a jewel of Web site design as well as a fascinating collection of a hundred of the finest examples of book culture in the

Netherlands. As the creators of this site acknowledge: "these objects, . . . except for temporary exhibitions, hardly ever leave their bookcases or cabinets because they are so extremely vulnerable. A most regrettable state of affairs, for what is the use of having such treasures if they can not be displayed and admired?"[108]

9. *The Classic Typewriter Page* at *http://xavier.xu.edu/~polt/typewriters.html* is the creation of Richard Polt, an assistant professor of philosophy at Xavier University and collector of antique typewriters. A rich and well-designed Web site on the history of typewriters.

10. *Charles Babbage Institute* at *http://www.cbi.umn.edu/* is a comprehensive source of scholarly information on the history of computing. The site is maintained by the Charles Babbage Institute Center for the History of Information Processing, a research and archival center at the University of Minnesota.

CHAPTER 2 | A Guide to the Geography of the Internet

BEFORE we get started on how the Internet works, it is important to understand that the different terms used to refer to this technology, including *Internet, cyberspace* and *online*, are not all interchangeable. The World Wide Web, e-mail and browsers are a part of the whole Internet package, but these terms describe different parts of a larger system. This proliferation of terms has led to confusion about the exact "geographic" layout of the Internet, leading one writer to describe it as "millions and millions of cars all being driven at top speed by people who barely understand road basics. Now, imagine them in a sprawling, mysterious city that has no apparent traffic regulations and street signs of only dubious meaning. Sound familiar? So you have visited New York . . . or been online."[1]

For the new user, even conversations about the Internet can be baffling. On the street, one can overhear scraps of conversations like "my ISP was down for three hours last night." Ads in magazines prominently display corporate Internet addresses. For example, TWA recently ran an advertisement solely promoting its Internet address: *http://www.twa.com.*

Despite its complexity, the Internet continues to attract new users. Even the queen of England "surfs the Web." In July 1997, the *Times of London* reported that:

> The Queen, after nearly a year of discreet practice with a home computer, has become a devotee of the Net. Coached by her husband, the Duke of Edinburgh, she has become a dab hand at surfing the global computer network and addressing a chosen few of her subjects by e-mail. . . . A Website about the monarchy has proved immensely popular. . . . The Queen . . . oversaw the site's design.[2]

On her fiftieth wedding anniversary in late 1997, the queen noted the highlights of her rule and observed: "What a remarkable fifty years they have been. . . . Think what we would have missed if we had never heard the Beatles or seen Margot Fonteyn dance: never have watched television, used a mobile telephone or surfed the Net (or, to be honest, listened to other people talking about surfing the Net)."[3]

Our daily language and even our social activities have begun to change in the wake of this technology. Characters have been resurrected with the new language of the Internet. For most of us the @ sign used to refer to something along the lines of "seven tomatoes @ five cents each"; now it is more likely that, along with a hastily scribbled phone number, a colleague or friend may also add something along the lines of *smith@anycollege.edu.* It seems clear that, like the recent introduction of the words *fax, video* and *beeper* into our day-to-day vocabularies, we are in the midst of another transformation in language that is incorporating the Internet into the way we communicate and conduct our daily lives. There is a barrage of new words and a general expectation that instead of being able to master one technology—a fax machine or word processor—we now must master a collection of technologies, from e-mail to the World Wide Web, in order to participate in this new world.

To alleviate some of this confusion, in this chapter we lay out the history of the Internet as a way to map this territory. As we discussed in chapter 1, by the end of World War II computers had evolved into number-crunching machines or giant calculators.[4] For much of the 1950s, these computers were used in "batch processing." Computer scientists who wanted to run a program had to stand in line, holding the program in a stack of punch cards until it was their turn to use the machine. Using the computer meant handing the stack of cards to an operator who fed them into the computer while the scientist settled in to wait until the program had run—a process that sometimes took a day or more. This process was frustrating for those who wanted to work more closely with the computer. The critical breakthrough of these years was the concept of time-sharing, one of the earliest precursors to computer networking. Fernando J. Corbató of MIT developed the first effective time-sharing system. In 1965, he explained the need for time-sharing:

As computers have matured during the last two decades from curiosities to calculating machines to information processors, access to them by users has not improved and in the case of most large machines has retrogressed. Principally for economic reasons, batch processing of computer jobs has been developed and is currently practiced by most large computer installations, and the concomitant isolation of the user from elementary cause-and-effect relationships has been either reluctantly endured or rationalized.[5]

Time-shared computers were the first interactive computers. Individuals working from different terminals could interact directly with the main computer. Time-sharing eliminated the lines and the need to run one program at a time. Time-shared computers could also be accessed from off-site terminals, much as we use electronic card catalogs today. Time-shared computers led directly to the development of a global computer network, which grew from a Department of Defense computer network in the late 1960s to the present-day World Wide Web.

Pioneers of the Internet

Five men stand out in the early history of the Internet for their ideas about interactive computing and a global collaborative network. Each saw the computer in terms of how it could both enhance the process of working with information and ease the process of information retrieval. Far from emphasizing the computer as a mathematical tool, these men envisioned it as a part of a vital scholarly network. This network would reduce the amount of clerical time involved in research and writing while providing intuitive and specific access to relevant materials from all the world's written and artistic material.

Emanuel Goldberg developed the prototype for such a system in 1927. In the 1920s, while working at Zeiss Ikon in Germany, Goldberg became intrigued by a problem posed by the use of microfilm. At this time, German businesses were actively transferring their records to microfilm. Indexing and retrieving records on the long spools of microfilm posed a significant challenge. Applying his knowledge of movie projector technology, Goldberg developed a "Statistical Machine" that could rapidly search through records.

Goldberg's machine was remarkable. It used an indexing scheme consisting of a series of opaque dots that were placed either alongside or beneath a microfilm record. A search card with a corresponding set of dots punched on it was mounted on a modified movie projector. The microfilm was then run through the projector. As the film scrolled by, light passing through the punched card focused into narrow beams that fell on the microfilm. As long as the holes on the card and the dots on the microfilm failed to line up, the light passed through the film, activating a low-voltage photocell that guaranteed that the film would continue advancing. Once the dots lined up, however, the beams of light were blocked and the current supplied by the photocell was cut off, stopping the projector and effectively displaying the desired record. Goldberg received patents for his machine and demonstrated it in 1931 before the Royal Photographic Society in London. In 1933, however, further work on the machine was interrupted when Goldberg was forced to leave Germany by the Nazis.[6]

In the late 1930s at MIT, Vannevar Bush developed a similar device called a "Microfilm Rapid Selector." When Bush applied for a patent, the examiner turned him down because his machine replicated Goldberg's concept for the "Statistical Machine." After World War II, inspired by the possibilities of the "Microfilm Rapid Selector," Bush wrote an article titled "As We May Think," which appeared in the *Atlantic Monthly* in 1945. Bush, who was now President Truman's science advisor, observed that a "growing mountain of research" was making it increasingly difficult to absorb information and that civilization might wipe itself out before it "learns to wield that record for [its] true good."[7] To counteract this glut of information, Bush proposed a device he called the "memex," by which people could assign numerical codes to microfilmed book passages, photographs and charts. He described the memex as a "device for individual use, which is a sort of mechanized private file and library . . . a device in which an individual stores all his books, records, and communications, and which is mechanized so that it may be consulted with exceeding speed and flexibility. It is an enlarged intimate supplement to his memory."[8] By pushing buttons and levers, a person working with a memex could instantly move from one text to related information contained in others. Bush argued that the memex could replicate the human mind's ability to create what he called a "web" of memory trails. Bush even predicted "a new profession of trail blazers, those who find delight in the task of establishing useful trails through the enormous mass of the common record."[9]

J. C. R. Licklider was closely involved with the development of the Internet from 1957 on. From 1957 to 1963, Licklider worked with Bolt, Beranek and Newman, the company that later successfully bid to build the computers for the first ARPANET connections. In 1960, he wrote the seminal paper "Man-Computer Symbiosis," inspiring the transformation in computer science that led to networking. He was recruited in 1962 to head the behavioral sciences division at the Advanced Research Projects Agency (ARPA) and lead the agency into computer research and into building ARPANET—the precursor to the Internet. In "Man-Computer Symbiosis," Licklider wrote that he spent the spring and summer of 1957 examining how he spent his time when he was "thinking" and concluded:

Throughout the period I examined . . . my "thinking" time was devoted mainly to activities that were essentially clerical or mechanical: searching, calculating . . . preparing the way for a decision or an insight. Moreover, my choices of what to attempt and what not to attempt were determined to an embarrassingly great extent by considerations of clerical feasibility, not intellectual capability.[10]

Licklider realized that a computer could perform many of these "essentially clerical" tasks. If a fast information storage and retrieval system were employed, the computer would be able to work in a symbiotic relationship with its operator. He argued that "the cooperative interaction would greatly improve the thinking process."[11]

Licklider went on to argue that by 1970 or 1975 "thinking centers" would exist that would function in many ways as libraries enhanced by computerized information storage and retrieval functions. Beyond these individual centers, he also envisioned "a network of such centers, connected to one another by wide-band communication lines and to individual users by leased-wire services." [12] In his vision of thinking centers, Licklider was off by about fifteen years. However, in his vision of a wide-area network, he was accurate to within a year—ARPANET, the first network, was launched in 1969.

One of the earliest written descriptions of "the social interactions that could be enabled through networking" is contained in a series of memos written by Licklider in the early 1960s. In 1963, Licklider addressed a memo to "Members and Affiliates of the Intergalactic Computer Network" in which he outlined his ideas about how computers could help researchers share information. He envisioned a day when communities of people with common interests would be able to discuss them online. In a series of memos, Licklider described what he called an "Intergalactic Network . . . through which everyone could quickly access data and programs from any site."[13] His concept clearly foreshadows the Internet.

Licklider's principle was to focus on the work of a creative group rather than on any specific hardware project. His idea of the creative group, however, went far beyond a small Ivy League brain trust. In his vision of an "Intergalactic Computer Network," such a "brain-trust" would be just one of many. He believed that only broad-based research could bring about significant progress in the field of computer sciences, and any such research required immediate access to a great deal of information, as well as timely and uninhibited communication. Being a behavioral psychologist, he argued: "If you are try-

Figure 2.1. Mainframe computer circa 1961. Console of the BRLESC-I mainframe computer (released March 1961), from the archives of the ARL Technical Library. "U.S. Army photo." Courtesy of Mike Muuss at *http://ftp.arl.mil:80/~mike/comphist/*.

Figure 2.2. The Engelbart Workstation circa 1964. Note the keyboard, monitor and mouse (the small dark box on the right). Image courtesy of the Bootstrap Institute and Christina Engelbart.

ing to find out where ideas come from, you don't want to isolate yourself from the areas that they come from."[14] In a 1968 essay, "The Computer as a Communication Device," Licklider began with the argument that "in a few years, men will be able to communicate more effectively through a machine than face to face."[15] He went on to explain:

> We have seen the beginnings of communication through a computer-communication among people at consoles located in the same room or on the same university campus or even at distantly separated laboratories of the same research and development organization. This kind of communication—through a single multiaccess computer with the aid of telephone lines—is beginning to foster cooperation and promote coherence more effectively than do present arrangements for sharing computer programs by exchanging magnetic tapes by messenger or mail.[16]

Douglas Engelbart of the Stanford Research Institute, best remembered as the inventor of the computer mouse, was also one of the early visionaries of the Internet. In 1962, he published "Augmenting Human Intellect: A Conceptual Framework," in which he, like Licklider, argued for the development of online libraries and for storing and retrieving documents electronically. Engelbart was influenced by Vannevar Bush, having read "As We May Think" while serving in the South Pacific during the war.[17] He was also influenced by Licklider's "Man-Computer Symbiosis." After completing his bachelor's degree in electrical engineering, Engelbart went to work as an electrical engineer at NACA Ames Laboratory (the forerunner of NASA). However, within a few years he became restless and started to think about how computers could be used to "solve the world's problems."[18] He recalled that while serving as a radar technician during the war, he had been fascinated by how information could be displayed on a screen and "began to envision people sitting in front of displays, 'flying around' in an information space where they could formulate and organize their ideas with incredible speed and flexibility."[19]

In "Augmenting Human Intellect: A Conceptual Framework" he laid out his argument for using computers as online tools for "improving the intellectual effectiveness of the individual human being."[20] Engelbart felt that the computer as a tool shows the "greatest immediate promise . . . when it can be harnessed for direct on-line assistance."[21] Echoing Licklider in "Man-Computer Symbiosis," Engelbart argued:

> In . . . a future working relationship between human problem-solver and computer . . . the capability of the computer for executing mathematical processes would be used

Figure 2.3. Computer-supported meeting, 1967. For this meeting of Engelbart's research sponsors—NASA, Air Force and ARPA—Engelbart and his engineers rigged up this meeting facility, including U-shaped table setup with CRT displays placed at the right height and angle. Each participant had a mouse for pointing. Engelbart could display his hypermedia agenda and briefing materials, as well as any documents in his lab's knowledge base. Image courtesy of the Bootstrap Institute and Christina Engelbart.

whenever it was needed. However, the computer has many other capabilities for manipulating and displaying information that can be of significant benefit to the human in nonmathematical processes of planning, organizing, studying, etc.[22]

This paper led him in 1963 to develop the technology he believed would be required to "augment human intellect." This work led to the development of the computer mouse in 1964 and a demonstration of an integrated system including a keyboard, keypad, mouse and windows at the Joint Computer Conference in San Francisco's Civic Center in 1968. In addition to the mouse and keyboard, Engelbart also demonstrated a word processor he had designed, as well as the first true working hypertext system and a system for remote collaborative work.

In the 1960s and 1970s, Engelbart and his lab worked on an elaborate hypermedia-network system called NLS (oNLine System). In the spring of 1967, it was announced that all the ARPA-sponsored computer research labs, including Engelbart's, would be networked to promote resource sharing. Engelbart saw this linking as an excellent vehicle for extending his online system in a wide-area collaboration. He also saw NLS as a natural to support an online directory of resources, so he proposed a Network Information Center. Since he had an early and active role in the formation of the ARPA community computer network, his computer lab site at Stanford Research Institute (SRI) was chosen as the second host on the network and literally became the first Internet site to be "logged onto."

Ted Nelson, who was influenced by Engelbart's work, is known for coining the terms *hypertext* and *hypermedia* in the mid-1960s.[23] However, his work as an Internet visionary stretches back to 1960, when, inspired in part by Vannevar Bush's essay, he envisioned a worldwide electronic database of interlinked artistic and literary works. Nelson came to computers from a humanities rather than a computing background. While a philosophy major at Swarthmore College, and encouraged by one of his professors, Nelson began studying systems for making and organizing notes. He went on to enroll in a master's program in sociology at Harvard. In 1960, while at Harvard, he enrolled in a computer course for the humanities. Early on in the course, he was struck by a vision. For his term project, he attempted to devise a text-handling system that would allow writers to revise, compare and undo their work easily (in effect, a system similar to our word processors). While thinking about this system, Nelson had a critical breakthrough: "It occur[ed] to me that the future of humanity is at the interactive computer screen, that the new writing and movies will be interactive and interlinked . . . and we need a world-wide network to deliver it."[24] In 1993, he recalled his excitement:

> As those weeks of fall 1960 passed, I tried to tell everyone my growing vision. It was obvious, unified and cosmic. We would not be reading from paper any more. The computer screen, with its instant access, would make paper distribution of text absurd. Best of all, no longer would we be stuck with linear text, but we could create whole new gardens of interconnected text and graphics for the user to explore! . . . Users would sit holding a light-pen to the screen, making choices, browsing, exploring, making decisions.[25]

Nelson coined the term *hypertext* to describe these connections in 1962. In an interview, he recalled that he was influenced by the vocabulary of mathematics, where the prefix *hyper-* means "extended and generalized."[26] Nelson described hypertext as "a combination of natural language text with the computer's capacity for interactive branching."[27]

Since the mid-1960s, Nelson has actively pursued his dream of a software framework called "Xanadu," which will serve as an information system resembling the thought processes of the creative mind, free of the constraints of files and documents and as fluid and intuitive as thinking itself. The metaphor of Coleridge's mythical Xanadu suggests for Nelson "the magical place of literary memory where nothing is forgotten."[28]

Nelson's vision of a worldwide database of interactive literary and artistic works to be delivered on demand and free of copyright restrictions is still in the works. His ideas, however, have been thought over by development teams from the 1960s on. In many ways, despite the fact that the infrastructure exists in the form of the Internet, the Xanadu system is still too sophisticated to implement. Nelson's system requires nothing less than the conversion of all the world's arts and literature into electronic form, as well as a more organic and fluid method of "linking" than we have now. (Currently, "links" on the World Wide Web are created by two mechanisms: the choices an individual Web author has made to include specific links in an online document and the filtering by "keyword" process produced by software agents in the service of online search engines.)

Someday, on the Xanadu network, a single document will have endless hypertext or hypermedia links to other documents, video clips, photos and sound files. The purpose of Xanadu is to establish Nelson's vision of what he calls the "Docuverse," a global online library containing, in hypermedia format, all of humanity's literature. In "What Is Literature?" (1987), Nelson argued:

> Our design is suggested by the one working precedent that we know of: literature. . . . By the term "a literature" we are not necessarily talking about belles lettres. . . . We mean it in the same broad sense [as] . . . that graduate-school question, "Have you looked at the literature?" A literature is a system of interconnected writings. . . . These interconnections do not exist on paper except in rudimentary form, and we have tended not to be aware of them. We see individual documents but not the literature. . . . The way people read and write is based in large part on these interconnections. A person reads an article. He or she says to himself or herself, "Where have I seen something like that before?" . . . and the previous connection is brought mentally into play.[29]

ARPANET
While Licklider, Engelbart and Nelson were thinking about the ways the network could be used, elsewhere during the late 1950s and early 1960s engineers and computer scientists were trying to create the technology to connect the computers on a network. The Internet as we know it today was preceded by ARPANET, a military computer network that was based on the innovative idea of "packet switching." In the late 1960s, the U.S. Defense Advanced Research Projects Agency (DARPA) began a project to develop a wide-area computer network based on this technology. ARPANET was launched in 1969 and consisted of a wide-area network connecting four sites. The need for such a network became clear in 1957 when the Soviet Union launched Sputnik, the first man-made satellite. The U.S. military was concerned that the Soviet technology capable of launching Sputnik could be adapted to launch a nuclear warhead at the United States. ARPA was formed to develop science and technology applicable to the military.

In the late 1950s, scientists and military analysts faced a serious problem. In the event of a nuclear disaster, command-and-control systems would be disabled if entire areas were destroyed. The command-and-control network depended on a centralized system with dependent hubs in cities and on military bases spread out across the United States. If a hub or the system center went down, the remaining hubs would either be out of action or have to be rerouted around the destroyed hub and relinked to central command. There was no way to shield the switches and wiring of these information hubs effectively in the event of a nuclear disaster or to automatically switch over in the event of a crisis, even if hubs were operational and physically unaffected by the crisis.

Figure 2.4. Centralized, decentralized and distributed networks, from Baran, "Introduction to Distributed Communications Network" (August 1964). Image courtesy of the Rand Corporation.

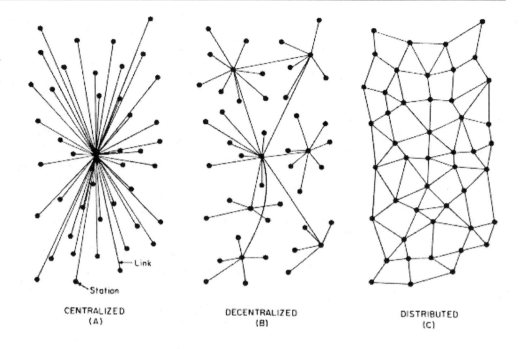

CENTRALIZED
(A)

DECENTRALIZED
(B)

DISTRIBUTED
(C)

An alternative was to break up the hubs and create a decentralized system with numerous critical command clusters. If one cluster went down, communications could be routed around the damaged cluster by way of the remaining hubs. (This is in fact how long-distance calling works today.) However, in the event of a nuclear diaster, even a decentralized network was open to catastrophic destruction, or at the very least, the loss of vital pieces of information. What was needed was a way to ensure that information would get through regardless of the condition of the network. The solution lay in distributed networks where no node or cluster would be more important than the next. The trick to such a network lay in splitting messages up into individual chunks of information—called packets—that would be sent out over a network that in design resembled a fishnet. These packets would travel through any strand of this net and be reassembled at the destination.

This solution was proposed simultaneously by Leonard Kleinrock of MIT, Paul Baran of Rand and Donald Davies of the British Particle Physics Laboratory, three researchers working without knowledge of each other's work in the early 1960s. Baran's work is significant because he saw that computers would play a critical role in the construction of this bomb-proof network. The Rand Corporation, one of the foremost Cold War think tanks, began research in distributed communication networks in 1962. In a proposal made public in 1964, Baran, who worked in the computer science division at Rand, proposed that the command-and-control system should "have no central authority" and should be "designed from the beginning to operate while in tatters."[30] Baran was the first to pose a solution on a theoretical basis, and he was "unquestionably the first to see that the way to solve it was by applying digital computer technology."[31] Baran was interested in how the brain worked, particularly its neural structures: "It struck him as significant that brain functions didn't rely on a single, unique, dedicated set of cells. This is why damaged cells can be bypassed as neural nets re-create themselves over new pathways in the brain."[32] In his proposal, Baran argued:

> In communications, as in transportation, it is more economical for many users to share a common resource rather than each to build his own system—particularly when supplying intermittent or occasional service. This intermittency of service is highly characteristic of digital communication requirements. Therefore, we would like to consider the interconnection, one day, of many all-digital links to provide a resource optimized for the handling of data for many potential intermittent users—a new common-user system.[33]

Baran explained that the system would depend on a packet-switching process analogous to the job of a postal carrier. Unlike point-to-point networks, the packet-switching networks would have multiple paths to get information from one point to another. "The switching process in any store-and-forward system is analogous to a postman sorting mail. A postman sits at each switching node. Messages arrive simultaneously from all links. . . . With proper status information, the postman is able to determine the best direction to send out any letters."[34] This analogy is the basis for the design of the Internet.

After winning support from Rand, Baran failed to convince AT&T, who held the monopoly on telephone services, that it was feasible to implement packet-switching over phone lines. AT&T officials were convinced that Baran did not know the first thing about

Figure 2.5. All digital network composed of a mixture of links, from Baran, "Introduction to Distributed Communications Network" (August 1964). Image courtesy of the Rand Corporation.

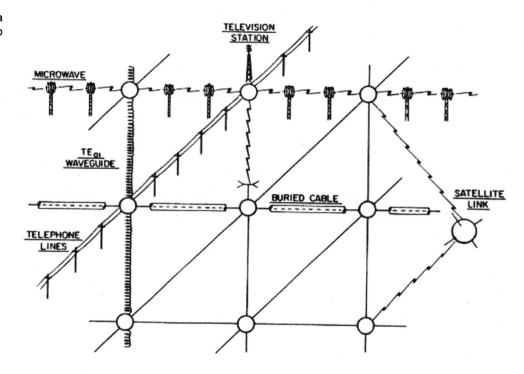

telephone lines and systems: "The idea of slicing data into message blocks and sending each block out to find its way through a matrix of phone lines struck AT&T staff members as preposterous."[35] Rand then approached the Air Force, which decided to go ahead and build the network without AT&T. However, the Pentagon intervened and decided to have the Defense Communications Agency (DCA) build the network. Baran was not impressed by the DCA, which was staffed by people whom he knew both had little or no background in digital technology and were about as enthusiastic about the project as AT&T was.[36] Baran decided to wait. Another agency and another group went on to build the network Baran envisioned.[37]

In 1965, the Defense Advanced Research Projects Agency (DARPA) sponsored

Figure 2.6.
"HAL9000" computer from Stanley Kubrick's film *2001: A Space Odyssey*. From HAL 9000 computer game by Nigel C. Eastmond. Image courtesy of Nigel C. Eastmond, University of Liverpool.

research into packet-switching computer networks, and in particular a cooperative network of time-shared computers. Lawrence Roberts remembers going to DARPA in the mid-1960s for research funds: "Bear in mind we're only talking about enough money to connect two computers over a dial-up line at 4.8 kbit/s."[38] (By comparison, as of January 1998 there were approximately thirty million computers connected to the Internet and average dial-up lines operating at 28.8 or 28,800 kbit/s [kilobytes per second] or greater.)[39] In the mid-1960s, only computers of the same kind could be connected to each other. Thus, "IBM mainframes could only connect to other IBM mainframes, Burroughs connected only to Burroughs, General Electric to General Electric, etc."[40] (Today we are more familiar with the discrepancy between Macintosh computers and IBM compatibles—however, a Dell computer can connect with a Hewlett-Packard computer, etc.) In the 1960s, the U.S. Defense Department wanted to develop a network that would connect computers, no matter what brand they were. To this end, the Defense Department commissioned ARPANET, which was launched the same year as the moon landing and a year after Stanley Kubrick's *2001: A Space Odyssey* was released.

It is interesting that the first steps toward the Internet coincided with the creation of a movie character that personified both the public's fears of and its perceptions about computers. Computers were seen as science fiction—mysterious machines waited on by a set of computer science priests and graduate student acolytes. With HAL 9000, the mainframe computer of the future, Arthur C. Clarke and Kubrick created a monster that in many ways resembled the one in Mary Shelley's *Frankenstein*. HAL served as a warning of the potential dehumanization of man through science. For many, HAL embodied the fear that computers would evolve into machines that would soon outstrip their masters.[41] This is a point that David Stork picks up on in an essay on the significance of HAL to his generation of computer scientists. "The fact that Frank takes his loss to HAL at chess without the slightest surprise reflects an attitude that is radically different from the public's perception in that decade when thoughts of a computer becoming world chess champion evoked anger and hostility."[42]

The Birth of the Internet   In the fall of 1969, after almost twelve years of research, what now is known as the Internet was born when a computer known as an Interface Message Processor (IMP)—a refrigerator-sized "network" computer at UCLA—linked up with a similar machine four hundred miles away at Douglas Engelbart's SRI lab at Stanford University.[43] The first

IMP was installed at UCLA on Labor Day weekend in 1969. The second arrived at Stanford a month later. The first communications over the ARPANET took place a few days after the SRI installation, when the host computer at UCLA logged onto the host computer at SRI, using a crude form of remote log-in. Leonard Kleinrock recalls:

> The procedure was to type "LOG" and the system at SRI was set up to be clever enough to add "IN." Charley and his counterpart at SRI had telephone headsets so they could talk. Charley typed in the "L" and asked SRI if they received it. "Got the L" came the voice reply. We typed in the "O," and they got it. Charley then typed in the "G" and the whole thing crashed! It was hilarious. On the second attempt, though, everything worked fine.[44]

By the end of the year, this expandable network became fully operational, linking four sites. After that, the ARAPNET grew dramatically. Within a year, the network included ten sites; by 1973, it was linked internationally. ARPANET was unveiled to the public in 1973. However, the term "Internet" would not be used to refer to this network until 1983.

Years later, Vinton Cerf, one of the architects of the Internet, recalled the early years of the ARPANET in a poem:

> *Like distant islands sundered by the sea,*
> *We had no sense of one community.*
> *We lived and worked apart and rarely knew*
> *That others searched with us for knowledge, too.*[45]

The early users of the ARPANET recall that from the beginning the "ARPANET and the Internet in the university research community promoted the academic tradition of open publication of ideas and results."[46] However, it was neither productive nor time-efficient to wait on traditional publication. What was needed was an informal exchange of working notes that everyone could contribute to as they worked on the ARPANET network. (Licklider's sense that only broad-based research could bring about significant progress applied here.) In April of 1969, the first step toward establishing this was taken by Steve Crocker of UCLA. Although the contents of the network working notes that Crocker introduced to the ARAPNET community may be arcane, it is interesting to note how immediately Crocker and others understood that the way to effectively communicate and rapidly disseminate information about the network was not through the formal mechanism of published observations and reports.

In April 1969, Crocker sent out the first of a series of working notes that he named "Requests for Comments"(RFCs). Initially the RFCs were distributed on paper and through the mail; later, they were available via FTP and now can be viewed on the World Wide Web, where they continue to be used today. In the first RFC, Crocker wrote: "I present here some of the tentative agreements reached and some of the open questions encountered. Very little of what is here is firm and reactions are expected."[47] Crocker elaborated on this further in RFC 3:

> The content of a NWG (Network Working Group) note may be any thought, suggestion, etc. related to the HOST software or other aspect of the network. Notes are encouraged to be timely rather than polished. Philosophical positions without examples or other specifics, specific suggestions or implementation techniques without introductory or background explication, and explicit questions without any attempted answers are all acceptable. The minimum length for a NWG note is one sentence.[48]

In a concept diametrically opposed to traditional scholarly interaction, Crocker encouraged spontaneity:

> These standards (or lack of them) are stated explicitly for two reasons. First, there is a tendency to view a written statement as ipso facto authoritative, and we hope to promote the exchange and discussion of considerably less than authoritative ideas. Second, there is a natural hesitancy to publish something unpolished, and we hope to ease this inhibition.[49]

January 1, 1983, marked the beginning of the Internet as we know it today. The Internet was not the beginning of a new network, but rather a change in the way the networked computers connected with each other. While ARPANET modeled the advantages of a packet-switched, decentralized network, it operated only when ARPANET machines communicated with other ARPANET machines.

The development of the Transmission Control Protocol/Internet Protocol (TCP/IP) in 1982 profoundly changed the way networked computers operated by providing a universal means of linking disparate computers. TCP/IP refers to the suite of communications protocols used to connect host computers on the Internet.[50] All communications between host computers require that the computers agree on the format of the data; the rules defining this format are called a protocol.[51] If you recall Baran's conception of packet-switching discussed earlier in this chapter, then you will remember that he used the analogy of a postman sending mail out over the network. TCP/IP can be understood using the same analogy. IP is "like the postal system. It allows you to address a package and drop it in the system, but there's no direct link between you and the recipient."[52] Combined with TCP, which allows two computers on the network to establish a connection and pass information back and forth, TCP/IP "establishes a connection between two hosts so that they can send messages back and forth for a period of time."[53]

TCP/IP was developed in 1982 by Vinton Cerf, popularly referred to as the "Father of the Internet," and Robert Kahn. After January 1, 1983, every machine connected to ARPANET had to use this protocol.[54] TCP/IP is literally the heart of the Internet. The remarkable thing about TCP/IP is that it works regardless of computer platform—Macintosh computers, PCs, UNIX workstations—TCP/IP connects them all.

In the early 1980s, inspired by ARPANET and especially by electronic mail, a number of research communities developed their own networks. Most of these networks were discipline specific and closed to the general public. These networks included, for example, MFENet, set up by the Department of Energy for its researchers in Magnetic Fusion Energy, which in turn sparked the creation of HEPNet, the Department of Energy's High Energy Physicists Network. NSA scientists worked on SPAN, and CSNET served the computer science community.

With the dissemination of UNIX came Usenet, based on UNIX's built-in UUCP communication protocols. In 1981, BITNET was created to link academic mainframe computers. The British JANET and the U.S. NSFNET, in 1984 and 1985, respectively, announced their intent to serve the entire higher education community, regardless of discipline. Indeed, a condition for a U.S. university to receive NSF funding for an Internet connection was that "the connection must be made available to ALL qualified users on campus." By 1985, the Internet consisted mainly of e-mail, Telnet, Usenet, FTP, and some other applications that allowed communication and file-sharing across the networks. At about this time, another development outside of the scientific community affected how people understood the Internet and defined it as a geographic space.

In 1984, science-fiction writer William Gibson coined the term *cyberspace* in his novel *Neuromancer* to describe the "matrix," an all encompassing computer network. Gibson was struck one day as he walked past a Vancouver video arcade by the way the players were hunched over the machines. He recalls: "I could see in the physical intensity of their postures how rapt these kids were. . . . You had this feedback loop, with photons coming off the screen into the kids' eyes . . . these kids clearly believed in the space these games projected."[55] Gibson defined this "cyberspace" as "the place where any telephone call takes place and we take that very much for granted. Otherwise I would say that when people use the Internet, that's when they're most obviously navigating in cyberspace. When you use the Internet you enter a realm in which geography no longer exists."[56] Today, when people talk about "cyberspace" they may be referring primarily to the World Wide Web and e-mail, but the term refers to the global network of interlinked computers that act as conduits for e-mail, Telnet, newsgroups, Internet Relay Chats (IRC), LISTSERV mailing lists, Usenet or newsgroups and Web pages.

In this book, we sometimes use the terms *Internet* and *World Wide Web* interchangeably, as is common practice. However, the Internet and the Web are in fact not the same thing. The World Wide Web is a smaller network of linked documents on the Internet that have been published using HTML and other Web-based mark-up languages and computer scripts. When people talk about the Web they are referring to a part of the Internet that serves up information published in this manner. Even though you will likely use these terms interchangeably, knowing the distinction between them will help you use the Internet and the Web for research, as well as talk to your students about the Internet.

Before the World Wide Web, the Internet was a diverse network that people navigated using a number of programs and tools—many of them oddly named and operated by using cryptic programming commands. Telnet, UNIX, FTP, e-mail, Usenet, LISTSERV, IRC, Archie, Gopher and Veronica were among the popular technologies of the Internet. Today, most of these appear to have been supplanted by the Web and browser-based programs such as Netscape and Internet Explorer. However, many of these programs are still widely used in their original form, and several, like FTP and Telnet, are critical to how information is accessed and moved on the World Wide Web.

While most Web users will not deal directly with UNIX, it remains the operating system for the Internet, now largely masked by the graphical Web browsers. E-mail has evolved to a point that a graphical interface and intuitive navigation have also hidden its UNIX foundations. Usenet, LISTSERV and IRC, while appearing to have been supplanted by the Web, are still extraordinary repositories of information of special interest to academics. Archie, Gopher and Veronica, while appearing to have been supplanted by search engines, still routinely reach into parts of the Internet that are filled with academic resources and into information repositories that have not been rewritten in HTML for the Web.

2.1 Components and Tools of the Internet

To help you understand these different components of the Internet, the sections that follow define the essential components and tools of the Internet.

2.1.1 UNIX

UNIX is to the network of interlinked computers what DOS is to personal computers. In short, UNIX is an operating system—a software program that controls the basic way the computer operates and directs the interactions between applications and hardware. UNIX is the only operating system to operate on supercomputers and desktop computers, PCs and Macs. In other words, UNIX is a multiplatform operating system that allows users to transfer files on one kind of computer to a completely different kind of computer, provided both are running UNIX. Since much of the World Wide Web is hosted on UNIX machines, the popularity of this operating system surged in the early 1990s.

During the 1960s, General Electric, MIT and Bell Labs worked on a time-sharing operating system called MULTICS. However, MULTICS grew too big and bulky, and in 1969, Ken Thompson of AT&T Bell Laboratories developed a single-user system called UNICS, which stood for "Uniplexed Operating and Computing System." Although the operating system has changed, the name stuck and was eventually shortened to UNIX.

For the first ten years, UNIX development was essentially confined to Bell Labs, though Bell did begin to offer UNICS to universities for a small fee in 1974.[57] In 1979, while on sabbatical from Bell Labs, Thompson worked with Bill Joy at the University of California at Berkeley and produced a new version of UNIX called "Berkeley UNIX" or BSD (Berkeley Software Distribution). From BSD came the "vi" editor, C shell, virtual memory, Sendmail and support for TCP/IP. These were critical to UNIX's eventual central role on the Internet. UNIX made networking capability part of a computer's operating system, and it was thus ideal for such things as e-mail and connecting to the Internet. UNIX was given free of charge to universities in the days when AT&T was still a regulated monopoly prohibited from competing in the computer market. Never market-driven, UNIX was distributed along with the source code so that programmers could tinker with the operating system and add enhancements. Since it was so widely available on campus, UNIX became the operating system of choice for teaching computer science.[58]

2.1.2 TELNET

Telnet, an application that lets you log on to a UNIX computer, is the main Internet protocol for creating a connection with a remote machine. Developed in 1972, it is one of the oldest Internet protocols. Telnet has been described as the "phone" of the Internet: "If you want to call someone, you need a phone. Telnet acts as the phone when you are ready to dial the Internet. It will let you log into other computers."[59] It allows a user to be on one computer system and do work on another, which may be across the street or thou-

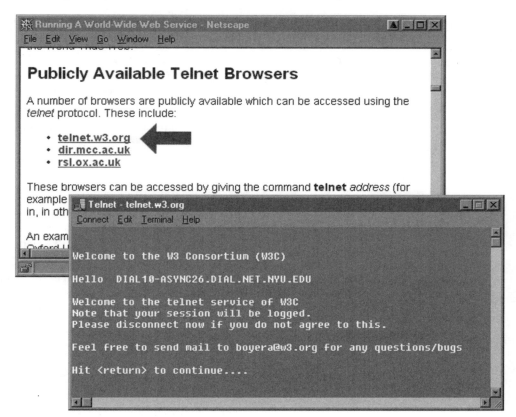

Figure 2.7. Opening up a Telnet session while connected to the World Wide Web. By clicking on the link in the Web page, a Telnet session is activated. Note the differences between the Web page and the black-and-white Telnet environment.

sands of miles away. Although Web browsers such as Netscape and e-mail programs such as Eudora now serve as the sole gateway for many Internet users, Telnet provides another way to access the Internet. Before PPP/SLIP software (a modern dial-up protocol like TCP/IP) created the interface necessary for graphical Web browsers such as Mosaic and Netscape, Telnet was how everyone accessed the Internet.

Before connecting to another computer on the Internet, you must install a Telnet client (software that runs a Telnet session) on your computer. You will also need the remote computer's Telnet address. Once you have connected to the remote computer, you may be prompted to choose a terminal type. Most of the time, choosing VT100 should be fine. Some computers will let you log on as a guest, while others require you to have an account. A Telnet link on a Web page will look like a normal hypertext link, but instead of connecting with another document on the Web, you will leave your Web browser and connect with another computer through the Telnet client. In order to make a Telnet connection, you must have Telnet capability. Most Internet connections have this capability. However, some SLIP and PPP commercial accounts do not include Telnet capability—though you may be able to pay extra for this service. If you are not sure whether you have Telnet options, contact your service provider or system administrator.

2.1.3 FTP Developed in 1972, FTP, or "file transfer protocol," allows users to upload and download computer files from the network. FTP is a quick, easy and error-free way of sending and receiving programs and data over the Internet. It was created to help scientists share data and utilities to further their research. Today, one can find millions of software programs at various anonymous FTP locations, or "sites," as most people call them. They are "anonymous" because anyone with a networked computer and the proper software can use them. As long as a program "speaks" FTP, it can send a copy of a file from one computer to another, receive files, and even rename and delete files on a remote computer (if the user has permission to do so). FTP was designed to allow users to copy files from remote computers, and most software and large text files are still moved across the Internet using FTP, although Web browsers hide it inside a graphical interface. FTP is the conduit through which Web pages are "published" or sent up to the World Wide Web.

2.1.4 E-MAIL In 1971, Ray Tomlinson, a scientist from Massachusetts, invented electronic mail—or "e-mail," as we know it today—to enable researchers to quickly send messages and ideas to other scientists on the ARPANET. In 1971, Tomlinson sent himself an e-mail between two computers in his office. He used the @ symbol to separate a user's name from the machine where the user can be found, a convention still used today.

Ian Hardy notes that "Tomlinson's email application was the first attempt to use the ARPANET as a medium for human communication."[60] The great popularity of electronic mail was a surprising development to ARPANET researchers. Hardy explains:

> Network email, a utility for human communication, never factored into early ARPANET plans. Its creation in 1971 proved completely unanticipated. After email's debut, however, the perceived function of the ARPANET shifted to encompass human communication. ARPANET email garnered stunning popularity and in the process changed the definition of what computer networks were good for.[61]

Analyzing the reasons for this unanticipated benefit from their ARPANET research, Licklider and Albert Vezza wrote: "By the fall of 1973, the great effectiveness and convenience of such fast, informed message services . . . had been discovered by almost everyone who had worked on the development of the ARPANET."[62] They noted that among the advantages of this new system were its speed and informality:

> In an ARPANET message, one could write tersely and type imperfectly, even to an older person in a superior position . . . and the recipient took no offense. The formality and perfection that most people expect in a typed letter did not become associated with network messages, probably because the network was so much faster, so much more like the telephone. . . . Among the advantages of the network message services over the telephone were the fact that one could proceed immediately to the point without having to engage in small talk first, that the message services produced a preservable record, and that the sender and receiver did not have to be available at the same time.[63]

Using an e-mail program, you can send text, or text with files attached, through your school's network or via an Internet service provider. E-mail is a cheap and fast way to correspond. Using e-mail was simplified by software known as Eudora, created by Steve Dorner in 1990 at the University of Illinois. Instead of logging on to a UNIX machine and reading mail online through a UNIX command-line interface such as "Pine," Eudora takes mail from the UNIX machine and saves it on your hard drive, allowing you to read your mail using only your computer. In an interesting aside, Eudora got its name while Dorner was writing the program. He became so immersed in the business of sending and receiving mail that he felt as if he was living at a post office, which reminded him of the short story "Why I Live at the P.O." by American author Eudora Welty.[64]

2.1.5 USENET AND NEWSGROUPS   Access to the ARPANET was originally limited to computer science researchers in universities and laboratories with U.S. Department of Defense contracts. A group of graduate students at Duke University and the University of North Carolina wanted to create a network that would be open to all those in the computer science community who had access to the UNIX operating system. In 1979, using a grassroots experimental approach to network development, these students launched Usenet News, which they nicknamed "a poor man's ARPANET." Stephen Daniel, who wrote part of the program, explains why they used this nickname:

> I don't remember when the phrase was coined, but to me it expressed exactly what was going on. We (or at least I) had little idea of what was really going on on the Arpanet, but we knew we were excluded. Even if we had been allowed to join, there was no way of coming up with the money. It was commonly accepted at the time that to join the Arpanet took political connections and $100,000 [though] I don't know if that assumption was true. . . . The "Poor man's Arpanet" was our way of joining the [computer science] community, and we made a deliberate attempt to extend it to other not-well-endowed members of the community.[65]

Usenet is a worldwide network of thousands of UNIX systems with a decentralized administration. Usenet enables people to post questions and share advice on more than twenty thousand special-interest discussion groups, better known as "newsgroups." Once an individual posts a message, several thousand people can view it. A regular poster to newsgroups has described them as "the town square of the Internet. . . . You can log onto newsgroups from anywhere that there is an Internet connection and can find a range of topics that span numerous fields of interest."[66] Newsgroups are organized by subject into eight major hierarchies or "trees." These include *comp,* or computer science; *news,* or Usenet information; *rec,* or hobbies, sports and recreation; *sci,* or scientific research; *soc,* or social issues; *talk,* or discussions on controversial topics; humanities, or literature, fine arts and other humanities; and *misc,* a catchall category. Each subject hierarchy is further broken down into more specific subcategories. There are also hundreds of *alt* or alternative hierarchies that are very similar to Usenet groups, but are not officially part of Usenet.

2.1.6 LISTSERV MAILING LISTS

LISTSERV mailing lists use the Internet to generate ongoing e-mail discussions on thousands of subjects and are similar to Usenet newsgroups. With Tomlinson's development of e-mail, it was not long before e-mail mailing lists were invented as "an ARPANET broadcasting technique in which an identical message could be sent automatically to large numbers of network subscribers."[67] The LISTSERV became an extension of this mailing list, and in 1986, Eric Thomas of BITNET, the main academic network of the time (ARPANET remained primarily a defense network), developed a program that allowed BITNET to run mailing lists on its mainframe computer. The program was developed by BITNIC, the Network Information Center at BITNET, and resided in an account called LISTSERV. One early subscriber recalls: "To join a mailing list, you would write to INFO@BITNIC (which, in spite of what the name might suggest nowadays, was a human being) and ask to be added to the list. . . . The BITNIC mailing list service became known as LISTSERV@BITNIC—the address from which all the mailing list messages were sent to subscribers."[68] The popularity of LISTSERV can be seen in the fact that by December 1997 there were 71,574 different lists with a total membership of 20,834,863 Internet users.

Unlike newsgroups, LISTSERV discussions are delivered by e-mail and can be responded to by hitting the "reply" button, which sends the message to everyone on the mailing list. Long a staple of academic Internet culture, LISTSERV mailing lists are often overlooked by new users of the Internet. As an example of the scale of academic LISTSERV mailing lists, H-Net (*http://h-net2.msu.edu/*), founded in 1992 as a history list, grew from one list and approximately a hundred members to more than fifty lists and thirty thousand individual subscribers by 1996. H-Net has grown so large that, as David Burrell notes in a 1996 essay on H-Net, "the 'H-' in 'H-Net' which used to represent 'History' is now taken as representative of all 'Humanities.'"[69] By 1997, H-Net was one of the largest organizations in the American Council of Learned Societies. Burrell argues that "this rapid growth suggests both the power of the medium and the preexisting desire among academics for its services. That is, the technology has not created a need, but is responding to it."[70] What LISTSERV mailing lists were responding to was the need for scholars to communicate with each other on a more immediate basis than that offered by juried journals and crowded conferences, which guarantee that only a minority of academics are heard. Burrell argues that this immediacy: "allows fruitful reaction and interaction in a culture of debate. Print journals take months to talk out. . . . Perhaps this is partly why an ethic of non-debate tends to reign in academic circles. . . . LISTSERV mailing lists, however, can transform that ethic."[71]

2.1.7 INTERNET RELAY CHAT (IRC)   IRC stands for Internet Relay Chat and has been described as "the CB radio of the Internet."[72] It was developed by Jarkko Oikarinen, a systems administrator at the University of Oulu, Finland, who set up the first IRC server, *tolsun.oulu.fi*, in August 1988.[73]

Chats occur in real time as people type messages to each other via a chat interface or "client." The typed comments appear onscreen for all to see. Some chats are moderated and some are free-for-alls. Because of time lags, chats can be a bit chaotic. Messages appear in the order that they are received, which may not be the order in which they make sense as conversation. In addition, if a number of people are online simultaneously, the conversation can begin to resemble a number of people in a small room all talking at the same time. If you are coming from America Online or Prodigy, you may already be familiar with "chat rooms." In IRC these are not called "rooms," but rather "Channels," with each Channel designated by a # or & in front of its name.

Although many computer users dismiss chat as simply a conduit for mindless chatter, IRC has served some important functions over the years. Logs of IRC chats are available on the Web and should prove rich research material for scholars. A sampling of the logs available includes logs for IRC chats from the 1991 Gulf War, the attempted August 1991 coup in Russia, the 1992 U.S. presidential election, the 1994 California earthquake and the October 1993 revolt in Russia. One observer has noted that "IRC . . . is mostly just people talking. It's the primary real-time activity on the Internet. Web pages may be weeks or months old, usenet posts might be days old, mailing-list messages might be hours old, but IRC happens right now. If you've seen someone using 'the Internet' on TV or in a movie, they were probably using IRC—it's the only thing on the Internet that really moves."[74]

In January 1991, IRC made a big splash for the first time during the Gulf War when it was the only source of information in Europe for four hours after the March 17 bombing of Haifa. International users relayed information they heard from local media while Israelis described what they were experiencing firsthand. Users in Israel remained online while donning gas masks, telling of air raid sirens, local news reports, and their growing apprehension. Many had terminals in their sealed rooms and continued typing throughout the crisis.

Figure 2.8. Bombing of Israel—IRC log. Archived at *http://sunsite.unc.edu/pub/academic/communications/logs/Gulf-War/Tel-Aviv-tidbits.*

wildstar nbc says launch undectected... missile hit in tel aviv POSSIBLE.

WinterMut reporting a 'very large explosion' in tel aviv

<Ely:+report> ok, i must go. radio instruct to wear mask immed.

<Nati> Alarm here too !

<Nati> Instructed to wear mask

<LuxYacht> Jerusalem correspondent putting on gas mask

->*nati* some type of non emission launch.

<Mustang:+report> ap report ....3 missles exploed in tel aviv

manson how'd they get through without anyone knowing?

<LuxYacht> Jerusalem correspondent putting on gas mask

<Nati> I am with mask now. Waiting. Room is sealed

<Mustang:+report> god speed nati

---

sjm I understood Nati is in Haifa, Israel ?

<Nati> All Israelis present- please come to +report

<Nati> To all ppl that are concerned: I am OK.

<Python:+report> nati, do you have your gas mask on? what city are you in?

<Stalker:+report> CBS says Pentagon confirms 5 missiles launched against +israel.

<Mustang:+report> glad to hear, Nati

<Nati> This is Nathan Srebro from Mount Carmel, Haifa, Israel in a live war

<Ryman:+report> 6 missle launches into Tel Aviv

>confirmation of 6 missiles launches into israel

<Nati> I have my mask on and am in a sealed room with my familly

The attempted coup in Russia in August 1991 was reported in much greater detail, with news flowing in from Swedish and Finnish as well as English-language sources. The most outstanding event to be followed on IRC, however, was certainly the standoff between Russian President Boris Yeltsin and parliamentary rebels in October 1993. IRC users in central Moscow were able to pass along information even before the major news reporting agencies could broadcast it.

In the late 1980s, the proliferation of Internet sites and the amount of material available online led to the dramatic and almost overnight—in terms of computer development—distribution and adoption of the World Wide Web as the main venue for Internet-based materials. The late 1980s and early 1990s also witnessed the evolution of indexing schemes such as Archie, Gopher, Veronica and Jughead—predecessors of today's popular search engines. In the academic computing scene, these indexes preceded the adoption of the Web in 1993. It is important to point out that though it may seem like these indexing schemes have been eclipsed by the Web, they are still in use today.

2.1.8 ARCHIE, GOPHER, VERONICA AND JUGHEAD

Archie was the first tool designed to index information on the Internet. Archie searches FTP sites and collates the results into an electronic directory. The Archie client connects to an Archie server, which in turn checks all the FTP sites in its database for files specified by the user. Archie makes the task of finding a specific file on the Internet much easier. The service began as a project for students and volunteer staff at the McGill University School of Computer Science. It was created in 1990 by Peter Deutsch, Alan Emtage and Bill Wheelan, to catalogue the contents of FTP sites all over the world. As of August 22, 1996, sixty Archie servers in twenty countries "were tracking over 1500 Anonymous FTP and World Wide Web archive sites containing some 5,700,000 files throughout the Internet, with additional information being added daily."[75]

Since its creation, Archie has been expanded to include an index of World Wide Web directories as well. In an interesting aside, the Archie name was derived from a UNIX truncation of the word "archive" into "archie." However, subsequent developers of tools for searching Gopherspace picked up on Archie the comic book character and named their tools after other characters from the strip. The original value of Archie is best demonstrated when there are major public releases of software applications online. For example, it is easy to get bogged down trying to download the latest version of Netscape right after a release. FTP sites are often overwhelmed with downloads. This is where an Archie search will ferret out the alternative locations for the latest version of the software.

Figure 2.9. October 3, 1993: Parliamentary forces attack Ostankino TV and major's office—IRC log. Log excerpted in Charles A. Gimon, "IRC: The Net in Realtime." Archived at *http://www.skypoint.com/members/gimonca/irc2.html*.

<slipper> cnn intl just now confiming report here 5 mins ago that russ tv off line!

<Bravo> Ok, people, I'm typing summary of what I know for the moment

<ginster> thanks

<Bravo> Today, around 15:00, people who were'demonstrating' their feelings, broke the chain of militsiya around white-house (the people were those on the side of Khasbulatov and K)

<Bravo> A bit later, they formed military units, and at the same time another group of people joined them

<geek> It should be noted that Bravo is in the former Soviet Union right now.

<Bravo> Around 16:00 (sorry don't have exact times) group of people arond 3-4 thousand started to move in the direction of Moscow municipal building

<Bravo> In about the same time by a machine-gun fire from hotel Kosmonavt two militia,en were killed.

<Bravo> They were standing in the chain around wehite-house, WITHOUT any weapons

<Bravo> Later, mayor building was stormed by a military forces of khasbula-tovites, main entrance broken by trucks

[Local time at AAPO.IT.LUT.FI is 19:20 +02:00 Sun 3 Oct 1993/#report]

<Bravo> Currently, first 5 floors of mayor-building (what the damn is the right word for it?) are taken, guards and remaining people locked above

<geek> If anyone has a frequency to tune to fo

<Bravo> Just about recently a troop of special forces has

arrived to the building and blocked all entrances. _This_ troop is armed but no special actions are being currently taken

<geek> r Moscow radio on shortwave, please let Engine know.

<Bravo> NB : No, I'm not talking about the parliament building, it is bulding where the mayor and municipal things are, whatever its name is...

<Bravo> Oh yeah, city hall!

<Engine> I don't have my shortwave radio anymore.

<ginster> i have a sw radio - what is the freqency?

<Bravo> Ok, somewhere a bit later in taime they has taken the Ostankino teletower, so it is not talking anymore

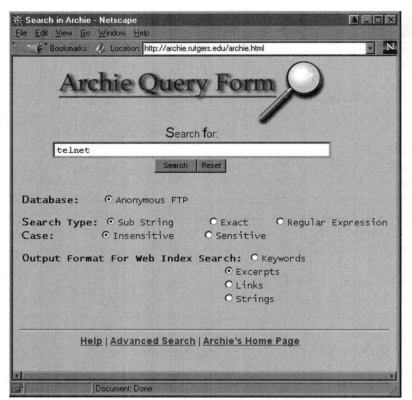

Figure 2.10. *(above)* Archie search page. Rutgers University Archie server at *http://archie.rutgers.edu/archie.html.* Figure 2.11. *(above right)* Gopher menu. Center for Computer Analysis of Texts at the University of Pennsylvania at *gopher://ccat.sas.upenn.edu:70/11/Archive.*

Gopher has been described as "the structure of information on Internet servers that preceded the World Wide Web."[76] When you access a server that uses the Gopher protocol, instead of Web pages you will see a hierarchically structured menu of viewable files. Gopher text files are plain files that lack the kinds of formatting control and font variation that HTML files have. Since many universities set up Gopher servers, you will find yourself working with these menus. Your Web browser can access these Gopher servers for you. However, you may find that your searches are enriched by using Veronica and Jughead, the two popular tools for searching "Gopherspace."[77] Gopher gets its name from the "golden Gophers" of the University of Minnesota, where the protocol was developed.

Like Archie, Veronica works to index the contents of all Gopher servers. "Veronica and Archie are perhaps of most use for serious researchers who have already tried the Web's main search engines first or who already know that the topic of their search is likely to be found on Gopher and FTP servers."[78] Jughead—for "Jonzy's Universal Gopher Hierarchy Excavation And Display"—is a subject-oriented search tool. Though similar to Veronica, Jughead is less sophisticated and can only search a small area of Gopherspace at a time. However, one user of Jughead recommends the tool because it is "faster for searching known Gopher sites or limited hierarchies."[79]

2.1.9 THE WORLD WIDE WEB

By 1980, students, computer science professors and other academics were the main users of the Internet. Ten years later, this state of affairs changed dramatically with the introduction of the World Wide Web. Within four years of its introduction, the World Wide Web eclipsed the Internet. Ben Segal notes that, "in the computer networking arena, a period of 10–15 years represents several generations of technology evolution." It is therefore surprising "that in a period of only three years there can be developments that radically change the whole way that people think about computer communications. This has just happened with the Web (prototyped in 1990–1, fully accepted over 1993–4)."[80]

Describing the critical difference between the Internet and the Web, one observer wrote: "the Web differs from the Internet, though it uses the Net as a highway. Explore the Internet and you find computers, routers and cables. Explore the Web and you find information."[81] The critical differences between the Internet and the World Wide Web are the use of "links" and the presence of graphics and text together. Web browsers in the 1990s hid the UNIX-based structure of the Internet under a layer of intuitive, graphically rich user interface. This is what permitted many people finally to use the Internet, much in the same way that the Windows operating system revolutionized personal computing for the noncomputer masses.

In 1979, Tim Berners-Lee, a British computer scientist working as a consultant at the Swiss particle physics laboratory (CERN) became frustrated with the inability of his computerized schedule planner to link between databases. His phone numbers were saved in one database, while his documents were stored in different databases. As a solution, he created a hypertext computer program called "Enquire-Within-Upon-Everything," which allowed "links to be made between arbitrary nodes."[82] Although never published, "Enquire" became the foundation for the development of the Web. In 1984, Berners-Lee accepted a fellowship at CERN to work on distributed real-time systems for the collecting and sorting of scientific data. During this period he began to expand on the ideas in Enquire and in 1989 proposed "a global hypertext project, to be known as the World Wide Web."[83] His main motivation for the project came from the fact that at CERN there was no easy way for his colleagues to access each other's notes and documents. Software and hardware incompatibilities made electronic collaboration almost impossible. He wanted to create a "global information space" that would be an electronic version of the coffee area where people at CERN gathered to exchange information and collaborate on projects.[84] In his proposal, he argued:

> The hope would be to allow a pool of information to develop which could grow and evolve with the organisation and the projects it describes. For this to be possible, the method of storage must not place its own restraints on the information. This is why a "Web" of notes with links (like references) between them is far more useful than a fixed hierarchical system. When describing a complex system, many people resort to diagrams with circles and arrows. Circles and arrows leave one free to describe the interrelationships between things in a way that tables, for example, do not. The system we need is like a diagram of circles and arrows, where circles and arrows can stand for anything. We can call the circles nodes, and the arrows links.[85]

We now call the circles "Web pages," while the arrows remain "links."
Berners-Lee went on to explain that

> several programs have been made exploring these ideas, both commercially and academically. Most of them use "hot spots' in documents, like icons, or highlighted phrases, as sensitive areas. Touching a hot spot with a mouse brings up the relevant information, or expands the text on the screen to include it. Imagine, then, the references in this document, all being associated with the network address of the thing to which they referred, so that while reading this document you could skip to them with a click of the mouse.[86]

In his personal notebook, Berners-Lee explored this idea further, articulating an indexing system as follows:

> Here are some of the many areas in which hypertext is used. Each area has its specific requirements in the way of features required.

- General reference data—encyclopaedia, etc.
- Completely centralized publishing—online help, documentation, tutorial, etc.
- More or less centralized dissemination of news which has a limited life
- Collaborative authoring
- Collaborative design of something other than the hypertext itself.[87]

He started work on this project in October 1990, and the program "WorldWideWeb" was first made available within CERN in December 1990 and on the Internet at large in the summer of 1991.[88]

Berners-Lee recalls that "there were three communities of users—the *alt.hypertext* Usenet newsgroup, Next [computer] users, and high-energy physicists. People started putting up servers, often writing their own software. This led to the development of various browsers."[89] Among the *alt.hypertext* users was a group of students at the University of Illinois. Led by Marc Andreessen, they took Berners-Lee's program and added graphics capability. Out of their experiments, they developed Mosaic in 1993. Mosaic turned Berners-Lee's text-based browser into the fully graphical Web browsers we are familiar with today. Andreessen went on to develop Netscape Navigator, one of the leading Web browsers today.

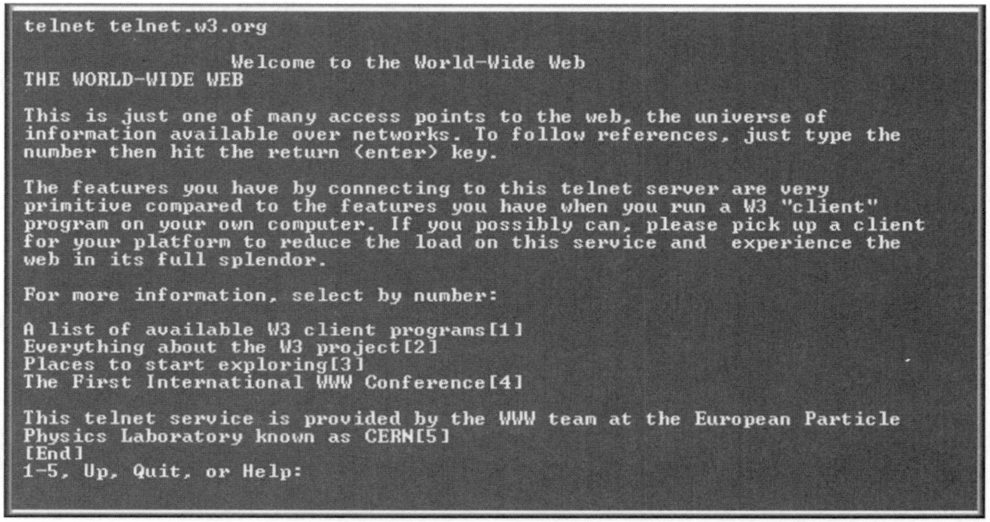

Figure 2.12. One of the first browsers to be developed was Tim Berners-Lee's CERN command-line browser. This example of the CERN command-line browser was re-created by Anne B. Keating.

```
telnet telnet.w3.org

                        Welcome to the World-Wide Web
THE WORLD-WIDE WEB

This is just one of many access points to the web, the universe of
information available over networks. To follow references, just type the
number then hit the return <enter> key.

The features you have by connecting to this telnet server are very
primitive compared to the features you have when you run a W3 "client"
program on your own computer. If you possibly can, please pick up a client
for your platform to reduce the load on this service and  experience the
web in its full splendor.

For more information, select by number:

A list of available W3 client programs[1]
Everything about the W3 project[2]
Places to start exploring[3]
The First International WWW Conference[4]

This telnet service is provided by the WWW team at the European Particle
Physics Laboratory known as CERN[5]
[End]
1-5, Up, Quit, or Help:
```

Mosaic was developed at the National Center for Supercomputing Applications (NCSA) at the University of Illinois Urbana-Champaign. It was the first public domain graphical Internet browser and turned the Internet into a place where a user could just point and click to retrieve information. This launched the rapid growth of Internet. For Andreessen, the lack of an easy-to-use graphically oriented interface for the Web was a critical omission. "There was this huge hole in the world . . . because a network existed with all these people hooked up to it, and the software was 10 years behind the hardware. This is typical of the personal computer industry today . . . perhaps because of people like me."[90] Andreessen argued that this was primarily due to the fact that programmers were daunted at the prospect of designing and building hardware. "Therefore the machines outstrip our capacity to use them."[91]

In the early 1990s, when Andreessen worked at the supercomputer center, he observed that

> Everyone at the center was hooked on the Internet, but there was this big disconnect between the 'Net and the rest of the world. You basically needed a Ph.D. in Unix to do anything. The Web existed then, but there were only 40 or 50 sites, and they were extremely hard to navigate. One of the other students, Eric Bina, and I were talking about this over lunch one day. We thought, wouldn't it be great if someone would sit down and write an interface that would make the Internet really easy to use?[92]

From the very beginning, Andreessen and Bina disagreed with Berners-Lee about the design for the Web interface:

> We thought making this interface graphical was the key. . . . Tim was looking for a way to connect a bunch of high-energy physicists, and he thought graphics were frivolous, unnecessary, and destructive. We didn't see it that way—we thought the information you see should be the interface. We wanted users to take over as much of the screen as possible and just put a navigational framework around that.[93]

They released the first beta version of Mosaic in March 1993. Andreessen recalls that, though initially there were only twelve users, "Within a few months we had 40,000 or 50,000. It was incredible. I graduated in December 1993 and . . . we started Netscape in April."[94]

The release of Mosaic marked the beginning of the widespread use of the Web. Within a few years, the Internet was transformed from a small, informal gathering place for tech-

Figure 2.13. An early NCSA Mosaic Web page, May 1993. One of the first virtual art exhibitions on the World Wide Web was the Library of Congress Vatican exhibition. This Web page is still active at *http://sunsite.unc.edu/expo/vatican.exhibit/ exhibit/Main_Hall.html.*

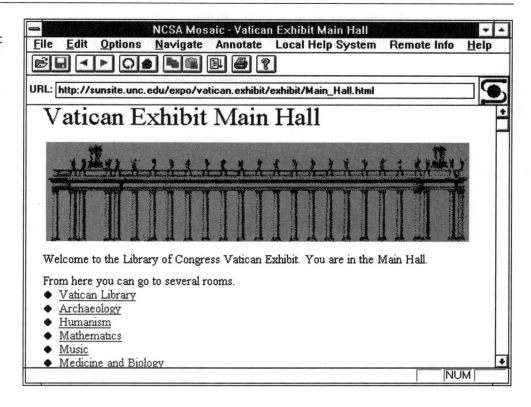

nically oriented users to a sprawling global gathering place for individuals who daily added to the wealth of information on the Web.

Research Links and Resources

1. In order to explore Telnet, you will need to get the Telnet program or "client." Telnet clients are available for free or as shareware from *Tucows* at *http://www.tucows.com* and *Shareware.com* at *http://www.shareware.com.*

2. To find libraries (and other resources) available via Telnet, look through the *Hytelnet database,* available online at *http://www.cam.ac.uk/Hytelnet/index.html.*

3. For available resources on Internet Relay Chat (IRC), see *IRC Central* at *http://www.connect-ed-media.com/IRC/.*

4. For general information on Internet chat, see David Barbieri's *Meta Chats: The Internet Chat Resource Guide* at *http://www.2meta.com/chats/*. Barbieri has a listing of historic IRC logs at *http://www.2meta.com/chats/university/*.

5. *Directory of Scholarly and Professional E-Conferences* at *http://n2h2.com/KOVACS/* is a database of academic listservs which can be searched by keyword, by subject or alphabetically by listserv name.

6. Usenet can be searched using any of the top search engines or by going to *Deja News* at *http://www.dejanews.com/*.

7. To search Usenet postings, use *Where is the archive for newsgroup X?* at *http://starbase.neosoft.com/~claird/news.lists/newsgroup_archives.html*.

8. *Liszt, the Mailing List Directory* at *http://www.liszt.com/*, another listing of newsgroups, "is basically a mailing-list spider; it queries servers from around the world and compiles the results into a single directory. This method ensures that the data Liszt provides is always up-to-date, since it comes direct from the list servers each week." Includes an education category.

9. *World Wide Web Consortium* at *http://www.w3.org*, directed by Tim Berners-Lee, is an open forum of companies and organizations with the mission of realizing the full potential of the Web. "Services provided by the Consortium include: a repository of information about the World Wide Web for developers and users; reference code implementations to embody and promote standards; and various prototype and sample applications to demonstrate use of new technology."[95]

10. *An Atlas of Cyberspaces* at *http://www.cybergeography.org/atlas/atlas.html* is an online atlas to the Internet and the Web. This collection of maps is a good way to visualize the "new digital landscapes on our computer screen and in the wires of the global communications networks."[96]

## CHAPTER 3

Online Research and Reflections on Building Course Web Pages

Critics who say that the potential of the Internet is over-hyped are either ignorant or arrogant (or both). The ability to have instantaneous access to almost any information you want, or to trawl for the cheapest air ticket, or study the Magna Carta in magnified form . . . is simply stunning. It will probably have more of an effect on more people and far more quickly than the discovery of electricity and the telephone.[1]

IN this chapter, we shift the focus from a general mapping of the geographic terrain inhabited by the Internet and World Wide Web to the twin aspects of many "wired professors'" lives: research and teaching. First, we focus on research on the World Wide Web. We then discuss the transformation that universities are undergoing as the Web is integrated into instructional technology. The remainder of the chapter presents a series of vignettes of a group of NYU instructors' initial experiences thinking about and posting course Web pages between 1995 and 1996.

3.1 Research on the Net

The other main gripe [is] information overload. This arises from the inability to find the right needle from the millions of electronic haystacks in Cyberspace. But there has always been too much information in the world to cope with; the Internet merely gives us a chance to get at it.[2]

For us, the discovery of the Internet and then the World Wide Web opened exciting possibilities for literally finding anything anywhere in the world on any subject and, best of all, at any time of the day or night. The Internet could satisfy our curiosity early in the morning over a cup of coffee or late in the evening long after the library was closed. We appreciated its speed as well. Traditional library research was a time-consuming and labor-intensive process—hours spent locating and then more hours spent sifting through multivolume indexes in the reference room. We would see leads and go away with slips of paper documenting possibilities only if our university library had the journal or volume, or if a distant research library was linked to ours by interlibrary loan. We still recall the steps in this process—locating possible sources and abstractly assessing these sources based on an abstract or review at best or a brief title at worst. Only after this stage would we actually get a chance to examine the content of the sources that made this cut. There were false leads and dead ends, and often the process of chasing leads went on for days without any solid information being retrieved. It was clear from the start that the Web was more a world of possibilities than of complete resources. However, we could see immediately that the fact that the research and retrieval process for information could be achieved within minutes rather than hours or days was a remarkable transformation of the traditional research process. While the research process on the Web still yields more than its share of false leads and dead ends, it has dramatically shortened the time it takes to retrieve information. In many instances, a research source can now be assessed on the merits of its content rather than on a review or abstract, or on the proximity of a library.

The computer's agility and speed amaze new users only briefly. We have witnessed friends make the transition from electric typewriters to personal computers, only to complain, within months, how slowly the computer boots up or loads a file. We have seen the same tendency with the Web as well. "It's a wonderful resource," our friends proclaim in the first flush of fascination with almost instantaneous information at their fingertips. But the glow wears off quickly, as they realize that the information they are seeking is not all out there, and that some of what they find was written by crackpots, which makes them doubt the accuracy of the information they found before. They are frustrated by the technology and the "intelligent agents" and "spiders" that work the Web to serve up the personalized results in search engines. This is especially true when the search engine serves up over a thousand hits on a subject, because all the words in the query are found somewhere in the documents retrieved, right down to the "a," "the" and so forth that were entered in the search string along with the keywords.

We have been amazed to see basic research skills honed from years of working with card catalogs go out the window when colleagues sit down in front of an Internet terminal. We have received blank looks when we mention the word "Boolean," as if we had just introduced some obtuse technical term into polite conversation. All of this has led us to ponder what it is about Web-based research that simultaneously amazes and annoys us. We have reached the following conclusion: to borrow from a currently popular television show, "the truth is out there," and in the case of the Internet, the information is out there if you know how to look.[3]

Search engines answer the critical question, "How do I find what I am looking for when there is so much information available on the Internet?" A search engine is a Web site that asks you what you are looking for and then points you to other sites that may be of interest. In most cases, you will get a list of Web pages containing a brief annotation of what you will find at each one. When you find one that looks promising, you click on the title and away you go. Of course, once you arrive at the site, you may find that it is not what you were looking for. In that case, you can either go back to the search engine to try again or scan the site for links to Web pages that are more promising.

Currently there are over a hundred search engines, and names like Yahoo, Alta Vista and Infoseek have become part of the Internet vocabulary. The first of these search engines was Archie, followed by Lycos.[4] Michael Mauldin, a computer science professor at Carnegie Mellon University in Pittsburgh, developed the latter search engine. Mauldin, who keeps a tarantula in his office, named his search engine Lycos for the wolf spider, which is known for both its mobility and its keen eyesight. Lycos, the computer spider, wanders over the World Wide Web searching for, then collecting and retrieving, all the information and material on the Internet.[5]

Online information retrieval dates back about twenty-five years to the launch of Lexis-Nexis, a commercial online database of legal information and news that could be accessed by dialing up a particular computer system. Other online databases soon began to spring up, some of which were publicly accessible through online services such as CompuServe. However, like Lexis-Nexis, these databases charged a basic commercial subscription fee of over a hundred dollars per month and were thus too expensive for many potential customers. In the early 1980s, the pre-Web Internet began to add another dimension to information retrieval. "We used the Internet before anyone knew there was an Internet," explains Barbara Quint, an independent information specialist. Initially, she said, the Internet's main value was in making it easier to contact experts at universities and making university archives more accessible.[6]

The reliability of information on the Web is a critical issue in Web-based research. A case in point that prompted a public forum on this topic was the controversy surrounding the information that was posted on the Web following the explosion of TWA Flight 800 over the Atlantic Ocean on July 17, 1996. As one reporter observed: "The first postings were speculation about the cause of the July 17, 1996, crash, but in the world of the Internet, where every viewpoint gets equal airing, the rumors took on an air of possibility, if not believability."[7] A 1997 poll revealed that "nearly half of Internet users doubt the reliability of the information acquired over the World-Wide Web. . . . Although familiarity with and usage of on-line services has increased steadily since 1994, an astounding number of consumers are not yet convinced of the accuracy of the information available."[8]

Kai Krause argues that librarians are poised to play an important role in sifting through online information.

> Validating the information available on the Internet is a critical task. Some librarians have created their own guides to databases on the Internet which meet their "Seal of Approval." Business Sources on the Net (BSN) is a good example of such a guide. Its conception grew out of the frustration of a group of academic business librarians with the vast number of business resources available on the Internet. Out of this frustration came an online bibliography of business information accessible at no cost on the Internet.[9]

Krause thinks that this process will follow traditional models for validating scholarly sources:

> Most librarians I spoke with about the problem of quality sources indicated comfort with information available from well established institutions and library services. I see this as equivalent to trusting the information found in a well-known reference book as opposed to one published by a small firm with no track record. It doesn't mean that the information in the latter is necessarily bad. It just means that reputation is an important indicator of quality on the Internet just as in print. Some of the most useful assistance in finding good sources of Internet information comes from listservs. They offer a good place to post queries when you're looking for a source or to read about good (or bad) Net sources. One librarian referred to them as "a godsend to the small library because so many experts are willing to share information, answer obscure reference questions, etc."[10]

Every major search engine includes a page explaining the different tricks and options that will help you to refine a search so that you do not receive back a listing of over a hundred thousand "hits" for your inquiry. There are search engine tricks that you should learn to help narrow your search, but every search engine uses different techniques. If you want to find how a certain search engine works, either visit that search engine's home page or stop by a Web site that specializes in search engine information.[11]

It is important to remember that there are two types of search engines: subject guides such as Yahoo, which permit you to limit your search to a specific subject before sending out your query; and all-over-the-Web search engines such as Alta Vista, which take what you submit and list all the "hits" for the keywords in your query. When working with keywords, it is important to have a working sense of Boolean logic. When you use a search engine, you are treating the contents of the Web as a vast computer database. Database searching is based on Boolean logic, which refers to the logical relationship among search terms and in particular works on a process of inclusion, exclusion and substitution. There are three logical operators in Boolean logic: OR, AND, NOT.[12] In most cases, using the words AND and NOT between keywords will go a long way toward limiting your search. For example,

Apples, Oranges and Pears will yield all pages listing all these.
Apples AND Oranges NOT Pears will yield only pages listing Apples and Oranges

Many search engines now use Implied Boolean plus (+) or minus (-) search operators to denote AND and NOT. Therefore, your query for the above example would look something like this:

+Apples +Oranges -Pears

Also, remember to use quotation marks around proper names and exact titles. A search for Bob Smith will yield results for all Bobs, Smiths and finally Bob Smiths. A search for "Bob Smith" will yield only results for Bob Smith.

3.2 The Role of Universities in New Learning Environments

Historically, universities have consistently been involved in information technology. The coincidence of the full emergence of European universities with the technological innovation of the printing press shows this relationship clearly, as does the increased role of stationers and copyists just before the print revolution. From the medieval period to the Information Age, the influence of universities has grown concentrically. As the means of scholarly communication moved from hand-copied manuscripts to printed books, the concept of the university changed. In the nineteenth century, the Industrial Revolution and especially Darwin's theories had an impact on the professionalization of the humanities and the social sciences and the refinement of graduate training. While these changes in the culture of the university have generally been slow, today universities have to adapt to and adopt innovations quickly in order to keep pace with the technological changes.

Planning, interaction, and management in academic computing centers used to work on an ad-hoc basis. Accounts and resources were provided on a case-by-case basis. The community of on-campus users was so limited that it would not be unfair to say in this period that the computing staff had a closer knowledge of peer groups at other universities than of people on their own campuses. The first change came with the introduction of personal computers, which created a new community of on-campus computer users who were outside of the computer science and physical science communities. This shift and expansion in the user base came in the late 1980s as personal computers made their way into academic departments, onto professor's desks and into graduate research seminars. Within ten years, e-mail had become a part of expected campus services, as had general access to the Internet and then the Web, in academic departments from anthropology to zoology.

This dramatic change affected not just academic departments and professors, but also university libraries as electronic catalogs began to replace card catalogs. Now we are in the midst of another transformation as digital libraries and electronic journals are beginning to coexist in the same information space—not just as digitized versions of concrete, real-world libraries or electronic versions of print journals. In recent years, this dramatic change has also reached into administrative areas as well. In-person registration has given way at many universities to online registration. In each case, a new campus center is in the process of being defined. Where before the library was a college professor's principle campus resource to access research materials, supplemented by academic conferences and professional contacts, now increasingly an academic computing facility acts as a critical gateway as these traditional avenues are supplemented and in some cases supplanted by online resources such as electronic libraries, journals and LISTSERV mailing lists.

Along with this new central role on today's campuses, academic computing centers have to meet a new set of operating demands. Before 1995, those of us who worked with e-mail and online resources were among a manageable handful of computer users outside the computer science and physical science fields, so the relationship between the academic computing center and faculty members could remain an informal one. How radical the shift was for academic computing centers can be seen in the jump in the num-

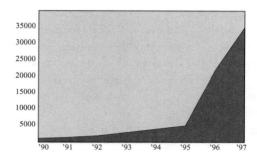

Figure 3.1. The growth of general computer accounts at New York University 1990–1997. Courtesy of George Sadowsky.

bers of computer accounts generated at New York University. In 1981, there were six thousand computer accounts at NYU. By January 1998, there were over forty-six thousand computer accounts and demand was still growing.

This change did not just increase the demand on the technical and administrative infrastructure of computing centers, it has also placed demands on the infrastructure of the university as a whole, as classroom space now has to be reworked and in some cases new classrooms need to be built. Classroom networks, course home pages and professors bringing laptops to class need to be accommodated. The classroom in some sense has always been the front parlor of the academy—the place where teachers and students come together to form "the university" in its most classical definition. In this front parlor, the tools typically have been a blackboard, an overhead projector and, more recently, a VCR. In today's classrooms and seminar halls, it is no longer enough to provide an overhead projector, much more is required. Fully wired classrooms, sophisticated projection systems and a central computing environment are quickly becoming the only way to provide the needed space to access the now twenty-four-hour virtual classroom. This virtual classroom is beginning to play not just an experimental role in higher education, but in some cases has become an entrenched tool and for many college teachers as much a part of course creation as writing the course syllabus.

In response to this unprecedented demand, universities must build and maintain industry-strength networking and computing environments. Campus-wide information networks need to be strengthened and in some cases updated to university Webs. The critical gateways to the outside world that comprise the modem pools, dial-up lines and on-ramps to the Internet need to be expanded and responsive to the need for speed. We have been fortunate at NYU to have the Innovation Center, a faculty computer lab set aside for the exploration of innovative technology and the acquisition of critical skills. It is our hope that such centers will become a ubiquitous part of the academic computing landscape at all universities. Financial investment in such a resource is crucial; if only one resource for the faculty can be set up, then this is far and away the best model. Faculty members need to have good tools, they need technical support, and they need to meet and interact with others involved in this process.

As faculty gravitate to placing materials on the Web, student computing services must also respond in kind. Walk-in general help centers need to be set up and centralized. Discipline-specific technical staff need to be hired, using the same model that libraries

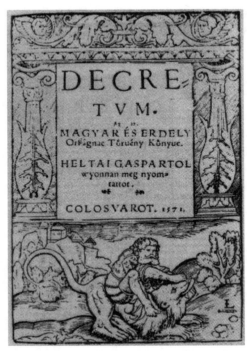

Figure 3.2. *Magyar és Erdély Ország Törvény Könyve* (Book of Laws of the Countries Hungary and Transylvania), printed in 1571, by Gáspár Heltai, Kolozsvár. Courtesy of the Teleki-Bolyai Library, Marosvásárhely, at http://www.nextron.ch/~teleki-teka/.

use of having a humanities reference librarian, a social science reference librarian and so forth. Since the Internet is rapidly evolving, there should also be a campus-wide and concerted effort, through seminars and workshops, to keep the campus community—students, faculty and administrators—informed about new developments in the technology as well as providing ways to update skills. On-campus computing laboratories—located around campus and in residence halls—need to be expanded from glorified writing centers to full-service multimedia centers. Internet access is critical here. Developing the necessary infrastructure to make information and rapid communication available will be a large step toward the ideal of a global university. If the Internet is used to its full potential, it will be as vital and necessary a linking device as the Internet's precursor ARPANET was when it connected university ARPA sponsored computer centers over twenty-five years ago.

New technologies, even those less dramatic than the Internet, have always worked to transform the way we see and explain the world and, by extension, have transformed the ways we learn and teach. The innovation of moveable type and the proliferation of printing presses, as seen in chapter 1, distributed information at rates of speed that were perhaps as remarkable then as the speed of Internet-delivered information now. As a result, libraries went through their first sustained period of growth since the fall of the Roman Empire. Whole new industries were created as printing houses emerged, and scholarly work and academic discourse were expanded and transformed. Exquisitely illustrated books, pictures, anatomical drawings and maps left locked monastery libraries and the private libraries of the wealthy and finally came into the hands of instructors and students alike. It is no coincidence that the period that followed the invention of the printing press was one of feverish production and that this technological revolution contributed substantially to the European Renaissance.

In the twentieth century, the development of radio, film and television ushered in a new age of what can be called early instructional technology. At first, these were used to make literal translations of written material. There was a natural lag between the time that radio, film and television were used primarily to "copy" print materials and when artists and technicians began to exploit the inherent power and creative range of the new media. The educational potential of these media was seen immediately, and there was a push to deliver class content via radio, film and television almost as soon as the bugs were worked out of each new media. With the new media, new ideas emerged. Educators and industry thinkers discussed the end of classroom-style education in favor of distance and

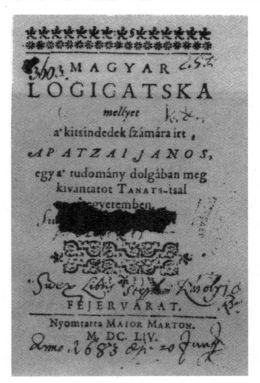

Figure 3.3. János Csere Apáczai, *Magyar Logigátska* (Small Hungarian Logic Book), printed in Gyulafehérvár, 1654, by Major Márton. The first Hungarian textbook on logic. Courtesy of the Teleki-Bolyai Library, Marosvásárhely at *http://www.nextron.ch/~teleki-teka/*.

distributed learning. Some questioned the role of educators in the learning process, or the negative effect of "information overload." Taken together, it is remarkable to see how closely the pedagogical issues of the television "revolution" foreshadowed those surrounding the Internet today.

Nonstructured and informal learning have been at the heart of the Internet since its inception. J. C. R. Licklider's broad research idea brought thousands of people together to share ideas, research and just plain information through e-mail and news discussion groups. As this network expanded, so did the knowledge base of the Internet community. Topic-specific newsgroups and information resources were created in dramatic numbers and their content was organized and archived for further study. As information was added and the Internet population kept growing, further organization took place. Specialized newsgroups evolved as offshoots of general newsgroups. A simple newsgroup like *rec.photo* cruised along for many years before it had to be split into smaller, more specific photography discussions focused around specialized areas to allow topic-specific browsing. Following the evolutionary model of the informal learning space created in newsgroups like *rec.photo*, it will ultimately be your job to facilitate structured learning. A carefully planned and executed Web page can act as both a microcosm of the Internet and a catalyst for discussion, exploration and further research. It can contain most of the tools you can find on the Internet, such as your class newsgroup for discussion, bulletin boards to discuss class issues, tutorials, tests, software downloads, and of course, if needed, links to other Internet sites. However, above all, you can inject some semblance of order and guidance into this seemingly unwieldy and ever-changing world.

Approaches to Web-based course-page creation reflect individual personal and teaching styles. We have seen three major approaches in the way instructors use the Web. The first is that of instructors who post their syllabus, office hours and telephone numbers online. This administrative approach is minimal and in some ways looks more and more to us like a basic service any department at a university should offer. The second group, and most people fall in this category, are instructors who translate their existing class routine to the Web with minor additions. This is a first real step toward providing meaningful educational material for the Web—a learning stage during which most instructors, like early silent film makers, acquire a feel for the new media. The third and traditionally most active group is made up of instructors who create educational material using Web-specific tools. These "wired professors" search high and low to create content that is unique and uses the latest Internet tools and ideas.

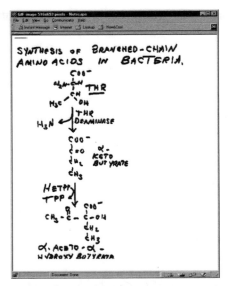

Figure 3.4. Synthesis of Branded-Chain Amino Acids, a simple science illustration for the Web. Courtesy of Professor Randall Murphy at *http://www.nyu.edu/classes/murphy/*.

While the search for a new angle to demonstrate a key concept or enhance the classroom discussion is both infinite and exhausting, the Internet and related technological breakthroughs do offer unique opportunities to show things in a way not seen before. Although the scientific community has led the way in the development and aggressive use of the new technology, the humanities and social sciences have actually been instrumental in leading the way to Web-based course design. The scientific community builds on tools older and more complex than hypertext; for them, entry to the Web as we know it today has been quite different. They were on the Internet long before most of us. In fact, many of them were actively involved in building the Internet, using applications, tools and delivery methods that predated HTML. This has led to an interesting duality: they were the first on the Internet, but are often the last on the World Wide Web. Some of this is due in part to the same sentiment expressed by Tim Berners-Lee that a graphical interface is frivolous and possibly destructive and what is key on the Internet is the ability to transmit and share technical text-based data. But the reasons are deeper even than this.

There has been a technology-enforced adherence to traditional tools in the sciences. Scientific research, visualization and typesetting methods are much too demanding in scope, complexity and detail to allow easy translation and posting to the Web. Scientific applications have been fine-tuned for decades and require computing power far beyond the reach of desktop computing. Browser plug-ins, Java applets and microcomputer-based "helper applications" could only in the most general sense register the end-result generated by high-end research, in the form of an image, or chart or a three-dimensional model. Only rarely would such an approach permit the user to "recalculate" data—the essential task performed by these scientific applications. However, while high-end scientific work on the Web may still be a few years down the line, science education has benefited from Web-based delivery. For example, Razmol, originally developed by Roger Sayle at the University of Edinburgh exclusively for high-end computer systems, now has a desktop version that offers a perfect way for students to look at and understand the spatial relationship of molecules. Some of these materials, in the form of images, charts and three-dimensional models, can be published on the Web as slides, animations and Java-based simulations.

Across the disciplines, much of the work posted to the Internet has involved translating existing content to Web-presentable content. Until 1993, the migration of material to the Internet was heavily text-oriented. The massive introduction of images around 1996 marked a turning point. We are now in the middle of a new wave as a whole new gener-

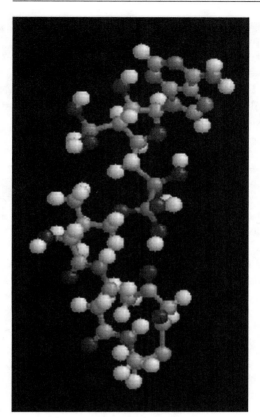

Figure 3.5. Acetoacetyl coenzyme in Razmol.

ation of software has been introduced that finally allows "complex" material that integrates interactivity, sound, animation and video to be presented on the Web.

For most professors, however, the initial step is still to translate preexisting materials to the Web. Although this approach does not tap into the creative range of the medium, the critical ideas that motivate instructors to take the plunge, the classroom metaphors they bring with them and how they handle the challenge of learning what is for many an absolutely new set of skills are critical first steps into the medium and continue to influence instructors regardless of how technically adept they become. First-stage Web design involves the refinement or discovery of new teaching metaphors, a heightened or renewed interest in pedagogy and an emphasis on learning and adjusting to the new technology. In some cases it also involves a degree of playfulness and exploration, which can colloquially be referred to as "hacking around"—inserting blinking text into a Web page or undergoing technical rites of passage like the first successful set of frames or the first image map. Some professors remain comfortably at this stage, eventually moving away from playing with the technology to focusing almost exclusively on content creation. However, others begin to mine the technology for its hidden strengths and creative potential.

Student involvement in the critique and refinement of these Web sites is a critical factor in designing effective teaching sites. It is especially important in first-stage design. Part of the excitement of working with the Web between 1995 and 1996 was that teachers and students faced a new technology together. For many students, a given professor was the first with a Web site, and students experienced the same anticipation, anxiety and exhilaration as their teachers. In ways that went well beyond end-of-term paper evaluations, students were an intense resource for feedback for teachers who asked: "Did this work?" "Did you understand it?" "Could you work with it?" In some cases, the excitement with the technology created unique opportunities in the classroom for nearly transparent collaborative learning.

This was certainly my experience with my adult students in the School of Continuing Education. Tackling the Web as a group, my students could observe my personal challenges on a weekly basis as I both learned and adjusted to this new medium. This in turn led to increased risk-taking and intellectual stretching on the part of my writing students. When I included interactivity on my Web site, this challenge increased as my students overcame their fear of posting a comment to a guest book or adding a link to a Web page. The psychology of success in this area (which I made clear was not going to reflect adversely on their grades as long as they made an effort to use the Web site) led to success with the course material. I can only conclude that the exhilaration combined with the acquisition of these timely skills led to greater self-confidence with the course material. I was teaching a course on writing a research paper at the time—a course that I had taught for several years before integrating the Web into my practice—and I saw both interest in the course material and writing skill levels rise dramatically when I introduced the Web as a research tool and partial extension of the classroom.

Christopher Mele observed similar responses in his classes:

> The growth of the Internet offers further encouragement for the effort it takes to conduct on-going or semester-length applied student research projects. . . . The notion of creating a public document visible to any number of people across the globe has a very positive effect upon student motivation. Made aware of both the exposure and possible uses of their research, students take keen interest in assuring high quality in their work both individually and collectively. The ease of mounting a project on the Web—in essence, making their work a reality in the public sphere—is not only appealing but instills a sense of responsibility upon the student researcher to do well.[13]

3.3 Faculty Experiences with First Experiments in Course Web Pages

In this section, we highlight the online work of a select group of NYU faculty between 1995 and 1997 in order to illustrate some issues of content or design that are pertinent here.

Initially, instructors at NYU came to the Innovation Center with simple ideas for translating their course materials to the Web. Caroline Persell, a sociology professor, was no stranger to using computers in her classes, and her research interests include the impact of computer technologies on education. Persell had used computers in her sociology courses before, and her students had already been exposed to computers and the Web through the Sociology Department's small computer network. They had primarily been working on computer-based statistical applications, but the network also gave Persell's students access to e-mail. However, creating a Web page for her course was a new departure for her. Persell arrived at the Innovation Center with a few pictures, a few graphs and simple idea. She wanted to create a starting page with a greeting and pertinent course information, followed by an elaborate description of each class as the semester progressed. On her home page, she wanted to list her office hours, class location, reading material and e-mail. In her class description, she planned to point out required readings, homework, pending test dates and student comments. She insisted on a simple

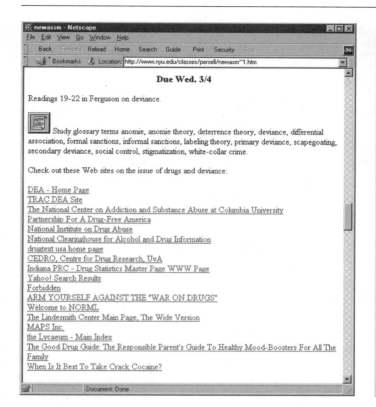

Figure 3.6. (*above*) Professor Caroline Persell's design philosophy allowed her to easily update her site (*http://www.nyu.edu/classes/persell*), as well as to make it transparent to her students.

Figure 3.7. (*above right*) "Garbage in Gotham" by Professors Robin Nagle and Thomas de Zengotita, at *http://www.nyu.edu/classes/garbage/*.

design that would allow her students to use a variety of browsers and fast downloads. This Spartan design also allowed for uncomplicated modifications, even by her teaching assistants, who took over the maintenance of her project.

Another early visitor to the Innovation Center was Robin Nagle, director of the Draper Interdisciplinary Master's Program in Humanities and Social Thought at NYU. Nagle had a strong desire to use the Web to create a "paperless classroom" for a course she was to teach in the fall term of 1995. By putting the bulk of her course "Garbage in Gotham: The Anthropology of Trash" online, Nagle wanted to "to avoid creating more trash, in the form of printed syllabi and typed papers. She required students to browse the Web, submit their papers via e-mail, and participate in an online class newsgroup.

Figure 3.8. Rene Gabri, a student in Robin Nagle's class, incorporated voice interviews, digital imagery and poetry in his assignment for Garbage in Gotham, at *http://www.nyu.edu/classes/garbage/renemonday/inter3.html*.

They also had the option of creating a Web page as the medium for their final research project."[14]

Joseph recalls some issues from the project. The first looming issue was student support. More than anything, Nagle's concept of a paperless classroom could be compromised by the lack of student training. It became clear at the Innovation Center that our previously narrow concentration on helping faculty to create materials for the Web had to be extended to include the needs of the students who would be using these materials. To ensure meaningful participation, it was critical that students both have a basic knowledge of Internet tools and be comfortable using them. To meet this need, the Innovation Center staff expanded its mandate and started to offer in-class tutorials using a very simple outline: a five-minute introduction to the history of the Internet; a hands-on tutorial on e-mail, FTP, browsers and search engines; and a quick HTML session.[15]

We also worked with individual students in the class. Among my most memorable moments participating in this project was working with Rene Gabri, one of Nagle's students. In many ways, the Web was the perfect outlet for his talents. Using his own work, including poetry, drawings, journal entries, photographs and soundclips from street interviews, Rene took full advantage of the Web's malleability and immediacy and created a unique project within a very short time. During staff meetings at the Innovation Center, we often talked about the discrepancy between ambition and reality in Web projects—that is, when the initial plans were ambitious but the reality fell short. Rene had gone the other way: from ambitious plans, he had created a sophisticated body of work.[16]

Nagle had two concerns when she sat down to create the course Web pages: "Will this let me teach the class without using any paper, and will this take me forever to create?"[17] Among the important issues she cited were: "How fully interactive can it be? How thorough are the links? How easy is it to maintain and update? How creative can the links be and still remain useful?—that is, can I be creative and still not get carried away with extraneous links?"[18]

At the end of the semester, she observed that her students had a "wide range of knowledge and affinities for the computer, and we spent too much time teaching basics. But once computers were integrated into the class dynamic, the technology quickly transformed from an obstacle to a helpful and even friendly tool."[19] The interactivity built into the Web site was an essential component of its overall success. The newsgroup in particular "was a vital way to continue discussions outside the once-a-week class meeting. Students especially appreciated and commented on our accessibility; through e-mail, my co-teacher and I were always around."[20] The final project requirement that everyone create a Web page was less successful: Nagle reported that out of twenty-three students, only four "composed Web pages as their final projects. This could have been more successful if I had worked with more students sooner on the mechanics of HTML and other Web-specific skills."[21]

Beyond the simple translation of print resources to a Web format to create a paperless classroom, Nagle discovered that the technology had an unexpected impact on the teaching of the course, especially in terms of how she thought of the structure of her course:

> One of the real pleasures of the course was the malleability of the syllabus; this would not have been possible without the electronic component. Some students liked that, but others felt that the class wasn't structured enough. This taught me the importance of the balance between allowing the class to take a shape of its own, and guiding the shape (and tone) it takes.[22]

In a final observation about her use of the Web in "Garbage in Gotham," Nagle wrote: "In a university, the Web allows teachers and students to dissolve classroom walls, continue conversations outside the boundaries of time, invite outsiders inside the discussion, and glean knowledge from people with similar expertise or curiosity from anywhere that the world is interconnected."[23]

Barbara Kirshenblatt-Gimblett, professor of performance studies at the Tisch School of the Arts had been using online discussion groups with her classes for several years and decided to develop a Web site for her class "Tourist Productions." She explained that there were two important issues that compelled her to integrate the Web into her course. First, she wanted to show how this medium was relevant to her style of teaching:

> I have always believed in a "resource-rich" approach to teaching and want my students to have their own first-hand experiences with varied materials and to interact with each other. . . . Discussion, collaborative projects, and peer learning are important to me. Using the Internet was a perfect match for my teaching style and my course material.[24]

Second, she wanted to show how this medium was relevant to the course's content. "Tourist Productions" explores how "we understand the world outside our own experience, as tourists, and how museum and tourist attractions present the world. . . . The growth of the World Wide Web has created another kind of tourist and another kind of museum . . . and students have access twenty-four hours a day to these resources and to each other."[25]

In form, her Web site was a simple one. It included a syllabus with links to the full text of some of the required readings, as well as links to bibliographies of recommended readings and other Internet sites related to each week's material. There was also a link to the class newsgroup and a form for sending e-mail to the professor. In addition to coming into the Innovation Center with a set of ideas for her course, Kirshenblatt-Gimblett also learned HTML skills and how to work with online resources so that she could update the "Tourist Productions" Web site.

Joseph recalls starting his first HTML session with Kirshenblatt-Gimblett:

> Barbara and I scanned an image in Photoshop. Sharpened it, resized it and turned it into a GIF. Then we started a document in a text editor. We put in our first tag: <IMG SRC="exo.gif"> Saved the document and called it from Mosaic. There it was. Barbara smiled, "This is it?" "Yes, that's all." It was clear that Barbara immediately understood the magic of the Web. The rest of the session went very much the same way. We put in some text. Looked at it. Added a little bold here a little extra size there, looked at it. We put in a link to other files, then a link within the document. We put in an e-mail link and to finish it off, a newsgroup for her class. While we admired her quickly growing page, we discussed the accessibility of her files for updates.[26]

Later, Kirshenblatt-Gimblett recalled her introduction to this medium: "It took me a while to realize what electronic/digital media were about. Then I had an epiphany with the Internet. I got it like a bolt of lightning." While on a leave of absence at the Getty Research Institute for the History of Art and the Humanities, Kirshenblatt-Gimblett worked with the institute's support person whose job, she recalls, was "to teach us whatever we wanted to know (I was the only fellow in my year to show any interest)." In hindsight she realized that her situation was fortuitous: "These are truly blessed conditions and without them I do not know if I would have ever gotten past the three-line messages I had been writing for years in VMS/VAX (I did not understand what a buffer was and that you had to hit ENTER at the end of each line, so the machine crashed if I wrote more than three lines)." With this introduction, she recalls, "the adventure began—mastering a tool that was at the same time a totally fascinating medium and phenomenon."[27]

As a scholar and a teacher, Kirshenblatt-Gimblett now uses the Internet on daily basis, primarily to stay in touch with colleagues and students all over the world.

> The factors that prompted me to keep going were the desire to (1) stay in touch with my students when I was away and they were all over the world writing their dissertations; (2) have access to online research resources; (3) understand the medium as a phenomenon in its own right, as a result of which I published "The Electronic Vernacular" in George Marcus, ed., *Connected* (University of Chicago Press, 1996); (4) develop my pedagogy and teaching to the fullest using every means available. I am a passionate teacher and pay close attention to pedagogy. I like to experiment and refine the pedagogy I use, which varies depending on the course, and to use all the resources I can command.[28]

After her initial introduction to the Internet and some years spent using it primarily for communication through e-mail and newsgroups, Kirshenblatt-Gimblett began to think about using the Web in her classes. She recalls her excitement:

> I was intimidated by the prospect but fantasized about [it]. For about a year I thought about what a wonderful thing it would be to create Web pages for my courses. When, without a hope in the world that such a thing would happen, I mentioned the idea to Vincent Doogan (associate director for user services), he surprised me. Not only did he say we could do it. He said that I could learn to do it myself and that it was not as daunting as I thought. It took less and more time than I thought. That is, I learned the basics quickly, though I had to deal with about 7 new elements—working on a Mac (I use a PC), scanning, Adobe Photoshop, Fetch, Pico, html, Webweaver, etc. But, then, once I saw how "easy" it was, I got ambitious and wanted to do more and more.[29]

In terms of solid design, the issues that Kirshenblatt-Gimblett keeps foremost in her mind when working on a course Web site are as follows:

> The site must be clear, easy to access, and useful—i.e. contain the essential information and full text of readings, where possible. The site needs to be rich, both in resources and in links, a place to come back to again and again, worth exploring, as well as fun thanks to images, surprises, and wit. Last, I try to make the site interactive through the newsgroup and by posting various kinds of material. Assignments often

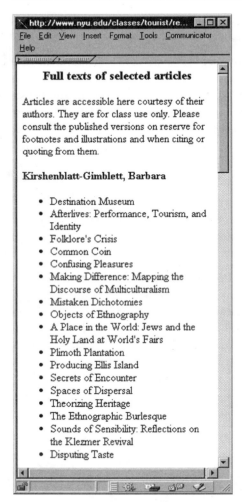

Figure 3.9. A page from the "Tourist Productions" Web site by Professor Barbara Kirshenblatt-Gimblett at *http://www.nyu.edu/classes/tourist/readings.html.*

include an online component, with links written right into the syllabus. Designing the course and designing the page are related, but they are not the same thing.[30]

Most of the instructors we interviewed believed in the positive effects of Internet-based education. We asked Kirshenblatt-Gimblett what observations and opinions she had about the possible negative effects of integrating the Web into classroom instruction. She began her answer by explaining that her perceptions of positive and negative aspects of using the Internet in teaching had changed over time. "It used to be that students were totally unfamiliar with the medium, intimidated by it, did not see the value of it, and resented the time and effort expended." Then, when the Web was becoming popular, she noticed a change in student attitudes: "They came in realizing they needed to get up to speed, but were not very adept."[31] In each of these stages, the negative effects of including Internet or Web-based material could be neatly summarized in terms of whether the effort on the part of the students to master the medium outweighed the value of the medium in instruction. However, Kirshenblatt-Gimblett observes that this situation has changed in the last year.

To my amazement, the latest generation includes many adepts and new expectations—that *everything* will be online! If it is not online there is no guarantee they will read it. And, as for research, they may even confine themselves to what can be found online. In other words, there is the danger of a sense of entitlement and an expectation of effortlessness.[32]

Kirshenblatt-Gimblett also has concerns that this medium may be used to replace traditional face-to-face teaching. "On the teaching side, I can see an abuse of the medium where it becomes a substitute for, rather than an extension of, face-to-face teaching. The corollary is the expectation that with this medium one teacher can service more students."[33]

We asked Kirshenblatt-Gimblett whether she believed the Web would change the role of professors and to summarize her own sense of how incorporating this medium had changed her teaching. She explained:

I am otherwise a low-tech person. I used a manual typewriter, never an electric one, before shifting to a computer. I do not own a car, dishwasher, washing machine, dryer, sewing machine, electric pencil sharpener, video camera, or any number of other technological conveniences. I use the Web to intensify the live face-to-face teaching. And,

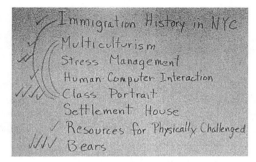

Figure 3.10. Professor Michelle Adelman's Communicating with Computer-Based Interactive Technology class started in an unusually low-tech fashion—on the blackboard. Photograph by Joseph Hargitai.

even as I learn the new technologies I like to think that I am getting a lot better at the old ones—talking to a class, leading discussion, chalk and blackboard, slides, films, handouts, lead pencils, a fountain pen, paper, books.[34]

Michelle Adelman is a doctoral student in the Educational Communication and Technology program in the School of Education. As a teacher at NYU, she is uniquely situated in the forefront of both incorporating and analyzing the impact of educational technology. Her course "Communicating with Computer-Based Interactive Technology" is aimed at helping students "develop skills to use interactive technology to support educational goals that they define."[35] Among her goals for the course are to foster a "basic understanding of the technology, a sensitivity to the evolving nature of the technology, an application of theory to a practical instructional module and an awareness of skills needed to produce interactive applications."[36] The course revolves around the development of a joint project.

Her approach to using the Web differs from that of the instructors above. "Since I want the students to determine the purpose as well as the look and feel of the class site, I do not start out with a Web site that I construct. This is a live, instructor-led class that meets once a week."[37] Her approach demonstrates some innovative solutions to the pressing problems faculty face when incorporating student Web projects in their courses. There are two critical problems. The first is the time outlay required by the medium. The second is that in any given class you will have students with different Web skill levels—a range that typically can include students who only use e-mail and the Web for research to those who have written their own Web pages. Adelman's approach emphasizes a collaborative learning model. At the beginning of the semester, she tells her students that they will be responsible for a major project:

I ask each student to submit an idea for the group project. We discuss it in one class session and select a few topics. In the following class session the class breaks down into small groups to discuss the selections and reports back to the class. The class reports on the topic. In subsequent sessions the class identifies the skills needed to accomplish the project. . . . They identify the skills possessed by each student and determine how to structure workgroups and establish workshops for students who do not have the basic production skills. Last year the students gave workshops on PhotoShop, HTML and Quicktime.[38]

Having the students work together in groups is a solid solution for the often pressing demands the technology makes on students. Adelman has developed a pedagogical strategy from what she sees as a real-world model: "In the real world, both in educational settings and commercial settings, distributed work groups are common. I also hope to model behavior that can be used in a classroom."[39]

The project that Adelman's students came up with was called "New York Around the Clock." In their description, Adelman's students wrote that their Web site was aimed at listing "fun things to do in New York at every hour of the day." On the opening page of the site, a visitor can either pick the a.m. clock face or the p.m. clock face. Clicking on an hour on the clock face takes one to a student page describing an event or place to go at that time in New York City. The site mixes descriptions reminiscent of *Village Voice* club reviews and tourist guides with more personal and even whimsical Web pages. For example, the 10 a.m. page is devoted to the class: "10am go to class and study."[40] After class, the noon page is a "Cyber Kitchen" with pictures of sushi and dim sum. At the end of the day, the 11 p.m. page is titled "Bad TV." This Web page opens with the following scenario: "Sometimes there's nothing better than locking your door, getting in bed and zoning out in front of the tube. Particularly when there is something utterly horrible on—a . . . made for TV movie."[41] Despite the design and technical sophistication of the Web site, which includes QuickTime movies and image maps, Adelman explains that she did "not dwell on production tools. I wanted the students to focus on needs assessment, purpose of the project, user need and application of educational theory."[42]

Students have been as involved in and excited about course Web pages as their professors. Jonathan J. Vafai was a student in Paul J. Gans's "Medieval Technology in Everyday Life" class. Gans is a professor of chemistry at NYU. However, as he explains,

as is not untypical of many members of academia, I have developed a number of disparate scholarly interests. . . . The "disparate scholarly interests" refers to my continuing association with NYU's Medieval and Renaissance Studies Program (MARS), where I teach a course titled . . . Medieval Technology and Everyday Life. . . . This course focuses on everyday life (and its technology) in western Europe during the period roughly from 1066 to 1347. This was the period of the "little" renaissance, the high Middle Ages, and the early stirrings of modernity. We discuss everything from clothing to armor, agriculture to cooking techniques, houses to cathedrals, and that ever-popular question: "did anybody ever wash in the Middle Ages?"[43]

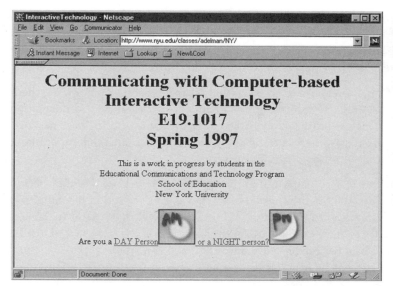

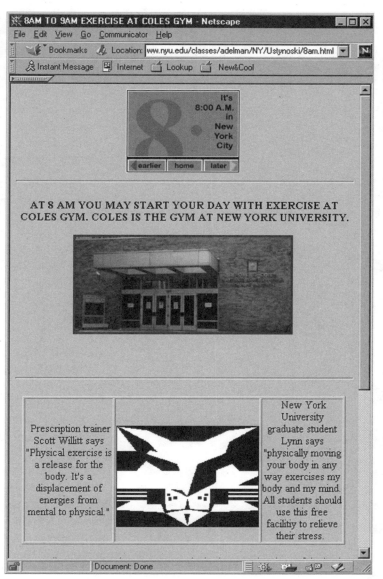

Figure 3.11. *(above)* "Communicating with Computer-Based Interactive technology" by Professor Michelle Adelman at *http://www.nyu.edu/classes/adelman/NY/*.

Figure 3.12. *(right)* Collaborative student page, *http://www.nyu.edu/classes/adelman/NY/Ustinoski/8am.html*.

Gans's course Web page was the first such page that Vafai saw as a student at NYU in the fall term of 1996. "My reaction to it was 'Oh neat!' I was not taking the class at the time, but by reading through the pages, I became very interested in the course, and later on decided to register for it."[44] Vafai believes that a good course Web site

> should have information about the class, with links to a syllabus, homework, schedules, etc, at the least. As extra information is included, such as links to information relating to the class, such as other people's Web pages, museums, etc, the page gets better and better. Course pages where there is unique information, such that other places might link to *our school* also rank high, in my opinion."[45]

Vafai believes that course Web pages add to the appeal of courses because they permit students to have an actual look at the course before they enroll, instead of having to rely only on the course description in the catalog. While he acknowledges that it will take a few years for all courses to have Web pages, he explains: "I'd like it if every class had a Web page. . . . It would be a reasonable expectation."[46]

However, as enthusiastic as he is about his teachers using this medium, Vafai is clear that the Web is a tool and should not necessarily become a stage where an entire course is conducted. "I don't know much about entire classes conducted on the net. I think a good course page is not confining. I like a page that goes beyond its own pages to outside sites, like Museums, or hobbyists. I like Prof. Gans' pages because he relies on other sites for many of the specifics."[47]

When asked whether he felt his learning style and experience as a student had changed since working with course Web pages and using the Internet as a collaborative medium, Vafai answered that he thought he learned the same way he did before the Web. "I still study from books, using notes from lectures, etc. I think that many aspects of the process have been streamlined with the Web. I am able to access a lot more information without leaving my room, and things that might normally take a few days to research might only take an hour or two."[48]

E-mail has been a particularly important tool for Vafai, who uses it to contact his teachers: "I e-mail them to ask about assignments, ask about the material, or simply to bounce ideas off of them, etc. I like it because I can do it at any hour of the day (2am in my pajamas), and the instructor or professor can get back to me whenever they want. Sometimes, even at 2am, I get a reply back in 2 minutes. That is pretty cool!"[49] However, he does see some limitations with e-mail: "It is hard to communicate with people who do not check their e-mail frequently—so when I really need to get something done, there is no substitute for a phonecall. Then again—there is no good way to really read and review a friend's 5 page paper over the phone."[50]

When asked to comment about teachers who were still uncomfortable with using this medium and what advice he would have for teachers in the preliminary stages of thinking about using this medium, Vafai observed:

> Some . . . young and old faculty members refuse to even use e-mail. Sometimes . . . I try and show them what is out there. Eventually, the students will all demand that there is some type of material on the 'net, and many faculty members will almost be forced to do something. Usually, in these cases, a TA does the dirty work, and establishes presence on the Web.[51]

However, he emphasizes what a valuable addition the Web and e-mail are to his studies at the university:

> I think that the World Wide Web makes an excellent complement to the classroom. Many of the faculty members that I have spoken to and worked with that have utilized this new medium felt that it was worthwhile. Most students that I know feel the same, and hope that this trend continues to increase. The internet makes it possible for classes to continue after the students go home. It is not uncommon for announcements, along with answers to frequently asked questions, or old exams to be posted at 12am, long after the library's reserve desk is closed. With e-mail, discussions can be conducted at everyone's leisure. Shy people who don't feel comfortable raising their hands in a big class can e-mail the lists without embarrassment. Card catalogs are a thing of the past—research can be done in 30 seconds by typing in a few keywords on Yahoo! It is a great time to be a student![52]

Julia Keefer, an adjunct assistant professor of humanities in the Liberal Arts Program of the Adult Degree Studies Division of the School of Continuing Education, uses the Web as a publishing medium in an approach that emphasizes creativity, performance and collaboration. She has made Web pages for classes that include "Language and the Body," "Major Twentieth Century Writers," "Writing Workshop I" and "Writing Workshop II." She explains that her Web site is an extension of her personality, but that she is also taken with

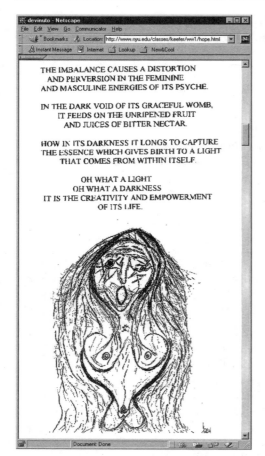

THE IMBALANCE CAUSES A DISTORTION
AND PERVERSION IN THE FEMININE
AND MASCULINE ENERGIES OF ITS PSYCHE.

IN THE DARK VOID OF ITS GRACEFUL WOMB,
IT FEEDS ON THE UNRIPENED FRUIT
AND JUICES OF BITTER NECTAR.

HOW IN ITS DARKNESS IT LONGS TO CAPTURE
THE ESSENCE WHICH GIVES BIRTH TO A LIGHT
THAT COMES FROM WITHIN ITSELF.

OH WHAT A LIGHT
OH WHAT A DARKNESS
IT IS THE CREATIVITY AND EMPOWERMENT
OF ITS LIFE.

Figure 3.13. Student work on Professor Julia Keefer's Writing Workshop I site: *http://www.nyu.edu/classes/keefer/*. Courtesy of Hope DeVennto.

the nature of the internet, a place where synapses fire all over the place without getting into cerebral ruts. The internet is also multidisciplinary, which makes me feel at home, because over the years I have taught anatomy, kinesiology, aerobics, literature, body sculpting, speech arts, argumentation, wrestling, acting, dance history, arthritic swim, French, screenwriting, multidisciplinary writing and now the theme courses in expository/creative writing that are presently on my Web site. While colleagues kept telling me that "A little learning is a dangerous thing," I insisted that having more disciplines deepened my knowledge and gave me more tools for analysis and creativity. Narrow specialization is antithetical to the fluid matrix of hypertext.[53]

Keefer believes that the range of her interests and avocations have carried over into her Web design. However, she also sees the Web as a collaborative space, and her Web sites are enhanced by her interaction with the staff and faculty at the Innovation Center as well as with her students:

I have a strong voice as a fiction writer and a strong presence as a performance artist so this has carried over to my Web design. However I see Web design as collaborative. My strong "presence" is enhanced by the wonderful people at ACF Innovation Center and my creative, enthusiastic students who are better poets and photographers than I am.[54]

Keefer has a keen interest in observing the results of that interaction, both in her own work and in terms of the impact of using the Web on traditional teaching methods. Working the Web into her teaching practice and, in some cases, as the object of study in her classes has led Keefer to ask: "Once you put your courses online, who needs you anymore? Why can't students just surf the net, write on their own and correspond with professors by e-mail?"[55] Among her answers is the following:

On-line courses can be enhanced and supplemented by the following: "To bring back theatre into the classroom: To offset the deleterious effects of cyberspace, the classroom should again become a theatre where debates, arguments, spectacle, role-playing once again occur as they did in classical Greece."[56]

As "organic professors," working with an "inorganic net where pixels may live forever," the key question for Keefer is how the Internet will change conventional education.[57] She believes that part of the answer lies in revitalizing traditional classroom practices, infus-

Figure 3.14. *(right)* Student work for Humans and Nature and Communication: A poem by Juliet Paez, at *http://www.nyu.edu/classes/keefer/nature/natlan.htm.*
Figure 3.15. *(far right)* Student work for Humans and Nature and Health, at *http://www.webhost.net/dwi/test/index-htm.htm.* Courtesy of Hope DeVenuto.

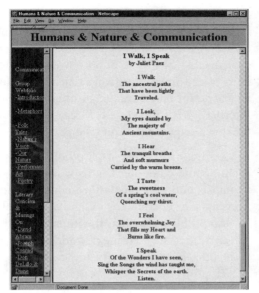

ing the "real" classroom with theater and generally enhancing the physical connections and interactions in "real time" so "that the body does not fall apart while the mind soars through cyberspace."[58] However, Keefer thinks the answer is more complex than simply balancing the body and the intellect. She argues that a successful integration of the Internet into teaching practice involves nothing less than the

> coordination of traditional and cyber rhetoric and a skillful use of cognitive domains and audience. The more non-linear I become the more classical literature and philosophy I read and the more Great Books show up on my reading lists. My objective is to help my students combine the best of our Western linear tradition with the nonlinear world of hypertext (and other cultures and media).[59]

Asked for a final observation on the integration of the Web into her teaching, Keefer said: "it is not a time-saving device. It enhances learning tremendously but it is more work for the professor."[60]

Jon McKenzie is an adjunct professor in the Department of Performance Studies at

Figure 3.16. StudioLab: thought, experiments, digital performance workshop, by Professor Jon McKenzie, at *http://www.nyu.edu/classes/mckenzie/.*

NYU. In 1996, he decided to tackle the question: "How does an artist perform technologically?" With this question in mind he taught "Electronic Performance" as a graduate course in the summer of 1996 and then as an undergraduate workshop in the fall. He explains that "the focus of both workshops was to explore electronic performance as the cross of cultural performance (such as theater, ritual, and performance art) and technological performance (ranging from clocks and answering machines to computers and the Internet)."[61] For this course, McKenzie created "StudioLab," a sophisticated Web site that became a stage for the workshops.

As the name suggests, StudioLab takes place in the environments of performance studio and computer lab. Its workshops explore connections between theory, performance, and new media through the production of actual and virtual events. These events are generated by individual and collective projects that investigate specific cultural problems, such as the impact of technology on everyday life and the role of the humanities in inventing new forms of sociotechnical interactivity. . . . Its productions include electronic theory, low-tech theater, performance art, and environmental and Web projects.[62]

We asked McKenzie how he came up with the idea of using the Web as a stage. He explained that both humans and technologies perform: "interfaces are thus always joint performances."[63] McKenzie believed that it was critically important for his drama students to experience and experiment with new media. He also admits that he was drawn to the Web because of his background in fine arts and cultural theory.

One project I use, "Interface in Everyday Life," combines performance art and Donald Norman's work on interface design. Students pick a common interface, explore the activities its design elicits, and create a live performance from this exploration. They then try to translate the performance back into a Web interface. Another project is a transformation of Brenda Laurel's *Computers as Theater,* which develops a theory of human-computer interaction using Aristotle's *Poetics.* Students create actual and virtual events by substituting another performance form for Greek tragedy: Kabuki, solo performance, Dada, Sumo, as well as the theater of Brecht, Artaud, Schechner, and LeCompte. In all cases, I give students lots of guidance and structure early on—and then try to get out of the way. Some experiments work, some don't, but that's what makes them experiments.[64]

Figure 3.17. StudioLab student work:
Homeless Home, at
*http://acf5.nyu.edu/~sjo1612/perfor-
mance_copy.html.* Courtesy of Abigail S.
Freeman and Stacey J. Oropello.

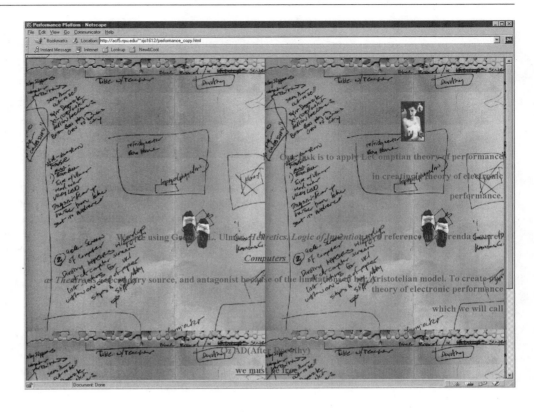

We asked McKenzie his opinion about the validity of collaborative student Web projects. He explained that theater has traditionally been a collaborative activity:

> If dramatic writing has traditionally been a solitary activity, producing theater has always been collaborative: actors, costume and set designers, technical crews, etc. It's this collaborative dimension that makes theater so applicable to creating new media, which requires integrating so many different skills and media. Again, not all collaborations work, but, then again, neither do all individual works. I think that the model of individual genius that has dominated modern aesthetics is giving way to collaborative modes of creativity. For me, *all* creativity is social and recombinant.[65]

Student participation is high in McKenzie's classes, and he has created a framework that permits students to add their own work. Like Adelman, McKenzie has organized his students into clearly structured Web project groups. He explains the role of the groups and his role as a teacher:

> StudioLab is designed to let students experiment: but it's not a free-for-all, it has a dynamic and interlaced structure. Students work in both performance studio and computer lab, moving from one to the other. In the collaborative projects, they work as "bands" in the studio, working on their performances and discussing the issues raised by the class. Each band is composed of a Hypertextualist, a Multimedium, and a Photoshopper, and these form "guilds" for working in the computer lab. It's like a rock band: the drummers get together, the bass players, the lead guitars, and they share techniques, so when they get back with their bands, they jam better. My function is like a producer: I give them advice about how to mix their tracks. Interlacing the bands and guilds was an important discovery for me, for it took the collaboration to a higher level.[66]

We asked McKenzie to talk about the process of updating and maintaining a large Web site like StudioLab. He joked that "Maintaining a Web site is artificial life!" He explains:

> It's a joke that makes sense on at least two levels. First, anyone who builds and maintains a site knows that it takes some effort and if you want it to be really interesting, it takes a lot of effort, so much that it can take over your life for a while. Second, the joke suggests Manuel De Landa's notion of inorganic life, which teaches us something important about human-computer interfaces, namely, that there are feedback loops and machinic processes everywhere, operating in all mediums—organic and inorganic—and doing so at very different scales and temporalities. Machinic processes are more than tools, more than mediums even: at a general level, they make up everything. Computers may make this generalized "artifice" more visible than it's been for a long time, at least in the West. Specific technologies such as tools, the alphabet, and spoken language have been feeding back on humans for millenia: just look at our thumbs and vocal cords![67]

I was also a member of this first wave of instructors who walked into the Innovation Center. Some, like Julia Keefer, taught in the same program as I did. Joseph introduced

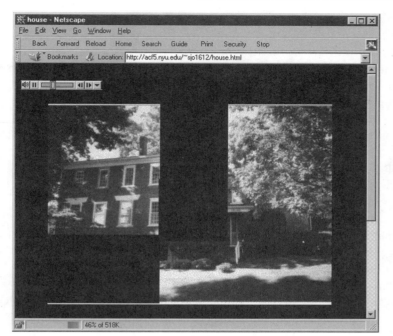

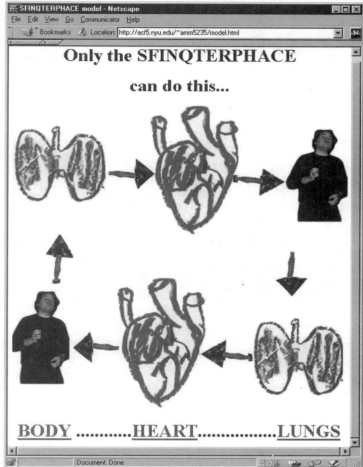

Figure 3.18. *(above)* StudioLab student work: *Homeless Home,* a clever visual pun using a GIF animation to "deconstruct" a middle-class home. Courtesy of Abigail S. Freeman and Stacey J. Oropello. Figure 3.19. *(right)* StudioLab student work: *Sfinqterphace* by the "heart people," who argue in their manifesto: "much too long audiences of western theatre have sat quietly in the dark so as not to disturb the performance." Courtesy of Marc Schmittroth, Anney Fresh and Bobbie G. Gossage.

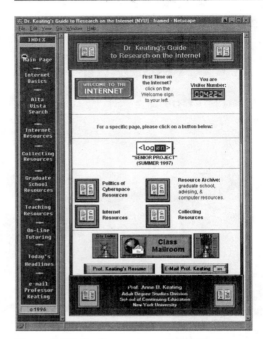

Figure 3.20. Professor Anne B. Keating's course Web site at
http://www.nyu.edu/classes/keating.

me to Jon McKenzie and the others. For several of us, Barbara Kirshenblatt-Gimblett provided the catalyst for own fledgling efforts on the Web. In the fall of 1996, she gave a symposium on her work with "Tourist Productions" to a standing-room-only audience of NYU faculty and administrators. Like many others, I was struck by the power of the presentation. Two months later, I walked into the Innovation Center for my first appointment with Joseph. When my first Web page went up, I was one of fourteen NYU instructors with Web pages. In the vignettes above, you have met the majority of the original group of faculty who pioneered the use of course Web pages at NYU.

My first course Web page was for my "Writing Workshop II" course in spring 1996. I had very simple goals. I wanted to introduce my students to research on the Internet. I felt that the Internet was becoming an important part of the research skills package I was teaching and could no longer be ignored. I also felt that students should start getting comfortable with e-mail, and that especially my adult students who attended classes after work would find e-mail a useful tool for communicating with me and with each other. As a teacher I also depended heavily on photocopied handouts and thought the Web page would be a neat way to keep copies of the handouts I was always passing out. I thought it would be fun to embellish these with graphics and with hypertext links. With these Web "handouts" my students could get both good diagrams and immediate clarification on different concepts. What I did not anticipate is how much of a collaborative effort the course Web page became and the dividends in terms of faster skill acquisition that I observed among my students. Learning about the Web translated into an explosion of intuitive learning in the classroom. My students were telling me that their kids had been trying to explain the Internet to them and now they were telling their kids about parts of the Web that they were discovering. I remember being told how proud they were to have sent their first e-mail messages. The self-confidence and zest for learning stimulated by the technology translated into a self-confidence with the course material. It was almost as if, after having conquered the Internet, writing a research paper was a piece of cake. It was an exciting semester.

In the spring of 1997, I taught a course called "Politics of Cyberspace." For many reasons, having a Web site for this course made sense. I needed a place to link to some of the sites and resources that were discussed in the books we were reading. However, I also wanted to make sure that we did not discuss the Internet without being regular visitors. So I set up some interactive elements on the "Politics of Cyberspace" page so my students

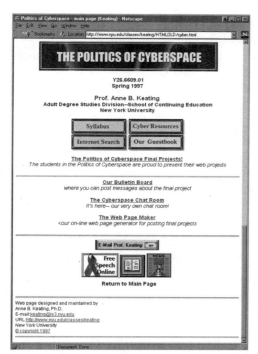

Figure 3.21. Professor Keating's "Politics of Cyberspace" class home page.

could continue their discussions online after class. Students also did their final projects as Web pages for this course. Using the Web as a platform for this class gave credence to the old adage "the medium is the message." Without this experience, it would have been very difficult not to fall into the trap of seeing the Internet in the terms that were being bandied about in the mainstream press that spring—as the domain of perverts and pornographers.

Using the Web as one of my tools has altered and enriched my teaching. I was young enough to have been exposed to ideas about collaborative learning when I was a graduate teaching assistant. However, I was generally unsatisfied by the artificiality of group projects and group work. Often as not there were problems, and students voiced their concerns about how they would be graded if the people in the group were working at different levels of commitment to the project. Something of value about the quality of an individual effort and engagement with the material seemed lost in the process. On the Internet, I had observed the culture of information sharing that evolved from the ARPANET Request for Comments (RFC). I was intrigued by the dynamically authored and constantly updated documents on the Internet embodied in Frequently Asked Questions (FAQs) and newsgroups, where many people came together on a regular basis to contribute valuable information to a communal store of information on a given subject. This was a critical resource on the Internet and a valuable teaching tool if the zest to share information could be reproduced in the classroom. In the last two years, the Web has provided this platform. Since the Web is a public space, it is a very real stage for the public performance of group projects. However, perhaps more importantly, the Web and the projects that are initiated there naturally bring the students in my classes together in groups, while at the same time preserving the individual inquiry I have come to value as a teacher.

In the next chapter, we show you how to build a course Web page. Before we get started, however, there are some preliminary tasks that you should complete before settling down to write HTML. Even if you are highly self-sufficient and like to do things yourself and your way, with the Web there exists a dependency that is very hard to circumvent. The Internet is the speedy agent of change. While most people are perfectly capable of learning HTML by themselves, there are more than a few unpredictable curveballs coming down the wire: exceptions, innovations, new concepts and bugs. To keep abreast of this effervescent technology, you need to rely on a dedicated team. Before you get start-

Figure 3.22. "Politics of Cyberspace Bulletin Board." Image by Keating/Hargitai.

ed, you should contact your campus computing center and talk to their accounts representative. You will need to explain that you want to set up an account on your school's server where you can post Web pages. While you are at it, you should also ask if there is anyone on staff who routinely works with faculty on setting up Web pages.

Plan to start the first class of a course where a Web page is a required class resource with a thorough hands-on introduction to the environment. If you are still shaky on how to do this, ask someone from your academic computing support team to do it for you. Also make sure your students have their accounts ready and working, and that they have a working knowledge of all the required tools.

Finally, write a personalized talk on the Internet so that you can articulate to your students what is interesting to you about the medium. They will be looking to you to set the tone for how the class uses the Internet. The Internet is not a self-explanatory space; one observer has even gone as far as to declare that, William Gibson aside, the Internet is not a separate space at all, but simply an extension of where we already are. "People don't really travel to the Internet, they are the Internet. When we're online, we're in the same place we always were."[68] This is a useful counterbalance to the hype about the Internet. Remember this as you go into the classroom—the Internet is a tool, a vehicle for the content you alone can provide: "All technology has a human measure; it is impossible to remove the human strand even from the most inhuman of technological devices. They are our creation, however eloquently we try to deny them."[69]

Research Links and Resources

1. *WebSonar* at *http://www.Websonar.com/Websonar/sonar.html* is a library of everything from classic literature to educational video transcripts. It is searchable by phrase and will find the exact source for the phrase or word.

2. The Central Intelligence Agency's *The World Factbook* at *http://www.odci.gov/cia/publications/nsolo/wfb-all.htm* is loaded with information on each country that is otherwise difficult to find in one spot.

3. The *Scout Report* at *http://www.scout.cs.wisc.edu/scout/report* is a weekly publication provided by the Info Scout and InternIC Information Service to provide a sampling of the best of newly announced Internet resources.

4. *Electronic Journals and Serials Subject Index* (University at Buffalo) at *http://ublib.buffalo.edu/libraries/e-resources/ejournals/* is an impressive list of journals available online. This list includes general interest periodicals, architecture and planning, biological sciences, computer science, earth sciences, education, engineering, genealogy, government information, health sciences, humanities and the arts, the internet, legal studies and human rights, library and information studies, management, music, physical sciences and the social sciences.

5. *Timelines Collection* at *http://www.canisius.edu/~emeryg/time.html* is organized by categories: history and cultures, science and technology, art and literature, popular culture and current events history and culture.

6. *ERIC Digests* at *http://www.ed.gov/databases/ERIC_Digests/index/* are short reports on educational topics targeted specifically to teachers. The ERIC Digests are produced by the sixteen subject-specialized ERIC Clearinghouses and are reviewed by experts and content specialists in the field. The extensive full-text database is searchable and is updated quarterly.

7. *The Librarians' Index to the Internet* at *http://sunsite.berkeley.edu/InternetIndex/* is a good starting point. This index is logical and well designed. The lack of intricate graphics makes it load quickly. Topics of interest have been categorized by subject to make them easier to find. The entries are annotated.

8. *The Michigan Electronic Library* at *http://mel.lib.mi.us/*, despite its Michigan orientation, is an intense site and certainly worth the visit. Included are extensive sections on humanities, health, science, and education.

9. *The Electronic References and Scholarly Citations of Internet Sources* (The World-Wide Web Virtual Library) at *http://www.gu.edu.au/gint/WWWVL/OnlineRefs.html* keeps track of materials dealing with the emerging standards for electronic references and scholarly citations of internet sources in both paper and online publications.

10. *World Lecture Hall* at *http://www.utexas.edu/world/lecture* is an extensive resource that indexes Web pages created by faculty worldwide who use the Web to deliver selected class materials.

## CHAPTER 4

Putting Together Your First Instructional Web Site

I presently have three courses online and love every minute of it. It provides a terrific continuity between semesters, a collaborative patchwork quilt that allows the subject to grow, expand and change with input and output. Multi-disciplinary teaching becomes easier and more effective; core material can be easily summarized and displayed; and individual paths followed with a click of the finger. The Internet also allows students to connect with similar courses all over the world, to supplement library books with up-to-the-minute research, and to publish as fast as they can think.[1]

THE process of creating materials for the Web is getting more complex all the time. New HTML enhancements, browser plug-ins, and Web-publishing tools are being introduced at a dramatic rate—even outpacing the standards that govern them. Formerly text-laden Web sites are metamorphosing into animated, splashy multimedia presentations. In many instances, the rules of advertising appear to have overtaken the orderly precision of Tim Berners-Lee's design for the Web with its emphasis on scholarly methodology. All too often these days, Web pages are consumed as "eye-candy" by avid "net surfers"—a quick stop here, a taste there and then it is time to move on.

While these fast-moving technological developments on the Web may seem both enticing and intimidating at first, the important thing to remember is that HTML, the core language of Web publishing, is simple and accessible to anyone who wishes to learn it. Fancy graphics and spectacular multimedia effects do not necessarily make for an effective Web site—and in fact may detract from the viewing experience by making pages slow to load and difficult to navigate. Regardless of the hype surrounding the Internet and the glitter of the Web, your academic Web site ultimately serves only one purpose: to effectively and clearly communicate the information you wish to provide for your students.

During introductory HTML sessions we conducted with faculty, we observed a certain degree of timidity, even on the part of people who were advanced in their fields. It is not clear whether this reserve came from the high visibility of the Web, the use of a completely new set of tools and publishing metaphors, pressure to have an online presence, or some combination of all of these. However, despite initial reservations, faculty members quickly acquired the necessary skills to publish their first Web pages. Anxiety was replaced with a growing sense of curiosity for the medium. Key among these challenges are establishing a clear rationale for choosing this medium, adapting print content, establishing clear and consistent design and integrating interactivity.

We focus on these design issues later in this chapter. However, as with any new medium—be it, for example, painting or carpentry—it is important to spend some time becoming familiar with the tools. To this end, we have created a hands-on manual beginning in section 4.1 with basic HTML and moving in section 4.2 to advanced HTML. In order to illustrate this manual, we have chosen to deconstruct a simple instructional Web site—in this case, the first series of Web pages for Anne's Writing Workshop II class that we collaborated on in January 1996. These are especially resonant for us because they demonstrate the evolution of our design for the Web.

All you need to publish your first Web site is to learn a few basic "tags." However, as many professionals and academics are now learning, once you become comfortable with basic Web publishing, you will likely become more involved, incorporating features and technologies into your site as your knowledge of this medium grows, and as your material dictates. You will discover that there are few limits to the flexibility and creative potential of this medium. The few limits that exist are currently hardware-based: older computers, slower modems and the growing traffic on the Internet infrastructure. However, these limitations primarily affect advanced design or graphics and video-heavy Web sites, not the kind of Web pages and sites you will initially be building. (Bear in mind that this technology is evolving rapidly. Current limitations will not be relevant five years from now as older computers are replaced, faster modems become mainstream and the infrastructure of the Internet is updated.)

4.1 Basic HTML
WHAT IS HTML?

By now, you are probably familiar with the term HTML—Hypertext Markup Language. Basically, HTML is the standard computer language used to create Web documents. HTML marks up documents so that a Web browser can interpret them and display them with paragraph breaks, bold text, italics, headings and so forth. HTML is a simple language to learn. The most basic component of HTML is the *markup tag*.

WHAT ARE TAGS? All documents can be broken down into their elements—heads, tables, paragraphs, lists, pictures and so forth. HTML tags are simply a way to mark the various elements of a file so that a Web browser will know how to interpret and display them. They consist of a left angle bracket (<), a tag name, and a right angle bracket (>). Tags are usually paired (e.g., <HTML> and </HTML>) to start and end the tag instruction. The end tag looks just like the start tag except that a slash (/) precedes the text within the brackets. Some tags include attributes, which provide additional information about the tag. For example, you can specify the alignment of images (top, middle or bottom) by including the appropriate attribute within the image tag. There are also unpaired or "empty tags," such as the ones for line breaks <BR> and paragraph breaks <P>.

HTML EDITORS Since HTML documents are plaintext (also known as ASCII) files, they can be created using any text editor. Such editors can be found both off- and online and are usually available free of charge. You can also use your word processing software if you remember to save your document as "text only" or "plaintext." You may also wish to use one of the many dedicated HTML editors that are now available. These editors come in many flavors. Some, such as Sausage Software's Hot Dog Pro, Allaire Homesite, or Coffee Cup, are essentially enhanced text editors. You have to type in the HTML code yourself, but the software gives you many "wizards" and shortcuts that make the job easier. Other editors belong to the newest generation of WYSIWYG (what you see is what you get) editors, such as Netscape Composer, Microsoft FrontPage, PageMill, and Macromedia Dreamweaver. These editors have a graphical "drag and drop" interface, much like desktop publishing programs. In some cases, you can create your pages without ever seeing the HTML code.

We recommend beginning with a simple text editor. By doing so, you will gain a solid understanding of HTML syntax from the inside out, you will retain good control over your pages and you will not need to tackle learning a brand new software program. We cannot emphasize enough the value of having such a foundation in this medium. It is a prerequisite to becoming comfortable with writing for the Web and later will help extend your creative reach. Once you have gotten your feet wet with HTML and published a few documents, however, you will probably want to move on to a more sophisticated editor, such as one of those mentioned above.

Simple text editors for UNIX include Vi, Pico, Emacs and Jolt; for Windows, Textpad and Notepad; for Mac-intosh, Bbedit, TeachText and SimpleText.

Figure 4.1. Editing an HTML file with Notepad, a text editor on a Windows machine.

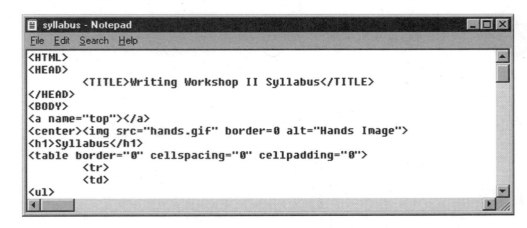

4.1.1 CREATING YOUR FIRST WEB SITE

To write a simple Web page, you will not need to know all the latest features of HTML, which is expanding all the time. This chapter is not an exhaustive guide to HTML. (There are many extensive HTML resources available, both in print and on the Web. At the end of this chapter and on the companion Web site to this book, *http://www.nyupress.nyu.edu/professor.html,* we list some of these.) Our goal is simply to get you started with your transition onto the Web, so that with a handful of tags, your Web site can be up and running in no time. Thus, we begin with a simple set of pages and build onto them gradually, using more and more HTML. The site we will build for you will serve as a useful template for your own course Web site.

Select Your Material

First, you need to decide what material you want to include. If you have a lot of material, this stage may involve some in-depth planning, which we discuss in detail later. Regardless of the amount of material you want to include, it is usually a good idea to storyboard your site. For this, a sharp pencil and a piece of paper will usually suffice.

In our sample class home page, we will include the following sections:

1. A Course Description
2. A Syllabus
3. Office Hours
4. An E-mail Link

The Minimal Components of
an HTML Document

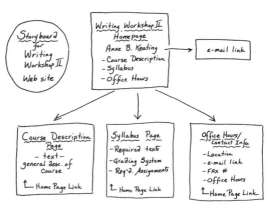

Figure 4.2. Storyboarding the Writing Workshop II Web site. Illustration by Anne B. Keating.

Every HTML document should contain certain standard HTML tags. These are:

1. The <HTML></HTML> tag, which identifies the document as HTML format.
2. The <HEAD></HEAD> tag, which identifies the header portion of the document.
3. The <TITLE></TITLE> tag, which is contained within the <HEAD></HEAD>tag. The title element contains your document title and identifies its content in a global context. The title is displayed in the browser menu, but not within the text area. The title is also what is displayed on someone's bookmark list, so choose something descriptive, unique, and relatively short.
4. The <BODY></BODY> tag, which contains the actual content of the page: paragraphs, lists, images and other elements.

These tags are all containers, which means that the elements they describe must be contained within them, and therefore they require an ending tag. Required elements are shown in this sample bare-bones document:

```
<HTML>
<HEAD>
<TITLE>Writing Workshop II Home Page</TITLE>
</HEAD>
<BODY>
(All Web page contents will go here.)
</BODY>
</HTML>
```

Because you should include these tags in each file, you might want to create a template file with them.

Naming Files

At this point, you should save your file. The file extension *.html* or *.htm* indicates that this is an HTML document and must be used on all HTML files. It is also a standard convention to call the main page of your site *index.html* or *index.htm.* This is because most Web servers are set up to recognize "index" files as "home" pages, so that if someone goes to your site they need only type the URL (Uniform Resource Locator) up to the name of the directory in which your index.html file resides. For example, in *http://www.mycollege.edu/professor/,* the index file will be called automatically. Other pages that you create may be named descriptively—for example, *schedule.html* or *syllabus.html.*

Adding Text

Now that we have our basic HTML template, it is time to add some content to our file. The important thing to remember when putting text in HTML documents is that browsers do not recognize carriage returns. You must use the paragraph <P> and break <BR> tags to insert paragraph and line breaks in your HTML file. When used within a block of text, the <P> tag will insert a blank line into the text block, separating it into two blocks of text, or paragraphs. The <BR> tag will simply force a line break in your text without inserting an extra blank line. Unlike the tags previously mentioned, the <P> and <BR> are empty tags and do not require ending tags. (Optionally, you may use </P> to end paragraphs. Some dedicated HTML editors add this closing tag automatically.)

When you name your files to be linked, it is always a good idea to do so in context. Unfortunately, you cannot always use a full description in file naming. PC operating systems prior to Windows 95, which do not support long filenames, limit you to eight-character filenames. In such cases, you can use a shortened version of the word that is still descriptive enough. (Thus, *F99syll.htm* should serve to help you to remember which syllabus version this file represents: "Fall 1999 syllabus.") If you are teaching more than one class, use a different directory for each. Dumping all files in the same directory will invariably result in overwritten files and orphaned links.

```
<HTML>
<HEAD>
<TITLE>Writing Workshop II Home Page</TITLE>
</HEAD>
<BODY>
Writing Workshop II <P>
Y20.7503.01/.04 / Spring 1996 <P>
Anne B. Keating, Ph.D. <BR>
Liberal Arts Degree Program—School of Continuing Education <BR>
New York University <BR>
</BODY>
</HTML>
```

One great aspect of HTML is the immediacy with which you can see the results of your work, and it is a good idea to do so frequently. To view an HTML file as you are constructing it, start up your Web browser, choose "Open File" from the File Menu and select the file from the directory in which you have saved it. (You do not need be connected to

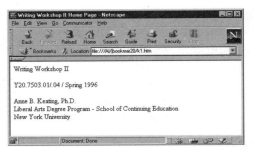

Figure 4.3. Basic template for Writing Workshop II page.

Figure 4.4. Preformatted text in the browser.

the Internet to view files locally.) Once you have loaded a file into your browser, you do not need to reopen it every time you make a change or addition. Simply save your HTML file, switch over to your browser and choose "Reload." Your latest changes will be viewable immediately. Most dedicated HMTL editors enable you to view your changes with even greater ease.

In addition to hard carriage returns, browsers also ignore multiple spaces within an HTML file—they are collapsed into a single space. For example, if the text within your HTML file contains indentation or other spaces, the browser will ignore this. There are tags you may use to format text so that it will be indented. One such tag is <BLOCK-QUOTE></BLOCKQUOTE>. Any text contained within this tag will display within a browser as an indented paragraph. Another formatting tag is <PRE></PRE>. Any text contained within this tag will display in your browser exactly as you type it, including all line breaks, paragraph breaks, and spaces. You may ask, why use HTML paragraph and line break tags when you can simply use the <PRE></PRE> tag? The reason is that, as you can see from Figure 4.4, preformatted text will always default to a fixed-width font, such as Courier, and does not allow you to specify any additional text formatting, such as headings, bold text, or italic. In these days of visually oriented Web sites, no one wants to read long blocks of preformatted text. While this tag can be useful in some instances, it should not be used as a general way to format entire pages.

Formatting Text   Now it is time to enhance our page with some formatting. We can do this by using some simple text-formatting tags:

1. The <H1></H1> tag, which marks text as a heading. There are actually six levels of headings that you can use: <H1></H1>, <H2></H2>, <H3></H3>, <H4></H4>, <H5></H5> and <H6></H6>. While different browsers will display headings slightly differently, <H1> is always the largest and <H6> the smallest.
2. The <B></B> tag, which makes text bold.
3. The <I></I> tag, which makes text italic.
4. The <U></U> tag, which underlines text.
5. The <CENTER></CENTER> tag, which centers text, images, or tables.

Here is how we can add some of these tags to our HTML file:

Figure 4.5. Formatted text in the Writing Workshop II page.

```
<HTML>
<HEAD>
<TITLE>Writing Workshop II Home Page</TITLE>
</HEAD>
<BODY>
<CENTER>
<H1>Writing Workshop II</H1>
<P>
Y20.7503.01/.04 / Spring 1996
<P>
<B>Anne B. Keating, Ph.D.</B><BR>
<I>Liberal Arts Degree Program—School of Continuing Education<BR>
New York University </I>
</CENTER>
</BODY>
</HTML>
```

Figure 4.5 shows how this page now looks.

4.1.2 ADDING AN IMAGE

Images can make your Web page more interesting and, in many cases, more informative. Scanning, manipulating and saving images will be covered in greater depth in chapter 5. For now, we focus on simply adding an image to your page. There is only one tag you will need to know for this—the <IMG> tag. It is an "empty" tag, like <P> and <BR>, and therefore requires no ending tag. However, the <IMG> tag has several attributes that are important to know.

As mentioned previously, tag attributes allow you to provide additional information about the page element that the tag is describing and are enclosed within the brackets that surround the opening tag. In addition, most attributes have values, which are usually surrounded by double quotation marks. For example, in <IMG SRC="picture.gif">, IMG is the tag, SRC is the attribute, and *picture.gif* is the value of the attribute. This tag instructs the browser to display an image file called *picture.gif*. Some <IMG> attributes that are good to know are:

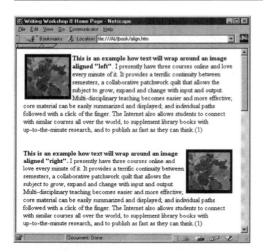

Figure 4.6. Image with text aligned in two different alignments.

1. SRC, which is the only required attribute. It identifies the image "source" file and is always set to the URL or filename of the image you would like to display.
2. ALT, which allows you to display text in place of an image when someone looking at your page has turned off "image loading" within his or her browser or is using a text-based browser such as Lynx. While it is not required, it is a good habit to provide alternate text for all your images, particularly if they are buttons that link to other pages or sites. In addition, some of the latest browsers actually display the alternate text when you pass your mouse over an image, which can be a nice feature of your Web page.
3. ALIGN, which allows you to define how an image should align with your text. It can be set to LEFT, RIGHT, TOP, MIDDLE or BOTTOM, the default value. (Figure 4.6 shows how some of these alignments display in a browser.)
4. BORDER, which allows you to specify a width for a border that will appear around an image if it is a "clickable" image. In HTML, widths, heights and sizes are always expressed in number of pixels. While this may be an unfamiliar measuring unit to you at first, with a little experience and experimentation you will soon get a good feel for setting pixel values. In most cases, you can set this value to "0" for no border to appear at all.
5. WIDTH and HEIGHT. These attributes may be used to specify the exact size of your image and, like the border attribute, are expressed in pixels. The advantage of using image height and width is that it may decrease the load time of your page, because the browser knows exactly what size image to expect, as opposed to determining the image size before rendering the page. It is not advisable to modify image size in your HTML file by using the height and width attributes. For best results, images should only be resized in an image editing program. (See chapter 5.) The height and width attributes in your HTML file should reflect the exact size of your image.

Using the image tag, let us go ahead and add an image to our class page:

```
<HTML>
<HEAD>
<TITLE>Writing Workshop II Home Page</TITLE>
</HEAD>
```

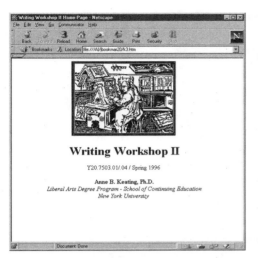

Figure 4.7. Writing Workshop II page with an image.

```
<BODY>
<CENTER>
<IMG SRC="illus1.gif" WIDTH="274" HEIGHT="205" BORDER="0"
   ALT="scriptor">
<H1>Writing Workshop II</H1>
Y20.7503.01/.04 / Spring 1996
<P>
<B>Anne B. Keating, Ph.D.</B><BR>
<I>Liberal Arts Degree Program—School of Continuing Education<BR>
New York University </I>
</CENTER>
</BODY>
</HTML>
```

Figure 4.7 shows how this looks in a browser.

4.1.3 ADDING A LIST

Now your page is really beginning to take shape. It is time to add a menu of our three subsections: "Course Description," "Syllabus" and "Office Hours." We will create the menu in the form of an HTML "list." HTML supports unordered, ordered, and definition lists. To make lists, use the following tags.

1. The <UL></UL> tag, for unordered, or bulleted lists. Within the <UL></UL> tag, which brackets the entire list, each individual list item must be marked using the <LI> tag, which is not a container and therefore requires no ending tag. The <LI> items can contain multiple paragraphs, as well as images, additional lists and tables. Indicate the paragraphs and line breaks with the standard <P> and <BR> tags.
2. The <OL></OL> tag, for ordered, or numbered lists. As with unordered lists, list items in an ordered list must be marked with the <LI> tag.
3. The <DL></DL> tag, for definition lists. Definition lists display much like dictionary definitions. You may specify a dictionary term, <DT>, and a dictionary definition, <DD>, within the list. This may be useful if you want to display a glossary of terms.

In our sample page we will use an unordered list.

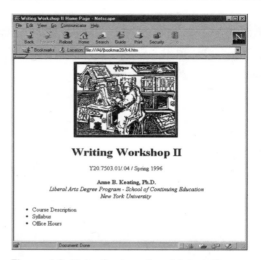

Figure 4.8. Note the unordered list at the bottom of the Writing Workshop II page.

```
<HTML>
<HEAD>
<TITLE>Writing Workshop II Home Page</TITLE>
</HEAD>
<BODY>
<CENTER>
<IMG SRC="illus1.gif" WIDTH="274" HEIGHT="205" BORDER="0"
   ALT="scriptor">
<H1>Writing Workshop II</H1>
Y20.7503.01/.04 / Spring 1996
<P>
<B>Anne B. Keating, Ph.D.</B><BR>
<I>Liberal Arts Degree Program—School of Continuing Education<BR>
New York University </I>
</CENTER>
<P>
<UL>
   <LI>Course Description
   <LI>Syllabus
   <LI>Office Hours
</UL>
</BODY>
</HTML>
```

Figure 4.8 shows how this page looks.

4.1.4 NAVIGATIONAL LINKS AND E-MAIL LINKS

The chief power of HTML comes from its ability to link text and images to other documents or sections of documents. A browser highlights the identified text with color and underlines it to indicate that it is a "link." Now it is time to add links to your page. HTML supports links to other files, to subsections of other HTML files, to subsections of the same file, to URLs, and to an e-mail address. To create links, you need to use the anchor tag: <A></A>. The <A></A> tag can surround either text or an image and make them linkable. It has several important attributes, including HREF, which specifies the name of the file or location to which you are linking.

The value of HREF can be set to:

1. A filename, if the file that you are linking to resides on the same server, in the same directory. For example, in <A HREF="home.htm">Return to Home Page </A>, the text "Return to Home Page" links to a file called *home.htm*, which resides on the same server and in the same directory as the page that contains the link. This is known as a relative link.

2. A filename with its complete relative path, if the file you are linking to resides on the same server but in a different directory. For example, in <A HREF="resource/books.htm">Book List</A>, the text "Book List" links to a file called *books.htm* located within a subdirectory called "resource." In this example, <A HREF="../home.htm"> Return to Home Page</A> the text "Return to Home Page" links to a file called *home.htm* located within a directory one level above the page with the link. Both of these are also examples of relative links.

3. A complete URL, if the file you are linking to resides on another server. The Web uses URLs to specify the location of files on other servers. A URL includes the type of resource being accessed (e.g., Web, Gopher, WAIS), the address of the server and the location of the file. The syntax is: *scheme://host.domain[:port]/path/filename* where scheme is *http:a file on a Web server.* For example, in <A HREF="http://www.nyu.edu/classes/keating/welcome.html">Welcome to My Course Web Site</A>, the text "Welcome to My Course Web Site" links to a file called *welcome.html* located on an NYU Web server within the *www.nyu.edu* domain.

4. An e-mail address, or "mailto,"—if you would like to allow people to send you e-mail from your Web page. In the example <A HREF="mailto:anne.keating@nyu.edu"> Send me an E-mail</A> clicking on the text "Send me an E-mail" will launch an e-mail client and fill in the "To:" field with the e-mail address *anne.keating@nyu.edu.*

5. A subsection or anchor of the same file, if you would like to provide links to other sections of your document. This is accomplished by using the NAME attribute of the <A></A> tag. First, you need to insert an anchor into your document at the point(s) that you want to link to. For example, if you wanted a link at the bottom of your page that pointed back to the top of the page, you would first insert the tag <A NAME="top"></A> at the top of the page. (Note that there is no text contained within the opening and closing tags. You do not need it because your are merely naming or

bookmarking that spot within your file.) Then go to the bottom of the page and insert the following tag: <A HREF="#top">Return to Top</A>. (Note that internal anchors are indicated by the # symbol, followed by the name of the anchor.) The text "Return to Top" would link back to the top of the page, where you inserted the "top" anchor.

Now we will add some links to our class page. We will make the text "Anne B. Keating" an e-mail link, and the menu choices (Course Description, Syllabus, and Office Hours) will link to external files.

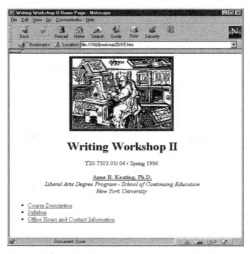

Figure 4.9. Writing Workshop II page with an e-mail link and three external links.

```
<HTML>
<HEAD>
<TITLE>Writing Workshop II Home Page</TITLE>
</HEAD>
<BODY>
<CENTER>
<IMG SRC="illus1.gif" WIDTH="274" HEIGHT="205" BORDER="0"
   ALT="scriptor">
<H1>Writing Workshop II</H1>
Y20.7503.01/.04 / Spring 1996
<P>
<A HREF="mailto:anne.keating@nyu.edu"><B>Anne B. Keating,
   Ph.D.</B></A><BR>
<I>Liberal Arts Degree Program—School of Continuing Education<BR>
New York University </I>
</CENTER>
<P>
<UL>
<LI><A HREF="course.htm">Course Description</A>
<LI><A HREF="syllab.htm">Syllabus</A>
<LI><A HREF="hours.htm">Office Hours and Contact Information</A>
</UL>
<P>
```

```
</BODY>
</HTML>
```

Figure 4.9 shows how our page looks now. Note that all the links are underlined. In your browser, your links will also be set off in a different color from the nonlinkable text.

4.1.5 SIMPLE TABLES   Before we create our subpages, we are going to make a slight design change to our home page. Notice that the list of subsections is flush left. While functionally this is fine, our page would appear more balanced if the list were centered. Unfortunately, the <CENTER> tag will not do the trick in this case, because it will center each individual line of the list, resulting in an unaligned list.

Instead, we will introduce a table. HTML tables are a great way to format many types of information, and one of the best ways to control the layout of page elements. To center our list of menu choices, we will place the list within a simple, single-cell table, and will then center the entire table on our page. This way, our list will remain properly aligned, but will be centered. The minimal table tags that you will need to know are

1. <TABLE></TABLE>, which will surround the entire contents of the table. Most browsers will automatically force a line break before and after tables, so that even if you do not put a <BR> into your HTML file, the table will appear below any previous elements, not next to them. Some attributes that can be used with the <TABLE></TABLE> tag are
   a. BORDER, which can be turned on by setting the border attribute to a numerical value that indicates the width of the border that will appear. As with image borders, table border widths are measured in pixels. When borders are turned on, or set to a numerical value, a border will appear around the entire table and around each table cell. You may experiment with different values to see how different sized borders look. If you set BORDER="0" there will be no visible border on your table. This is a feature commonly employed in HTML to lay out page elements in a specific way. This type of table is sometimes referred to as an "invisible" table. If you do not include the border attribute at all, then its default value will be "0" and no borders will appear on your table.

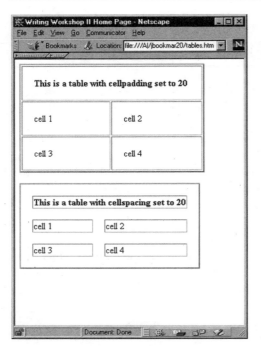

Figure 4.10. Tables in the browser.

b. CELLSPACING, which can be set to a numerical pixel value and allows you to define the space between table cells. This attribute may be used whether you are using table borders or not, and its default value is two, which means that even if you do not use the attribute there will be a two-pixel-wide space between your table cells.

c. CELLPADDING, which can be set to a numerical pixel value and allows you to define the space around data within table cells. Think of using this attribute as setting margins within a table cell. Again, this attribute may be used whether you are using table borders or not, and its default value is two, which means that even if you do not use the attribute there will be a two-pixel-wide space around the data in your table cells. While the cellpadding and cellspacing attributes may seem similar, they can be used quite cleverly to control how data displays within a table. If your borders are turned off, cellpadding and cellspacing can be used somewhat interchangeably to the same effect. If your borders are turned on, however, you will see the difference between the two quite clearly.

2. <TR></TR>, which indicates a table row. Tables must have a minimum of one row, but they may have as many rows as your data requires. The <TR></TR> are contained within the <TABLE></TABLE> tags.

3. <TD></TD>, which indicates table data. Each <TD></TD> tag forms a table cell within a row. Table rows must have minimum of one table cell, but you may have as many table cells as your data requires.

All of the table tags above may be modified with many attributes that can give you further control over how your table and table data are displayed. We have only introduced the basics here to get you started. Tables will be covered in more detail later in this chapter. Now it is time to add the table tags to our class Web page:

```
<HTML>
<HEAD>
<TITLE>Writing Workshop II Home Page</TITLE>
</HEAD>
<BODY>
<CENTER>
```

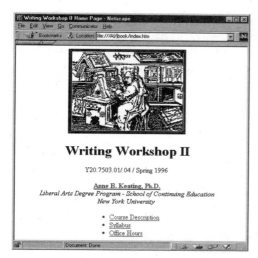

Figure 4.11. Writing Workshop II page with the addition of an "invisible" table.

```
<IMG SRC="illus1.gif" WIDTH="274" HEIGHT="205" BORDER="0"
   ALT="scriptor">
<H1>Writing Workshop II</H1>
Y20.7503.01/.04 / Spring 1996
<P>
<A HREF="mailto:anne.keating@nyu.edu"><B>Anne B. Keating,
   Ph.D.</B></A><BR>
<I>Liberal Arts Degree Program—School of Continuing Education<BR>
New York University</I>
<P>
<TABLE BORDER="0" CELLSPACING="0" CELLPADDING="20">
   <TR>
   <TD>
   <UL>
   <LI><A HREF="course.htm">Course Description</A>
   <LI><A HREF="syllabus.htm">Syllabus</A>
   <LI><A HREF="hours.htm">Office Hours</A>
   </UL>
   </TD>
   </TR>
</TABLE>
</CENTER>
</BODY>
</HTML>
```

Notice that we have set the table border to "0." Figure 4.11 shows how our table looks.

4.1.6 CREATING SUBPAGES

At this point, you have enough knowledge of HTML to complete the first draft of your class Web page. By employing some of the HTML tags that we have just introduced, we are now going to create the subpages for our site: the "Course Description" page, the "Syllabus" page and the "Office Hours" page. In the HMTL file for our "Course Description" page that follows, note that we have added a link at the bottom of the page that links back to our class home page. It is always a good idea to provide "cross-navigational" and/or "Return to Home Page" links on your pages so that users will not get to a page and become "dead-ended." Note also that we have revised the <TITLE> of our page. This is not functionally necessary, but it is a good habit to form. (In order to help you focus on the HTML, the text portions of each HTML example from now on will be truncated, though they will appear in full in the illustration.)

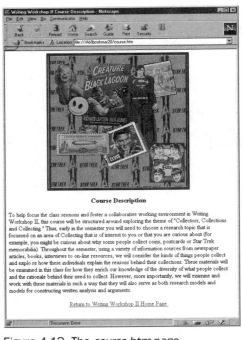

Figure 4.12. The *course.htm* page.

```
<HTML>
<HEAD>
<TITLE>Writing Workshop II Course Description</TITLE>
</HEAD>
<BODY>
<CENTER>
<IMG SRC="collage.gif" BORDER="0" ALT="collecting collage">
</CENTER>
<P>
<CENTER>
<H3>Course Description</H3>
</CENTER>
To help focus the class sessions and foster a collaborative working environment
    in Writing Workshop II, this course will be structured around exploring the
    theme of "Collectors, Collections and Collecting."
. . . . . . . . . . . . . . . . . . . . . . . . . . . . . . . . . . . . . . . . . . .
<P>
<CENTER>
<A HREF="index.htm">Return to Writing Workshop II Home Page</A>
</CENTER>
</BODY>
</HTML>
```

Figure 4.12 shows how our page will look.

Now we turn to our "Syllabus" page. This is the most complex page so far, because it contains three internal subsections: "Required Texts," "Grading System," and "Assignments." Here are the steps we employed to create this page:

1. We copied the format of our home page menu to create a menu of subsections for the "Syllabus," a centered single-cell table and a bulleted list of links.
2. We anchored all of our subsections and set up our menu choices to link to these subsections.
3. We employed one new tag—the <HR> or hard rule tag—to insert lines between our sections. The <HR> tag produces a horizontal line the width of the browser window. This is a useful tag, and makes this page much easier to read and navigate.
4. We used an anchor at the top of our page and inserted links back to the top of the page and back to the home page at the end of each subsection. This will enable users to find their way around our site quickly and easily.
5. We employed a numbered list by using the <OL></OL> tag in the "Required Text" section.

Here is how our HTML file for this page looks:

```
<HTML>
<HEAD>
<TITLE>Writing Workshop II Syllabus</TITLE>
</HEAD>
<BODY>
<CENTER>
<IMG SRC="hands.gif" BORDER="0" ALT="Hands Image">
<H1><A NAME="top">Syllabus</A></H1>
<TABLE BORDER="0" CELLSPACING="0" CELLPADDING="0">
<TR>
<TD>
<UL>
<LI><A HREF="#texts">Required Texts</A>
```

Figure 4.13. The *syllabus.htm* page.

```
<LI><A HREF="#grades">Grading System</A>
<LI><A HREF="#assignments">Required Assignments</A>
</UL>
</TD>
</TR>
</TABLE>
</CENTER>
<P>
<HR>
<CENTER>
<H3><A NAME="texts">Required Texts</A></H3>
</CENTER>
<OL>
<LI>Turabian, Kate. <U>A Manual for Writers of Term Papers, Theses, and
    Dissertations.</U>6th edition.
```
. . . .
```
<P>
<HR>
<CENTER>
<H3><A NAME="grades">Grading System</A></H3>
</CENTER>
Computer-aided research skills, the proposal, outline and working bibliography
    will not receive letter grades, but will be marked as accepted on the following
    basis
```
. . . .
```
<P>
Final Draft of Research Paper – 20%
<P>
<CENTER>
<H3><A NAME="assignments">The Assignments </A></H3>
</CENTER>
All work assigned in class and as homework must be completed and turned in on
    time.
```

```
<P>
All of these assignments lead up to or are drafts of the final ten to fifteen page
    research paper due at the end of the semester.
<P>
<CENTER>
<A HREF="#top">Return to top of page</A><P>
<A HREF="index.htm">Return to Writing Workshop II Home Page</A>
</CENTER>
</BODY>
</HTML>
```

Figure 4.13 shows how our page looks.

Finally, we will create our "Office Hours" page—a very simple page. We will just use some of the formatting and list tags that we have used above as well as the <A HREF="mailto:"> </A> to make an e-mail link. Here is how the HTML file will look:

```
<HTML>
<HEAD>
<TITLE>Writing Workshop II Office Hours </TITLE>
</HEAD>
<BODY>
<P>
<A NAME="hours"></A>
<CENTER>
<H3>Anne B. Keating: Office Hours and Contact Information</H3>
</CENTER>
<UL>
<LI><B>Location: </B>Shimkin Hall, Room 225
<LI><B>E-Mail:</B>
```

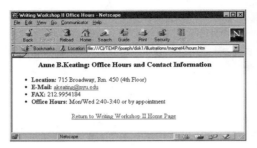

Figure 4.14. The *hours.htm* page.

```
<A HREF="mailto:anne.keating@nyu.edu"> anne. keating@nyu.edu</A>
<LI><B>FAX: </B>212.995.4184
<LI><B>Office Hours: </B>Mon/Wed 2:40-3:40 or by appointment
</UL>
<CENTER>
<A HREF="index.htm">Return to Writing Workshop II Home Page</A>
</CENTER>
</BODY>
</HTML>
```

Figure 4.14 shows how the page will look.

4.1.7 Publishing Your Page

Congratulations! You have now created your first complete, functional set of HTML pages. Your files are named, organized and saved. At this point it is always a good idea to copy them into a backup directory or onto a disk. In order to see your files on the Web, you need to publish them. In other words, you have to move your files to a place where your university's Web server can see them. How does this work? At this point, it is best to pause and do some administrative footwork. By now your university must have a policy regarding instructors publishing course pages. This policy will give you the proper guidelines on where your files should reside in relationship to your university's Web server. This policy will also describe what kind of account you will need to host your files. This account will most likely be on a time-sharing system, very likely a UNIX system. Talk to your university's computer accounts office, because you may possibly be using such an account already.

Once you know where to place your files, the rest is just mechanics. The application—or, as technical people call it, the "client"—for doing this is called "FTP." As you will recall from chapter 2, FTP stands for "File Transfer Protocol," and there are different types of FTP software for different platforms. In principle, they all perform the same routine:

1. They establish a connection between your machine and the remote machine.
2. They allow you to log in as an authenticated user.
3. They allow you to transfer files between the two platforms.
4. They allow you to log out and break off the connection.

One popular file transfer tool for the Macintosh platform is a product called "Fetch." Fetch has been around for many years. It is extremely user-friendly and function-rich, and allows you to move entire directories in one swoop. A popular tool for the Windows platform is WS_FTP, which is similar to Fetch.[2] (Instructions for using FTP on the two platforms named above are included in the Appendix.)

Common Mistakes and Problems with Uploading

If you encounter problems when uploading your files to a server, here are some possible causes:

1. Incorrect data type is selected. Remember, "binary" is for images, "ASCII text" for text.
2. Incorrect file is uploaded. Quite often people working with WordPerfect or Microsoft Word forget to save their HTML files as ASCII text. Even if they subsequently upload these files as ASCII, the result is unreadable by browsers.
3. Larger image files can get corrupted during uploads. While this rarely happens, make sure that your original is working fine by viewing it directly from your browser. Then upload the file again and watch for error messages during transmission.
4. UNIX is case-sensitive. Make sure your actual filenames reflect the correct case in the HTML code. If you are calling the file *BigPicture.gif* using the code <IMG SRC="BigPicture.gif">, your file will load correctly. If you call it *bigpicture.gif* using the code <IMG SRC="BigPicture.gif">, your image will not load.
5. Putting files in wrong directories. Be sure to upload files to the directories where your HTML file is expecting to find them. In other words, if your HTML file contains a reference such as <IMG SRC="images/picture.gif"> but you send the *picture.gif* file to the root directory instead of the images subdirectory, you will not see your image when viewing your file.

Testing Your Page

Now that we have created a complete Web site, it is always a good idea to check our page for errors and make sure that all of our links work. Fortunately, HTML is a solid performer and its immediate visual feedback allows you to apply rapid remedies. Here are some pointers to follow when checking your page.

1. *Spelling.* First and foremost, test your writing for typos and spelling errors. Luckily, most dedicated HTML editors offer spell checking. Once your file is online and you

have easy access to it, you may do a spell check from the UNIX command line or from within the simple UNIX text editors Pico or Emacs. While neither offers visual sophistication on a par with Microsoft Word, they do pick up on outrageous spelling errors.

2. *Links.* There is nothing more annoying to a Web user than broken links on a page, so make sure that all of your links work. Make sure they are active and that they go to the right place. Since the Web is a dynamic medium, verify from time to time that your intended targets have not changed. Since all of the links on our sample class page are local, relative links, this is easy to do. Simply load the *index.htm* page into your browser and test each link you have created, including the e-mail links. If any are not working properly, double-check all of your filenames in your HTML file. Also, check your tag syntax. A missing bracket or open tag may be enough to cause a problem in your file.

3. *Images.* If your image comes up with a broken-image icon, most likely this error is the result of one of three things: (1) an incorrect filename or path, (2) your file was uploaded as ASCII text rather than binary, or (3) there is a misplaced or omitted quotation mark in the HTML file.

4. *Unclosed tags.* A missing bracket may only affect a small section of your page. However, in some cases, especially with unclosed end tags, the results can be startling. For example, all text in bold after that tag—or, in the case of a link, all the text after the link—will seem to disappear from your Web page.

5. *Cross-platform related problems.* "I did everything right. I checked my links, I checked my images, I even tried my page on my machine and everything worked fine." Well, what may work perfectly fine on one machine, may look slightly different on another. This is a fact of life. Here are some issues to ponder:

   a. *Resolution.* Resolution is a function of the monitor and video card used on a particular platform. Different computers can therefore have different resolutions and pixel shapes. Macintoshes use 72 dpi, Windows around 80 dpi and UNIX can drive resolution as high as 115 dpi. This means that graphics that look perfectly arranged on the Mac may look different on other machines. Is there a cure for that? No. Research your target audience. If their preferred platform is UNIX, create your pages on a UNIX machine.

   b. *Cross-platform file naming.* This has been the cause of many headaches and rewrites. When you are writing your HTML file on a Macintosh or Windows machine, you may be tempted to pay little attention to how you name your files. However, once your files are uploaded to a UNIX-based Web server, links that worked perfectly on your original machine suddenly will come up with errors. This is because UNIX is case-sensitive. The code <A HREF="CLASS.HTML">class page</A> will send a UNIX server looking for a file *CLASS.HTML* in your directory. If you have a file named *class.html* or variations like *Class.HTML* your link will not work.

4.2 Advanced HTML

Now that you have mastered the fundamentals of HTML, you are probably ready to move on to some of the more advanced features. These features can give you more control over your pages' appearance, and, when used correctly, can make your site much more effective.

4.2.1 BACKGROUND AND TEXT COLORS

One relatively easy way to make your site more visually appealing is to add color. Just as in print publishing, color can make your Web site more effective and more readable, and can even set a mood for your site. Conversely, misuse of color can make your site hard on the eyes, difficult to read, and downright unattractive. While colors are largely a matter of taste, for the sake of your students, we strongly suggest adhering to a couple of basic rules:

1. *Limit the number of colors.* In the early days of HTML, only background, text and link colors could be specified, which was a natural deterrent to using too many colors. Now HTML allows you to specify table colors for individual cells and text colors anywhere in your document. This has created great possibilities for designers, but can be used ineffectively by those with limited design experience. Play it safe—use only a few colors.
2. *Choose conservative colors.* Use soft, muted colors, rather than bright ones. If you are not good with colors, pick white as a background color. White is conservative, simple and very easy on the eyes.
3. *Make sure your text is readable.* For example, you may choose a color for your links that is very visible on your background, but your visited link color is not. Test your pages thoroughly for readability.

Colors are identified in HTML in one of two ways:

SOME HELP CHOOSING COLORS

There are some good utilities available for testing colors, which allow you to see how various text colors will look on various backgrounds. One such utility is a freeware program called "ColorFinder". You can find it on the Web at *http://www.acmetech.com/* and download it. It allows you to test and select colors and provides you with the color codes, which you can copy right into your HTML file.

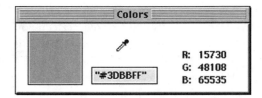

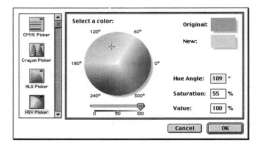

Figure 4.15. A freeware color picker program such as ColorFinder (*http://www.acmetech.com*) helps you to convert RGB values to hexadecimal equivalents.

1. Every color on the computer has a red, green and blue (RGB) component (the values of which range from 0 to 255), which can be represented by a two-digit hexadecimal number consisting of the value of each of these components. In HTML, these values are represented as a triplet of RGB values that takes the form "RRGGBB." There are many resources available, both in print and on the Web, which provide complete listings and, in many cases, examples of colors with their associated hexadecimal values.

2. You can also identify a color simply by using its name, such as "red," "blue" or "white." There is a short list of colors that have these reserved names (see the Appendix) and can be interpreted by most browsers by this name instead of the hexadecimal value.

Colors can be specified in HTML documents in several ways:

1. You can set up color tags within the <BODY></BODY> tag that will apply to the entire document. The color elements you can specify within the <BODY> tag are:
   a. Background color, using the BGCOLOR attribute. For example: <BODY BGCOLOR ="white"> or <BODY BGCOLOR="#FFFFFF"> ("#FFFFFF" is the hexadecimal value for white).
   b. Text color, using the TEXT attribute. For example: <BODY BGCOLOR="white" TEXT="blue">.
   c. Link color, using the LINK attribute. For example: <BODY BGCOLOR="white" TEXT="blue" LINK="red">.
   d. Active link color, using the ALINK attribute. Links become active when you click them. The ALINK color punctuates this transition. For example: <BODY BGCOLOR ="white" TEXT="blue" LINK="red" ALINK="brown">.
   e. Visited link color, using the VLINK attribute. You have probably noticed that when you click on a Web site's link, the link will change color when you return to that original page, indicating that you have already been down this road. This is known as the visited link color. For example: <BODY BGCOLOR="white" TEXT="blue" LINK="red" ALINK="brown" VLINK="green">.

2. You can set colors for individual words or portions of text within your document, using the <FONT> tag with its "color" attribute, as follows: <FONT COLOR="color-name"> </FONT>. When you use this tag, text contained within the opening and closing tags will display in the color you specify. This will override any text color that

you have specified within your <BODY> tag. (Please note that you cannot use this tag to change the color of links. It can only be used on nonlinkable text.)

3. You can specify colors within tables. This will be covered later in this chapter, when we discuss some advanced table tags.

Now it is time to go ahead and add some color to our class Web pages. For the sake of simplicity, we will work with some colors from the list of reserved names and will stick to a muted, earthy palette of khaki, black, red and brown. Generally, the best way to pick colors is by trial and error, adhering to the general principles outlined above. To set the text and link colors on our site, we will add attributes to the <BODY> tag within each of our documents. Remember, we want to retain consistency throughout our site: <BODY BGCOLOR="khaki" TEXT="black" LINK="red" VLINK="brown" ALINK="black">. Another common way to use color is to differentiate headings. Let us go ahead and add one more color to our site to make our headings stand out. Once again, we will choose an "earthy" color—"darkolivegreen"—to match our palette. Using the <FONT> tag, we will then add it to all headers on our pages. For example, here is how the HTML file on our home page will look:

```
<HTML>
<HEAD>
<TITLE>Writing Workshop II Home Page</TITLE>
</HEAD>
<BODY BGCOLOR="khaki" TEXT="black" LINK="red" VLINK="brown"
    ALINK="black">
<CENTER>
<IMG SRC="illus1.gif" WIDTH="274" HEIGHT="205" BORDER="0"
    ALT="scriptor">
<FONT COLOR="darkolivegreen"><H1>Writing Workshop II</H1></FONT>
Y20.7503.01/.04 / Spring 1996
<P>
<B>Anne B. Keating, Ph.D.</B><BR>
<I>Liberal Arts Degree Program—School of Continuing Education<BR>
```

```
New York University</I>
<P>
<TABLE BORDER="0" CELLSPACING="0" CELLPADDING="0">
<TR>
<TD>
<UL>
<LI><A HREF="course.htm">Course Description</A>
. . . . . . . . . . . . . . . . . . . . . . . . . . . . . . . . . . . . . . . . . . . . . . . . . . . . . . . . . . . . . . . . . . .
</TD>
</TR>
</TABLE>
</CENTER>
</BODY>
</HTML>
```

If you are following along with your version of this HTML exercise, go ahead and load it into the browser to see how the colors look. If you have substituted your own colors for the ones we used in our example, be sure to test all pages and links—including visited links—for readability.

4.2.2 ADVANCED TABLES We now have an easy-to-read, easy-to-navigate, aesthetically pleasing and consistent Web site. It is time to think about expanding your resources. One useful element on an academic Web site is a class schedule. Chances are you will be handing this out anyway, so why not include it online? It is easy to update, and students who tend to lose papers will have no excuse for not being prepared for class discussions. We assume that you already have your semester schedule typed up and that it looks similar to this one for Anne's class (for this example we will be working with the first month of her syllabus):

SEPTEMBER
Week 1 (9/5) Introduction to Writing Workshop II. What is a research paper? Choosing a research topic. Brainstorming techniques.
Week 2 (9/10, 9/12) Bring brainstorming charts to class. Introduction to Research

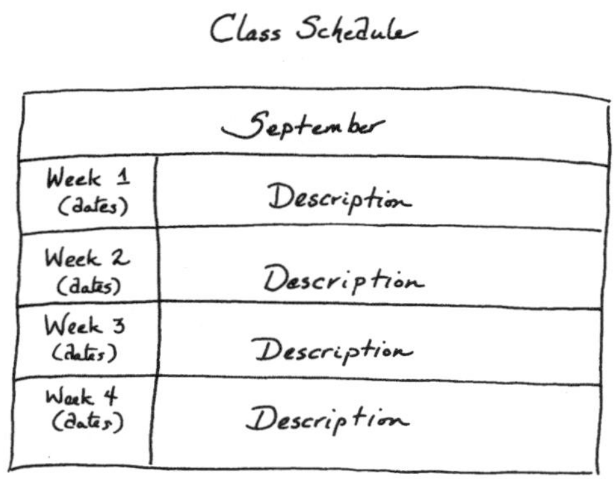

Figure 4.16. Pencil rendering of table with September portion of class schedule. Illustration by Anne B. Keating.

Methods. Using library resources. Introduction to the Reference Room. The Library of Congress Subject Headings. Fact Tools and Finding Tools. Preparing the proposal.

Week 3 (9/17, 9/26) Research methods continued. Using online research resources effectively.

Week 4 (9/24, 9/26) Proposal due. The importance of a thesis statement. Introduction to the outline. Using the outline to project time and resources needed to complete the research paper on time.

We introduced the basic table tags earlier in this chapter. You may recall that we included simple, single-cell "invisible" tables on the Writing Workshop II home page. If you do not remember these tags, now would be a good time to review them, as we will be using them here. The first issue to consider when formatting information for display on the Web, whether using tables or not, is how you would like your information to display. It may even be helpful to do a quick pencil sketch before you begin coding. Figure 4.16 is a sketch of how we might display our class schedule in a table, using just the month of September as a sample.

Now let us create this table in HTML. We begin by creating an HTML template for our new page. We can do this easily by saving one of our existing pages, *hours.htm*, with a new name—in this case as *schedule.htm*. Edit the title with a new description (Writing Workshop II Class Schedule) and delete the rest of the code and text up to the "return to home page" section. Your HTML file should look like this:

```
<HTML>
<HEAD>
<TITLE>Writing Workshop II Class Schedule</TITLE>
</HEAD>
<BODY>
<P>
<CENTER>
<FONT COLOR="darkolivegreen"><H3>Writing II Workshop: Class
    Schedule</H3></FONT>
</CENTER>
```

```
<CENTER>
<A HREF="index.htm">Return to Writing Workshop II Home Page</A>
</CENTER>
</BODY>
</HTML>
```

Now, let us add some of the text of our class schedule. Now our rough HTML file will look like this:

```
<HTML>
<HEAD>
<TITLE>Writing Workshop II Home Page </TITLE>
</HEAD>
<BODY>
<P>
<CENTER>
<FONT COLOR="darkolivegreen"><H3>Writing II Workshop: Class
    Schedule</H3></FONT>
</CENTER>
September
Week 1 (9/5) Introduction to Writing Workshop II. What is a research paper?
    Choosing a research topic. Brainstorming techniques.
Week 2 (9/10, 9/12) Bring brainstorming charts to class. Introduction to
    Research Methods. Using library resources. Introduction to the Reference
    Room. The Library of Congress Subject Headings. Fact Tools and Finding
    Tools. Preparing the proposal.
Week 3 (9/17, 9/26) Research methods continued. Using online research
    resources effectively.
Week 4 (9/24, 9/26) Proposal due. The importance of a thesis statement.
    Introduction to the outline. Using the outline to project time and resources
    needed to complete the research paper on time.
```

```
<CENTER>
<A HREF="index.htm">Return to Writing Workshop II Home Page</A>
</CENTER>
</BODY>
</HTML>
```

In order to create a table such as the one we have sketched out, we will need to open with the <TABLE> tag and set our cellspacing and cellpadding. We will center the table this time by using the table ALIGN attribute, which may be set to left, center or right. In addition, we will separate the components of our document into table rows as we want them to appear, using the <TR></TR> tag. Note also that we have set the width of the table border to three pixels. Here is how the table portion of our document will now look:

```
<TABLE BORDER="3" CELLSPACING="0" CELLPADDING="5" ALIGN="center">
<TR>
September
</TR>
<TR>
Week 1 (9/5)
Introduction to Writing Workshop II. What is a research paper? Choosing a
    research topic. Brainstorming techniques.
</TR>
<TR>
Week 2 (9/10, 9/12)
Bring brainstorming charts to class. Introduction to Research Methods. Using
    library resources. Introduction to the Reference Room. The Library of
    Congress Subject Headings. Fact Tools and Finding Tools. Preparing the pro-
    posal.
</TR>
<TR>
```

```
Week 3 (9/17, 9/26)
Research methods continued. Using online research resources effectively.
</TR>
<TR>
Week 4 (9/24, 9/26)
Proposal due. The importance of a thesis statement. Introduction to the out-
    line. Using the outline to project time and resources needed to complete the
    research paper on time.
</TR>
</TABLE>
</BODY>
</HTML>
```

Next, we need to divide each row that contains a week description into two cells using the <TD></TD> tag. The first cell of each row will contain the number of the week and corresponding dates, and the second cell will contain the explanatory text. Here is how the table portion of our HTML file will look now:

```
<TABLE BORDER="3" CELLSPACING="0" CELLPADDING="5" BORDER="1">
<TR>
September
</TR>
<TR>
<TD>Week 1 (9/5)</TD>
<TD>Introduction to Writing Workshop II. What is a research paper? Choosing a
    research topic. Brainstorming techniques.
</TD>
</TR>
<TR>
<TD>Week 2 (9/10, 9/12)</TD>
<TD>Bring brainstorming charts to class. Introduction to Research Methods.
    Using library resources. Introduction to the Reference Room. The Library of
```

```
Congress Subject Headings. Fact Tools and Finding Tools. Preparing the pro-
  posal.
</TD>
</TR>
<TR>
<TD>Week 3 (9/17, 9/26)</TD>
<TD>Research methods continued. Using online research resources effectively.
</TD>
</TR>
<TR>
<TD>Week 4 (9/24, 9/26)</TD>
<TD>Proposal due. The importance of a thesis statement. Introduction to the
  outline. Using the outline to project time and resources needed to complete
  the research paper on time.
</TD>
</TR>
</TABLE>
```

Before we look at our table in a browser, we need to complete the table row that contains the word "September." Recall from our original pencil sketch that this title should span across the entire table as a centered heading. There are several ways to achieve this effect; in this case, we are going to use a new tag and an associated attribute. First, instead of using the <TD></TD> tag in this row, we will use the table heading <TH></TH> tag. This tag is identical to the <TD></TD> tag except that it identifies the contents of the cell as a table heading, which simply means that it displays the text bolded and centered. In all other ways, the <TH></TH> tag behaves exactly as the <TD></TD> tag and may be modified with the same attributes. Second, we are going to modify the <TH></TH> tag with the COLSPAN attribute. This attribute allows for the creation of table cells that span across several columns. Because this row of our table only contains one item—the title "September"—we need to indicate that this table cell will span across two columns. Here is how our HTML file will look now (here you will see just the modification and the text for the first week as a comparison):

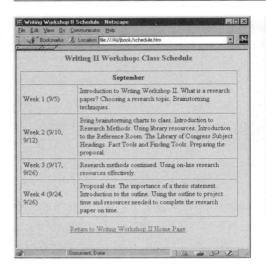

Figure 4.17. The table in the browser.

```
<TABLE BORDER="3" CELLSPACING="0" CELLPADDING="5" BORDER="1">
<TR>
<TH COLSPAN="2">September</TH>
</TR>
<TR>
<TD>Week 1 (9/5)</TD>
<TD>Introduction to Writing Workshop II. What is a research paper? Choosing a
    research topic. Brainstorming techniques.
</TD>
</TR>
```

Figure 4.17 shows how our table will appear within a browser.

With the addition of this simple table, our class schedule has become an easy-to-read quick reference for students. Another useful feature of tables is the ability to select a background color. HTML allows you to specify background color for an entire table as well as for individual rows and cells, using the BGCOLOR attribute. You may recall that this is the same attribute we used to set the background color of our document within the <BODY> tag. If you set a background color for the entire table, this will be the default color for the table, but you may override this color in individual rows or cells. HTML also allows you to set the border color of a table, row or cell using the BORDER-COLOR attribute.

Let us go ahead and add some color to our table, this time using hexadecimal numbers to represent some of our color choices. We will choose one color as our default table background color and then set off the table heading ("September") and the "number of the week" column with two additional colors by inserting the BGCOLOR attribute into the appropriate <TR>, <TH> and <TD> tags. In addition, we will set our border color to black. Here is how the HTML for the first part of this page will look:

```
<TABLE BORDER="3" CELLSPACING="0" CELLPADDING="5" BGCOLOR="white"
    BORDERCOLOR="black">
```

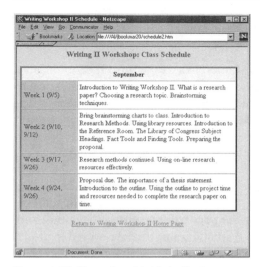

Figure 4.18. The colored table in the browser.

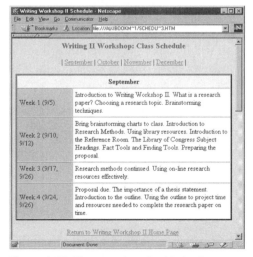

Figure 4.19. The completed table in the browser.

```
<TR>
<TH COLSPAN="2" BGCOLOR="#FFFF80">September</TH>
</TR>
<TR>
<TD BGCOLOR="#E2C670">Week 1 (9/5)</TD>
<TD>Introduction to Writing Workshop II. What is a research paper? Choosing a
    research topic. Brainstorming techniques.
</TD>
</TR>
```

Figure 4.18 shows how the table will look in the browser.

Now that we have one portion of the class schedule completed, the rest may be added by simply copying the HTML that we just created for September, and creating four similar tables for each month of the semester. In addition, we can make our class schedule even easier to navigate by inserting anchors and links to each table at the top of our file. Figure 4.19 shows how our completed page will look.

There are many more ways to use tables in your HTML files. As you experiment, you may find the following attributes helpful:

1. WIDTH, which can be used to set the width of tables or individual cells. Table and cell widths may also be set to absolute pixels or as a percentage of the page or table. For example, a table width may be set to 80 percent, and the table will expand or contract to 80 percent of the width of the browser window. In addition, a table cell width may be set to a percentage of the entire table width.
2. BORDERCOLORLIGHT and BORDERCOLORDARK, which may be used within a <TABLE> tag, <TR>, <TD> or <TH> tag to set a light and/or dark border color. Experiment with this to achieve a more three-dimensional effect on your tables.

Keep in mind that tables may contain images, lists and even other tables. You may find that using "invisible" tables is an effective way to lay out your page elements; in fact, it is often the only way to control page design. Additionally, be sure to leave plenty of "white space" in your HTML files when coding large tables, because, as you can see, the code may quickly become quite complex, and editing it can be difficult when your table row and cell tags run too closely together.

4.2.3 FRAMES

Another more advanced feature of HTML is frames. Just as the introduction of tables changed the fundamentals of page layout, frames have completely changed Web site navigation. In a Web site without frames, such as the one we have just created, navigating means jumping from one page to another, and completely leaving the other page behind. Recall that we had to include a link to our home page on every subpage so that our users would not become dead-ended. If we redesign our site using a frame-based navigational system, we can deposit all navigational tasks to one frame, or section of the visible browser window, which can remain static at all times. This enables users to navigate to any page in our site at anytime, without having to backtrack to a home page. In addition, it frees us up to focus on providing and laying out page content, rather than on providing navigation back to other points in our site. A second frame can be reserved to display all of our site content. Here again, a simple hand-drawn sketch (Figure 4.20) may clarify this concept and help you to design your own frame-based site.

Initially, coding frames may seem a daunting task, but once you understand that all you are really doing is writing a Web page to control the placement of other Web pages, working with frames will make sense. Here is a simple recipe for a framed version of our class site that has two frames—one on the left that will fill about a quarter of the browser window, and one on the right that fill the remaining three-quarters. Even though all you will see when you view the site are the two Web pages, you will write three pages to create the effect.

Setting Up the Frame

First, we need to create an HTML page that works behind the scenes to set up the two frames in our site. We will call this page "frames.htm." Note that there is no <BODY> tag in this HTML code. The <FRAMESET></FRAMESET> tag takes its place. The FRAMESET tag may be modified by several attributes. The most important are:

1. FRAMEBORDER, which may be set to a pixel width, or to "0" for no border to appear.
2. FRAMESPACING, which controls the spacing between the frames within the frameset. When frameborders and framespacing are both set to "0" for a frameset, there will be no visible separation between frames, which creates a seamless appearance.

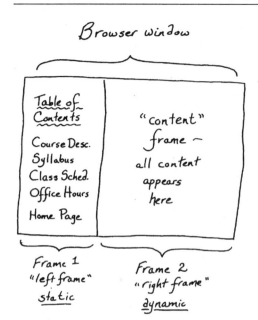

Figure 4.20. Pencil rendering of frames. Illustration by Anne B. Keating.

3. ROWS and COLS, which divide the browser window into vertical or horizontal frames. The ROWS attribute divides a window into horizontal frames, the COLS attribute into vertical frames. The size of each frame may be specified in absolute pixels or in a percentage. Within the <FRAMESET> tag, frames are referenced from left to right (if horizontal) and from top to bottom (if vertical). For example, in the HTML code <FRAMESET COLS="100,*">, the left frame will be 100 pixels wide, and the right frame will consist of the rest of the browser window, indicated by the asterisk. In the HTML code <FRAMESET ROWS="*,20%">, the bottom frame will take up 20 percent of the browser, and the top frame will consist of the rest of the browser window, again indicated by the asterisk symbol.

The <FRAMESET> tag contains the <FRAME> tag, which allows us to specify information about each frame within the frameset. The <FRAME> tag may be modified by several attributes. The most important are:

1. NAME, which gives the frame a name. The reason we need to identify frames by name will become clearer when we create our links.
2. SRC, which identifies the source HTML file that will be called into the frame initially.
3. MARGINWIDTH and MARGINHEIGHT, which allow you to specify, in pixels, margins within each of your frames.
4. FRAMEBORDER and FRAMESPACING, which work the same way they do for the <FRAMESET> tag, but can be applied at the <FRAME> level as well.
5. SCROLLING, which may be set to "yes," "no," or "auto." If you set scrolling to "yes," the frame will always have a scrollbar, regardless of how long its contents are. If it is set to "no," it will never scroll, even if the contents of the file in the frame are too large to fit in the frame. If it is set to "auto," the frame will automatically scroll when the contents of the frame are too large to fit into it. Unless you have a specific reason for controlling the scrolling yourself, it is a good idea to set scrolling to "auto" most of the time.

As a courtesy to those who may still be using a browser that does not support frames, HTML also supports a <NOFRAMES> tag, which appears when the page is viewed in a browser that does not support frames. Use this space to provide a link to a non-frames-based page. For example, the code <A HREF="index.htm">View a non-frames-based

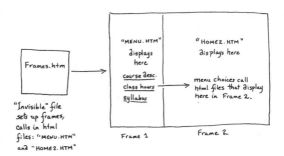

"Invisible" file sets up frames, calls in html files: "MENU.HTM" and "HOME2.HTM"

Figure 4.21. Pencil sketches can help you visualize the action of frames. Illustration by Anne B. Keating.

home page for Writing II Workshop</A> can take users to our original home page. Here is how we might set up a frameset for our class Web site. Note that we will need to create a *menu.htm* file and a *home2.htm* file in order for this file to function properly:

```
<HTML>
<HEAD>
<TITLE>Writing Workshop II Frameset</TITLE>
</HEAD>
<FRAMESET COLS="25%,*" FRAMEBORDER="1" FRAMESPACING="0">
<FRAME NAME="left_framed_window" SRC="menu.htm"
    MARGINWIDTH="10" MARGINHEIGHT="10" SCROLLING="auto">
<FRAME NAME="right_framed_window" SRC="home2.htm"
    MARGINWIDTH="10" MARGINHEIGHT="10" SCROLLING="auto">
</FRAMESET>
<NO FRAMES>
<BODY><A HREF="index.htm">View a non-frames-based home page for
    Writing II Workshop</A>
</BODY>
</NOFRAMES>
</HTML>
```

Our *frames.htm* file provides directions for the browser on what pages to call and how to arrange them in the browser window (see Figure 4.21).

Preparing Pages to Be Called into Frames

Now that we have created the frames page, we need to create the pages that will be called into it. For our left frame window, we will create a page of menu choices. Basically, we can borrow the list of menu choices from our home page and create a page that contains only this list. We will simply add the heading "Table of Contents" to the page and save the page as *menu.htm*. (Note also that we have added a link to our new section, "Class Schedule.") Here is how the HTML file will look:

```
<HTML>
<HEAD>
<TITLE>Writing Workshop II Menu</TITLE>
</HEAD>
<BODY BGCOLOR="khaki" TEXT="black" LINK="red" VLINK="brown"
  ALINK="black">
<CENTER>
<FONT COLOR="darkolivegreen"><H4>Table of Contents:</H4></FONT>
<TABLE BORDER="0" CELLSPACING="0" CELLPADDING="0">
<TR>
<TD>
<UL>
<LI><A HREF="course.htm">Course Description</A>
<LI><A HREF="syllabus.htm">Syllabus</A>
<LI><A HREF="schedule.htm">Class Schedule</A>
<LI><A HREF="hours.htm">Office Hours</A>
<LI><A HREF="home2.htm">Home Page</A>
</UL>
</TD>
</TR>
</TABLE>
</CENTER>
</BODY>
</HTML>
```

However, now we need to make one important change to the way our links are set up. Remember in the HTML above how each FRAME tag was followed by a NAME attribute just before the SRC attribute (for example: <FRAME NAME="right_framed_window" SRC="home2.htm">)? You will need to add the TARGET attribute to your links in *menu.htm.* (for example: <A HREF="course.htm" TARGET="right_framed_window">). If you do not add the TARGET attribute, the pages you link to in *menu.htm* will auto-

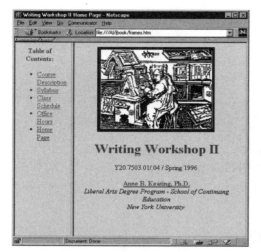

Figure 4.22. The complete "framed" version of the Writing Workshop II home page.

matically open in the frame reserved for *menu.htm* with sometimes unexpected results. You can be creative in the "directions" you give to the frame, but most of the time you will be sending the Web page you are calling to the larger window, which in this example is called "right_framed_window." Here is how our modified links will now appear in *menu.htm*:

```
<UL>
<LI><A HREF="course.htm" TARGET="right_framed_window">
    Course Description</A>
<LI><A HREF="syllabus.htm" TARGET="right_framed_window">Syllabus</A>
<LI><A HREF="schedule.htm" TARGET="right_framed_window">
    Class Schedule</A>
<LI><A HREF="hours.htm" TARGET="right_framed_window">Office Hours</A>
<LI><A HREF="home2.htm" TARGET="right_framed_window">Home Page</A>
</UL>
```

Now we can modify our original home page, *index.htm*, by stripping off the menu of choices—we will not need them because our choices will always be visible in our left frame—and save the file as *home2.htm*. Then, when we call up our *frames.htm* file, it will in turn call up our *menu.htm* file and *home2.htm* file into the appropriate frames. If all has gone well, the menu choices in the left frame should be visible at all times, and the content pages should appear in the right frame. Keep in mind that our subpages still contain links back to the home page. If you choose to stick with our new frames-based design, it would be a good idea to delete those links. Figure 4.22 shows how our home page will now appear in our browser.

Though it may seem like a lot at the beginning, this is all there is to it. As you get comfortable with frames, you can extend your use of them by making multiple-framed documents. However, bear in mind that on a smaller monitor framed windows will become progressively smaller, so you should try to avoid using frames as a layout tool—tables are probably better suited for this. Frames can be a great addition to your site, but think carefully about how you use them.

Also, because not everyone likes frames, it is always good to include a "No Frames" escape tag. (We have included a range of these escape tags in the Appendix.) An escape tag should always be included if you are calling up a page of links to Web sites other than your own. Your students will inevitably want to bookmark these sites, only to discover that they have bookmarked your framed page because the bookmarking function will only mark the page that is currently displayed by the browser—namely, yours. Here is how you write the "escape tag." We will assume that your page of links is called mylinks.htm. Open *mylinks.htm* and, right beneath the <BODY> tag, insert the following tag: <TARGET="_top">.

Fun with Frames   In this section we include some variations you may find useful.

Here is a recipe for a "three-window" frame:

```
<FRAMESET COLS="25%,75%">
<FRAME SRC="menu.htm" NAME="menu">
<FRAMESET ROWS="75%,25%">
<FRAME SRC="page1.htm" NAME="main">
<FRAME SRC="bottom_row.htm" NAME="bottom">
</FRAMESET>
</FRAMESET>
```

Once you are comfortable working with frames, try the following variation to see another frame that places a navigation bar at the top of the browser window:

```
<FRAMESET ROWS="15%,*">
<FRAME SRC="navigation_bar.htm" NAME="top" SCROLLING="no"
MARGINHEIGHT="1" MARGINWIDTH="2">
<FRAMESET COLS="20%,*">
<FRAME SRC="menu.htm" NAMES="menu" SCROLLING="auto"
MARGINHEIGHT="4" MARGINWIDTH="0">
```

```
<FRAME SRC="welcome.htm" NAME="main" SCROLLING="auto"
    MARGINHEIGHT="1" MARGINWIDTH="8">
</FRAMESET>
</FRAMESET>
```

Here is another frame that uses hidden frame (border, marginheight, marginwidth, etc.) elements to achieve an interesting effect. (In effect, this is very similar to setting the BORDER attribute in the <TABLE> tag to "0.") Try it out by setting the background color for *head.htm*, *whatsnew.htm* and *navigate.htm* to the same color. (Note that there is a new attribute in this example. NORESIZE is a useful attribute when you want to set the look of your frames so as not to give your audience the option of resizing your framed pages. Without the NORESIZE attribute, your audience can widen or narrow your framed windows.)

```
<FRAMESET ROWS="56,*" BORDER="0" FRAMESPACING="0"
    FRAMEBORDER="no">
<FRAME NAME="head" SRC="head.htm" NORESIZE MARGINWIDTH="0"
    MARGINHEIGHT="0" SCROLLING="no">
<FRAMESET COLS="150,*" BORDER="0" FRAMEBORDER="no"
    FRAMESPACING="0">
<FRAMESET ROWS="58,*">
<FRAME NAME="new" SRC="whatsnew.htm" NORESIZE MARGINWIDTH="9"
    MARGINHEIGHT="0" SCROLLING="no">
<FRAME NAME="nav" SRC="navigate.htm" NORESIZE MARGINWIDTH="0"
    MARGINHEIGHT="0" SCROLLING="no">
</FRAMESET>
<FRAMESET ROWS="50,*" BORDER="0" FRAMEBORDER="no"
    FRAMESPACING="0">
<FRAME NAME="dochead" SRC="dochead.htm" MARGINWIDTH="0"
    MARGINHEIGHT="0" SCROLLING="no">
<FRAME NAME="content" SRC="page1.htm" FRAMESPACING="0"
```

```
MARGINHEIGHT="0">
</FRAMESET>
</FRAMESET>
</FRAMESET>
```

4.3 Web Site Development and Design

With the simple tools presented in this chapter, you should be able to post any number of course-related Web pages. We recommend careful planning for the overall design of your Web site, considering your audience, the purpose of your site, navigation and design aspects.

4.3.1 THE PURPOSE OF THE WEB SITE

Planning a Web site typically begins with the awareness that you need to provide more information than is currently contained in the handouts and other written materials provided for your students. While it is easy to post everything you have in print, in the end this is neither an efficient nor cost-effective way to set up a Web site. Though Web sites in many ways resemble classic print resources such as books and magazines, students have a specific set of likes and dislikes when it comes to online material.

Some of these tastes are dictated by the technology itself. For example an article in a journal may command a reader's attention, while online the same article may either take a long time to load or be too long to read onscreen. Web-surfing students typically move rapidly from site to site. Critical, well-indexed, graphical Web pages that make use of bulleted bursts of text will help capture and hold the relatively short attention span of the first-time visitor to your site. Review your rationale for having a Web site: What purpose will it serve beyond currently available resources? What exactly do you want your Web site to accomplish? Do you want your site to serve as a clearinghouse for information related to your field? You can accomplish this by including bibliographies, directories and lists of links to related online resources in your field. Do you want to stimulate an online dialogue about the issues raised in your course? Do you want to post administrative issues? Do you want to work on a preservation process? Once you have a clear idea of where you are going, decide on the immediate framework of your site. Do you want to create a course page, a departmental page, an online departmental newsletter, or a research-oriented page?

4.3.2 AUDIENCE The students who enroll in your class most likely will represent a wide range of skills. Some may have strong scientific training, while others will be stronger in multimedia and humanities. In such cases, tread carefully. If you are teaching graduate classes, you can assume a good level of proficiency in handling specific software and communication tools. In this case, allow for self-guided learning, offer pointers versus lengthy explanations, incorporate more links and encourage wider searching. If you are teaching undergraduate classes, take the time to evaluate your students' level of expertise in using computer equipment and software, use a transparent interface, follow strict structure and keep your links to information within your site. In addition, offer detailed descriptions of new items, terms and language and offer easily printable material.

4.3.3 DESIGN CONSIDERATIONS One of the most gifted calligraphers of this century, Edward Johnston, began teaching lettering and illumination at London's LCC Central School of Arts and Crafts in 1899. Later, he recalled: "Through years of practice, I had achieved such mastery that I seemed to write on a blackboard as a medium for expressing my art itself and not merely for explaining something about it."[3] This image is particularly resonant for us and has shaped a number of discussions we have had about the World Wide Web as a medium for design. It is possible with the tools currently at hand to achieve an excellence of design without the many years of preparation a craftsman like Johnston would have had to spend learning to steady his hand or cut the perfect quill pen. The Web as a medium offers greater and faster access to a proficiency with the tools of the trade. Many academics, especially those from the humanities, have taken to the graphical and typographic design elements of the Web with a hunger that we can only explain by the absence of such "handwork" in most academic work.

The majority of academics working with the Web as a creative medium have no formal training in design. Photocopy shops and publishers have done the work of designing and preparing our print materials for us. This challenge—combined with the fact that as a medium, the World Wide Web was primarily constructed to facilitate quick delivery of structured text as opposed to well-laid-out pages—means that we all face significant obstacles to good design. Will this pose an insurmountable problem for you as you post your materials to the Web? Not at all. Here, briefly, are the basic design principles for the Web, as well as some general ideas on how to design a functional yet elegant Web page.

Consistency and the "Look and Feel"
of a Web Page

The general look and feel of your pages should remain consistent. This assures students that they are still within your site. Never lose sight of the fact that, as much as working with the Web resembles working with print, it cannot duplicate the concreteness that a bound book or photocopied course packet imposes on your course materials. You must establish this order through design consistency. In other words, do not make each page a uniquely designed entity. If you have used large headings for the main sections and smaller headings for your subsections on one page, continue this convention throughout your site. As you get into some of the more advanced features of HTML, such as font size, color, and more extensive use of images, consistency becomes even more crucial. Icons and buttons should be consistent on all pages. Do not use the same icon as a metaphor for different concepts, or make the same type of icon clickable in one place but not in another.

Navigation

Your site should be organized logically and clearly. We mentioned earlier that it is a good idea to storyboard your site before you begin to create your pages. The more extensive your site, the more important this becomes. First, establish a hierarchy of sections, going from the most general to the most specific, much like you would create an outline when writing a paper. Determine which subsections belong within which major sections and work your way down until you have drawn out or storyboarded a complete site map.

Next, determine what links you will need on each of your pages. Just as in our sample site, it is usually a good idea to provide a link back to your home page on each subpage, so that users will not become lost or dead-ended. This may be all your site requires. On the other hand, as you become more adept at HTML, you may choose to use a frame-based "navigation bar" that remains visible on your site at all times. There are many ways to design the navigation on your site, but the important thing is that every button or text link has a clear description of where the link is going. Furthermore, include enough navigational cues to guide your visitors back to your central page or to other pages.

You should be patient with your first efforts. Do not become so focused on practical issues that you are not free to experiment at this stage. Take a step-by-step approach to learning how to write for the Web. Try not to do too much at once, and remember to have fun with this hands-on work. In the next chapter, we continue the discussion on design and cover working with images as well as incorporating interactivity into Web sites.

Research Links and Resources

1. *Yale C/AIM Web Style Guide* at *http://info.med.yale.edu/caim/manual/contents.html* is a detailed and extensive style manual for Web authors designed by Patrick Lynch and Sarah Horton of Yale University School of Medicine's Center for Advanced Instructional Media (C/AIM).

2. Sandra E. Eddy's *HTML in Plain English* (MIS Press, 1997) is an A–Z guide to all the standard HTML tags.

3. *Web Page Builder's Resources Online* at *http://www.nowonline.com/resources.html* offers an extensive list of HTML editors, Web sources for HTML help, Web sites for help with HTML and Web sites with free art for Web pages.

4. *Builder.com* at *http://www.cnet.com/Content/Builder/* is Clnet's Web design area and is an extensive and excellent collection of resources, interviews and reviews of current Web site building tools.

5. *The Webmaster's Reference Library* at *http://www.Webreference.com/* is an up-to-date collection of articles and resources for professional Web designers. However, there is much of value for newcomers to Web design here as well.

6. *Web Developer.com* at *http://www.WebDeveloper.com/*, a companion Web site for *Web Developer.com* magazine, is another extensive professional Web design site. In addition to articles and resources, there are also threaded discussions on all aspects of Web design.

7. *The Web Developer Virtual Library* at *http://www.stars.com/* includes articles by leading Web designers and programmers, as well as an extensive list of resources and links.

8. *Project Cool: Anyone Can Build a Great Website!* at *http://www.projectcool.com/* provides an index of the best-designed sites on the Web. Its philosophy is that if you want to build great Web sites, you first have to look at great Web sites.

9. Jennifer Niederst's *Designing for the World Wide Web* (O'Reilly, 1996) provides the basics you need to hit the ground running. Although written for graphic designers, it covers information and techniques useful to anyone who wants to write for the Web. It is especially relevant for those working on Macintosh computers.

10. Crystal Waters's *Web Concept and Design: A Comprehensive Guide for Creating Effective Web Sites* (New Riders Publishing, 1996) is an excellent overview for beginners. Waters gives a quick and colorful overview of the main issues in Web design. She has a Web site at *http://www.typo.com/*.

CHAPTER 5 | Second-Stage Instructional Web Design

The most powerful learning takes place when there is a passion, joy, and excitement experienced by the learner. There is absolutely no reason why learning needs to be synonymous with boring, hard work. New generations of students do not need to learn in exactly the same ways as previous ones.[1]

THE first stage of your online career should be spent learning the building blocks of Web publishing. Learn the medium. Ask questions. Try things out. Make mistakes. Explore new ways to look at things. During this stage, set aside design manuals and focus on what feels comfortable. Try different pages, different colors, different fonts and type sizes, flow text in tables, expand tables, delete tables. Save a few files and print them out. Analyze the result. Make pencil changes. Draw storyboards. Slowly build up a portfolio of your own. Grab a few appealing pages from the Web and study their design, concept and interface. Ask yourself, why do these pages work? How do they help convey the content? Share your thoughts with peers and students as well—like you, they too are daily challenged by this medium.

If you are interested in multimedia, spend some time at your school's media center learning how to scan images, digitize sound and grab clips from a videotape. As you will see in this chapter, using multimedia in today's technical environment is both forgiving and relatively easy. Once you are comfortable with your new tools, you can start thinking about fresh concepts and ways to integrate your material on the Web.

What Is Second-Stage Instructional Web Design?

Second-stage instructional Web design implies higher involvement on the part of your audience. The Web, which started out as a text- and image-based communication and educational tool, today is turning more and more into a total immersion, multisensory learning space. With this shift, your tools will change and your involvement in creating material will grow dramatically. Second-stage design will be rich in metaphor, experimentation and interaction. The initial goal of presenting information to your students shifts to a reciprocal relationship with them—a collaborative effort. Your students now will take the initiative in both the design and creation of course projects. They will be the ones exploring new ways, dictating their own pace and directions. In order to facilitate such a role reversal and to create a framework within which your students can contribute material and expand their knowledge, you will first need to understand these new tools and concepts.

Metaphor, Motivation, Multimedia

Successful integration of technology into your coursework is often based on intuition. Since so much is dependent on your own personal vision and ability both to plan long term and to improvise as the class progresses, it is difficult to spell out exactly how to build a successful site. Yet we would say that such sites are built around a unifying theme or metaphor. As you have seen from the examples of "Garbage in Gotham" and "StudioLab" in chapter 3, the use of strong metaphors quickly translated to heightened student alertness for the material and in class. These sites also provided a solid structural framework for collaborative projects—and student interest in these projects facilitated motivation and therefore learning. The use of effective metaphors for your site and the incorporation of multimedia tools may also bring forth students' curiosity about your subject and stimulate in-depth study that more closely resembles your own.

Therefore, you will need to look at your subject with a brand-new eye. More than ever, you will have to cater to students' often narrow, fleeting but nonetheless vital "interest." Your professorial role will increasingly become a form of "performance art" that the Web and the use of multimedia can both enhance and continuously extend.

Taking Risks

Whereas older forms of computer-aided instruction almost completely failed to involve students in other than mandatory activities, from its very early days the Web has offered students self-paced, spontaneous learning. Perhaps the most stunning aspect of the Web today is the student participation, production and knowledge creation that it engenders. This sudden change is coming from the fact that this technology—unlike the technologies employed by computer-aided instruction—in many instances has been chosen by the students. In part due to its informality, many students feel right at home using Internet technology, and many are longtime Internet users who were involved in Internet Relay Chats (IRC) and Multi-User Dungeons (MUD) long before the advent of the Web. A number of creative writing instructors have also found that their students are more likely to share work in progress online than in a classroom. This sudden burst of student creativity has continued to evolve with the arrival of multimedia to the Internet and to the classroom.

If you take a look at your university's course offerings, you might find that, in addition to traditional courses, there are more and more technology-related courses offered every semester. Where an introductory class in computer applications a few years ago would cover Microsoft Word, Excel and perhaps HyperCard, today the same general student population will be learning how to use multimedia tools such as Director, PhotoShop and Premiere. In addition to multimedia, there is equally great interest in Web-development tools such as Adobe's PageMill and Macromedia's Dreamweaver. In many ways, this new generation of students are much closer to technology than their instructors are. In order to work this paradox in your favor, you will need to assume a relaxed posture about the heart and soul of the Internet that is always dynamically changing while becoming infinitely detailed. In this new virtual world, you cannot know everything, so you will have to develop points of reference and a certain amount of courage to dive into things you have not explored before. Learning is becoming more dynamic, and to teach in this new environment you will have to acquire new knowledge daily. In order to be an effective teacher, you will have to immerse yourself and learn ways to interact with your students on terms that more closely resemble peer-to-peer communication.

Interactivity and asynchronous communications are at the heart of second-stage instructional Web design. It is wise to decide during the early stages of course development the kind of interactivity you would like build into your Web site. Would you like a newsgroup for your class? A bulletin board? An IRC channel? Would you like to create self-guided tutorials? Test your students online? Require that assignments be e-mailed to you or posted online? All these issues come with different sets of problems. Web publishing, while a flexible medium, requires time, attention and administrative effort. You will need to plan ahead and discuss relevant issues with your computing center's Webmaster and system administrator.

Although in practice there is significantly more technology involved in creating second-stage instructional Web sites, technology is not a prerequisite to enter this stage. Course concepts and metaphors can be delivered just as well through text-based interaction such as e-mail and discussion boards. Undoubtedly, written text and speech still remain our most profound vehicles of expression. However, both developmental and creative writing classes can benefit from shared ideas and continuous peer exposure previously impossible with traditional teaching methods. Simple, text-based discussion boards can serve as outlets for such discussions, while encouraging writing practice as well as providing archives through which your students can track their own postings and their progress. These archives will also provide a fixed place where student work is preserved—unlike returned papers all too often destined for the wastebasket.

As you have seen, for many people being online means being part of a large human network, and this has many gratifying points. But the uninhibited and spontaneous interaction of the Web also promotes experimentation. Freed from having to be perfect, your students will create more work faster than before and be more willing to take chances even at the cost of making mistakes. They will use technological tools, even as you will, for pure experimentation. They will try out concepts, often fail, and yet they will not veer from their fascination and joy with this medium. Neither should you.

You should not think of second-stage instructional Web design as a technological tour de force. Rather, regard the tools we discuss in this chapter as vehicles for experimentation and let them serve your shifting ideas and creative plans.

Using Multimedia Components in Your Web Page

As the name suggests, multimedia is the combination of components, namely images, sound, movies, animation, three-dimensional models and authored environments. For a number of years, multimedia was primarily confined to the computer desktop in the form of CD-ROM encyclopedias, games and catalogs. What has changed during the past year or two is the presence of multimedia on the Web. Early in 1998, modem speeds began climbing to 56k for many home users while most universities supported high-speed T3 network lines, resulting in sufficient speed to deliver properly compressed images and audio in a timely fashion.

At the same time, the power and diversity of desktop computers increased. Today, even an average multimedia PC will have the built-in capacity to capture sound from CD players, through a microphone supplied with the computer, or from a tape recorder connected through the built-in sound card of the computer. For a modest investment, a video-capture card can be added that will capture movie clips from a VCR or a video camera.

In such a technically rich environment, it is relatively easy to incorporate multimedia components into Web presentations. Careful preparation of material—which means editing and compression in the case of images, audio and video, and sometimes working in authoring and modeling environments such as Director and VRML—can still be difficult and time-consuming. Here is where you will need to pause and evaluate the rationale for using multimedia components. What is the scope of the project? How will using multimedia help? What are the limitations?

Despite advances in hardware development, many feel that bandwidth limitations are still too restrictive for meaningful multimedia use. Rather than offering this excuse to postpone production of your own material, you should use these limitations to your advantage. Think creatively; constrain media use, not content; use smaller and shorter files; use black-and-white images where color would be superfluous; use animated images and sound where a video clip would be redundant.

In addition, explore alternative methods of multimedia delivery. The first and most overlooked method is local use. As you know, browsers do not distinguish between files on your hard drive and files coming from the Web. HTML, while primarily the authoring language of the Web, can also be deployed in a "local" situation, such as on stand-alone machines and local area networks. The advantages of such local delivery are twofold: first, there is dramatic increase in speed; second, there is significant control over your computing environment. The increased speed will allow the use of large, detail-oriented images, movies and sound files especially useful for sciences, art history, music appreciation and cinema studies. The ability to control the computing environment will allow for task-specific configurations that would be very hard to achieve for a wider, more general audience. Such task-specific configurations may include the uniform installation of multimedia components, such as audio and video cards, headphones, special software, browser plug-ins and helper applications.

5.1 Working with Images

As you develop your Web site, it is very likely that images will become an integral part of it. Here are some of the ways that you can incorporate images onto your pages. Initially, you may want to replace HTML text links with graphical buttons or small images that link. Later, you may want to use images to display information that pertains to your field or course, such as diagrams, photos, x-rays, microscopic images, charts and so forth. Finally, you may simply want to make your site more visually appealing with some decorative images or bullets. (For updates, additional information and dynamic examples of the techniques in this chapter go to the companion site for this book at *http://www.nyupress.nyu.edu/professor.html*.)

5.1.1 CREATING DIGITAL IMAGES

How you use images on your pages will initially be dictated by the format of the images you begin with. If you have images that are currently on paper, in books, or in slide or negative form, you will most likely want to convert them to computer-readable format using an image scanner. (See "Scanning Basics" later in this chapter.) Once an image is scanned into digital format, the image file may then be further manipulated using an image-editing program, such as Adobe PhotoShop.

5.1.2 DIGITAL CAMERAS

Another way to obtain images is to take photographs using a digital camera. Digital cameras are tailor-made for the Web. Instead of using film, they store images on removable memory cards. The memory cards are erasable and can be reused after transferring the images to your computer via a serial or parallel port. The transferred images then can be manipulated in image-editing programs.

5.1.3 IMAGE ARCHIVES AND OTHER DOWNLOADABLE IMAGES

If you are using images as buttons or decorative elements, you may want to use some of the many images that are available on the Web in free clip-art archives. To download an image from a clip-art archive, just place your cursor over the image as you are viewing it in your browser and right-click on your mouse button. (On the Macintosh, click and hold the mouse button down.) A browser menu will pop up, and you will need to select the "Save as Picture" option to save a copy of the image to your hard drive. (Be aware of copyright issues when you copy images from the Web. Most clip art is in the public domain. However, an image at your favorite Web site may be protected by copyright. Although most Web sites with copyrighted images will have a statement to that effect on the home page, even without such a statement, copyright law applies to any image "fixed in a tangible medium.") If you would like to create your own personal collection of digital images, CD-ROMs of Web-ready clip art and photographs are available and are relatively inexpensive. Generally speaking, however, you will find plenty of useful images for your Web site online.

5.1.4 CREATING YOUR OWN IMAGES

You can create your own images using one of the many image-editing programs available, including Paint Shop Pro and Adobe PhotoShop. All of these programs are powerful image-editing programs and will take some time to master. Fortunately, there are many resources available for learning them, both on the Web and in print, and if you decide that high-quality images are an important part of your Web site, it may be worth your while to invest time and effort to learn the basics of these programs.

5.1.5 HOW TO INCORPORATE IMAGES ON YOUR WEB PAGES

There are four ways to incorporate images into your Web pages: as inline images, external images, background images and image maps.

Inline Images An inline image is any image that actually displays on your Web page and can be anything from a tiny, brightly colored bullet to a large illustration. As you may recall from chapter 4, inline images are included in your HTML file using the <IMG SRC="filename"> tag.

External Images An external image is one that the user links to from your Web site, just as he or she might link to an external Web site or to another part of your site. Thus, you can link to an image file using the standard <A HREF="filename"></A> tag. In the following example, the text "Click Here to View Image" links to an image called *picture.jpg*: <A HREF= "picture.jpg">Click Here to View Image</A>.

When you link to an image, it will display within the browser window by itself—that is, outside of the context of the Web page that the link is on. Some older browsers may actually launch a separate image-viewer program. In fact, one quite common use of images is to combine inline and external images by inserting inline thumbnail images of a larger image, making these thumbnails "clickable" as links to the full-size images, which are called externally and open as new Web pages. This gives the reader of the Web page the option of viewing the image or not. If your Web page must include a number of large images, this is a good design approach.

Background Images You can also specify a background image for your page. This is done using the background attribute within the <BODY> tag on your page. The appropriate syntax is: <BODY BACKGROUND="FILENAME">. (You may recall from chapter 4 that the full <BODY> tag specifying colors looked like this: <BODY BGCOLOR="khaki" TEXT="black" LINK="red" VLINK="brown" ALINK="black">. When you include a background image, you will need to remove the BGCOLOR attribute. The example would look like this: <BODY BACKGROUND="splendid_border.gif" TEXT="black" LINK="red" VLINK="brown" ALINK="black">). Background images are automatically "tiled" by the browser, so they may actually be very small in size. "Tiled" refers to the process by which a single small image is repeated across and down a Web page as many times as is required to fill the page—in effect, like a mosaic. The advantage of background tiling is that a rich backdrop is set up on which to display other images and text. However, a word of caution when working with background images: it is important that your text remains legible on top of the image, so always be sure to test your Web pages carefully. A background image that is rich and high in contrast or very close in color to your text may render your page completely unreadable.

Image Maps An image map is an image that has designated "hot-spots" that link to other Web sites, pages or sections. To create an image map, you need to specify certain areas of an image, defined by their vertical and horizontal coordinates, to link to a specific file or URL. You may hear about "server-side" image maps, which require a special program running on your Web site's server in order to function. However, most browsers now support "client-side" image maps, which are easy to create and do not require any extra programs.

The first thing you need to do when creating an image map is to put an attribute in your <IMG> tag called USEMAP. The value of the USEMAP attribute will be the name of the actual image map that you will create, which will include the hot-spot coordinates and the linking information. In the following example, the file *hombres.jpg* will be an image map, and the coordinates will be defined in a map titled "hombres": <IMG SRC="hombres.jpg" USEMAP="#hombres">.

Next, you will need to create the image map, which may be done using any number of available utilities and HTML editing tools. Image-map programs figure out the coordinates of each of your hot-spots, and then generate the basic HTML code using the <MAP></MAP> tag, which you can then cut and paste into your HTML file. These utilities allow you to pick a shape for your hot-spot area—typically, a circle, square or polygon. For each area that you define, the image map program will prompt you for a URL to link to. Once you have completed defining your hot-spots, the program will create the HTML code for you to save. You can place this map code anywhere in your file, but it is customary to place it right beneath the <IMG> tag that calls the image map. Here is a sample of what the <IMG> tag and completed image map code will look like:

```
<IMG SRC="hombres.jpg" USEMAP="#hombres">
<MAP NAME="hombres">
<AREA SHAPE="rect" COORDS="9,139,105,407" HREF="man1.html">
<AREA SHAPE="rect" COORDS="110,101,244,419" HREF="los1.html">
<AREA SHAPE="circle" COORDS="313,152,61" HREF="man3.html">
<AREA SHAPE="circle" COORDS="410,165,25" HREF="man4.html">
<AREA SHAPE="default" NOHREF>
</MAP>
```

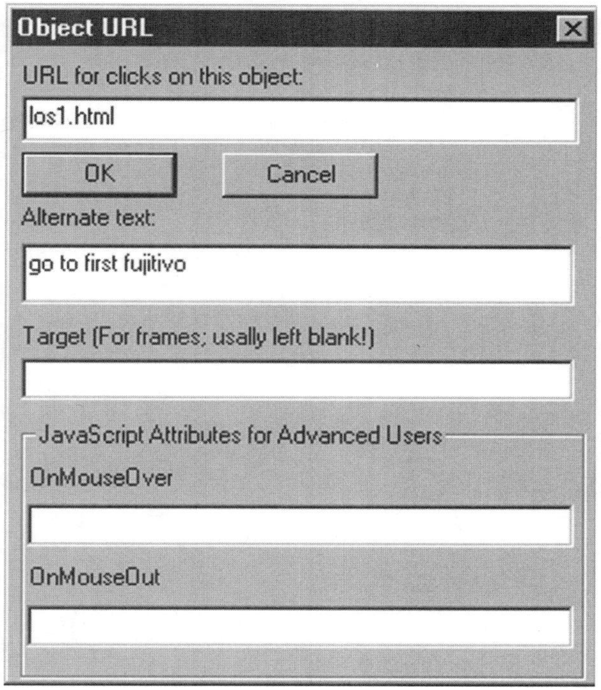

Figure 5.1. *(above)* Checking the hot-spots with MapEdit. Image by Joseph Hargitai.
Figure 5.2. *(above right)* Defining the URL for the selected hot-spot in MapEdit.

You may have noticed that this map includes an area with a shape called "default." This optional feature allows you to define a link if a user clicks his or her mouse anywhere outside of the defined hot-spots.

Once you have created your image map, remember to upload the image complementing the map to the server. In addition to dedicated "mapping" utilities such as MapEdit, sophisticated HTML editors like FrontPage and Dreamweaver can also be used to create image maps.

5.1.6 FILE FORMATS FOR THE WEB

Once you start working with images, it is important that you save them in a Web-compatible format. While image format standards for the Web continue to evolve, the two most common formats are GIF and JPEG.

GIF   GIF, which stands for "Graphics Interchange Format," is the most common image format on the Web. It was developed by CompuServe in 1987 to deliver images over telephone lines. GIFs are ideal for flat color components and images that contain a limited range of tones. The basic palette of a GIF image is 256 colors, so in order to save a file to a GIF format, you first need to reduce the number of colors to 256. To do this in PhotoShop, you first need to change the "mode" of your file to "indexed colors." You can do that by selecting "Indexed Colors" from the "Mode" item of the "Image" menu. Then, you will be able to save the file as a CompuServe GIF.

Transparent GIF   In addition to the CompuServe GIF format, Web browsers also support a slightly modified GIF format known as GIF89a. This format allows you to define one of the colors in your image as "transparent." This is an important format to use because pixel-based images always default to rectangular shape, and in many cases, the image you are working with will not be this shape. If you mask a selection of an image and turn the masked portion to a solid, transparent color, the background color will show through the transparent area and result in a nonrectangular image. Most graphics programs have the option for creating transparent GIF89a images.

Animated GIFs   Another type of GIF format that is supported by many browsers is the "animated" GIF. Basically, GIF animation allows you to string together a sequence of GIFs into one image file that when viewed will create an animation. This animation is included in your HTML file just like any other image file. However, a browser will display all the frames of the animation at a set speed, determined when you create the GIF. Animated GIFs may be created with any number of available programs, many of which offer fancy transitions and interesting visual effects such as wipes and zooms. Some of these programs are available as shareware and can be downloaded easily from the Web. When creating animated GIFs, bear in mind that each "frame" you add to an animation will also add to the total size of the resulting file.

JPEG Files   JPEG, which stands for Joint Photographic Experts Group, is the other commonly used Web-compatible image format. It is the best format for displaying complex images such as photographs. To reduce file size, JPEG offers a "lossy" compression scheme. The more you compress, the more detail your image will lose. Nevertheless, a JPEG, unlike a GIF, is always a full 24-bit color image, which means that the subtle gradations in color that

Figure 5.3. Saving a photograph as a GIF image in PhotoShop, using a "browser-safe" palette. Image by Joseph Hargitai.

Inline images should weigh in somewhere between 10 and 50k. This may seem small for an individual image, but if you have five or six such images the overall size of the page—text and images—might end up being quite large.

are so rich in photographs are better preserved than by using GIFs. Though images will be dithered by the browser (that is, pixels will be mixed to simulated colors missing from the color table) on any monitor displaying less than 24-bit color, JPEGs will generally be of higher image quality than GIFs. When saving files as JPEGs, you will be asked what type of compression you would like—low, medium or high. Choosing medium is always a safe bet. If you need the highest possible image quality, use the "maximum" setting. If you need the fastest possible download time, use the "low" setting.

5.1.7 THE BROWSER-SAFE PALETTE   Another issue that complicates the process of creating Web-compatible images is that Macintosh and Windows machines display colors somewhat differently due to their 8-bit color tables. From the available 256 colors for an 8-bit display, Macintoshes and

Figure 5.4. Saving a photograph as a JPEG file in PhotoShop, using a "medium" compression setting. Image by Joseph Hargitai.

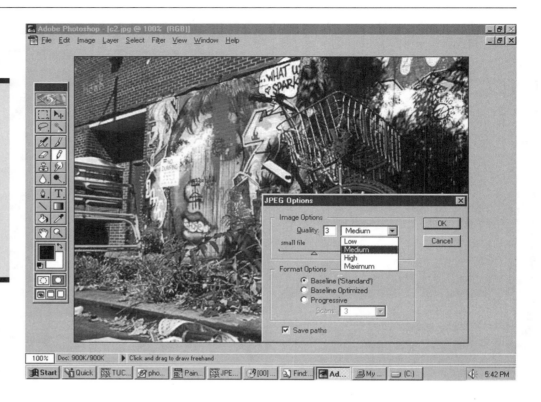

Occasionally, when you try to save a file as a JPEG in PhotoShop, this option will be unavailable. In this case, you will need to "flatten" your file. In case of PhotoShop, this refers to the image layers used automatically by the program, which need to be combined into one, or "flattened," in order to save your image as a JPEG file.

Windows share only 216 colors. The remaining forty colors are interpreted slightly differently by browsers. The so-called browser-safe palette, often popularly referred to as the "Netscape Palette," contains only the 216 colors that Macintosh and Windows machines share. If you eliminate the forty variable colors by opting to create and save your GIF files using the browser-safe option, which can be done in PhotoShop as well as several available image utilities, you can eliminate cross-platform shifts of color.

5.1.8 IMAGE SIZE

Another important issue when creating images for the Web is the total byte size of the image. (You may recall a description of byte size in chapter 1.) While text files are typically small in terms of total byte size, even small image files can be made up of a large number of bytes. For this reason, it is a good idea to avoid using a number of large images on the same Web page, as they will slow down the loading of your page. When you must use large images, try to use the thumbnail technique described above accompanied by a brief description of the image, including how large it is in terms of byte size. A sample description might read "Pieter Brueghel, *Tower of Babel*, 1563 [60kilobyte JPEG]." If this is not feasible in terms of your design for the page, try to compress the image as much as possible in your graphics program to reduce the size of the file.

5.1.9 SCANNING BASICS

If you have course material that you would like to add to your site which currently exists only on paper, in slide format or as photographic negatives, you will want to learn how to use a scanner. Image scanning requires dedicated software that in most cases is supplied by the manufacturer of the scanner and is often integrated into image-manipulating tools such as PhotoShop. However, the scanning software itself is not an image-manipulating tool. While you can use scanning software to perform a few simple tasks, such as sharpening, adjusting contrast and brightness control, for serious image manipulation you need more versatile tools such as PhotoShop.

"Flatbed" scanners are the workhorses of image scanning. Quick, efficient and very

SCREEN RESOLUTION

While theoretically you could use images of any resolution, 72 dpi (dots per inch) is often agreed upon because that is the highest resolution most monitors can display. When scanning and manipulating images, it is best to set the resolution in your scanning and image-editing software to 72 dpi.

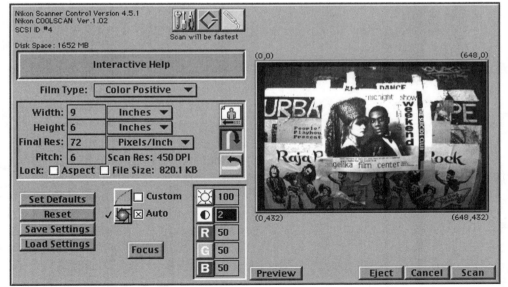

Figure 5.5. Using a Nikon CoolScan to scan a slide. Remember to set the resolution to 72 dpi, also known as "screen" resolution. Image by Joseph Hargitai.

Figure 5.6. *(right)* OmniPage Pro uses three automatic steps to turn a typewritten page into a computer readable form: scanning, zone or block-recognition and character-recognition.

Figure 5.7. *(below)* OmniPage Pro can convert your optically recognized characters to a wide variety of word processing formats.

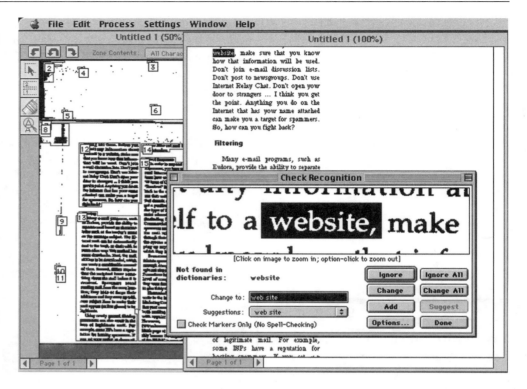

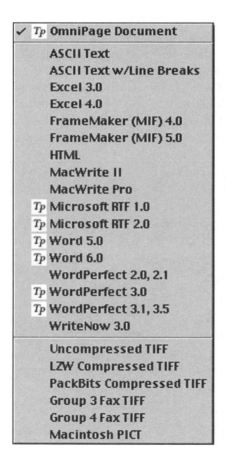

easy to use, these machines yield clear, crisp and accurate digital facsimiles of print-based materials. It is possible to scan originals as large as eight-and-a-half-by-eleven, making this type of machine incredibly versatile.

If you have large collections of slides and negatives, you will need to use a "slide" scanner. In order to get a good quality digital image from a slide, you will need to make sure your slides and negatives are clean and that the emulsion side of your material is facing the direction indicated in the scanner's manual.

Another type of scanning you may find useful is OCR, or "optical character recognition." Instead of creating digital images, OCR scans material containing text and, using special algorithms, translates these text images into an electronic text file that can then be opened up in any word processing package. OCR is useful in cases where you only have a paper copy of an original text—for example, pre–personal computer handouts and lessons, photocopied excerpts from books, newspaper clippings and so forth—and you do not have the time or inclination to sit down in front of your word processor and manually key in the text. While OCR works with regular image scanners, it requires the use of specialized software such as OmniPage Pro from Caere Corporation. It is important to note that, as good as OCR scanning is, the results must be proofread, especially if the original material contains any special characters—accented letters and mathematical symbols may often fail to scan correctly.

5.1.10 PRINTING RESOLUTION

While screen resolution is fine to display images on monitors, in printed matter such resolution produces poor results. Acceptable printing resolution starts at 300 dpi and can even exceed 2,400 dpi. You may be in a position where an image will do double duty both on your Web site and in printed form in a book or departmental newsletter. In that case, the best thing to do is to run multiple scans on the image. For print publication, ask your editor what file format and resolution are required. If you can, scan the image at that resolution. Currently, the standard for images for print publication starts around 300 dpi. Once you have saved your image at 300 dpi, then save it a second time under a different name at 72 dpi for your Web page. (In some graphics programs, you can do this using the "resize" function, which in addition to resizing, can also "resample" your image's resolution.)

5.1.11 ANTI-ALIASING

Computer-generated images such as logos, type and simple drawings should be anti-aliased. Popularly referred to as "removing the jaggies from an image," anti-aliasing is the process of adding intermediate colors to smooth out the jagged edges between areas of solid color. While this process sounds complicated, most graphics programs such as PhotoShop will do it automatically when prompted.

Figure 5.8. Here are two large typefaces with anti-aliasing on and off.

5.1.12 BATCH PROCESSING IMAGES

The power of batch image-processing tools may not be obvious to you when you are working with a few images. However, if you get to a point where you have twenty-five or more images that you are preparing for the Web, batch-processing utilities will eliminate having to manipulate each image individually. The advantages of batch processing include the ability to reduce and crop a group of images to a user-specified size; convert a group of images to almost any file format; rename, reorder and catalog entire directories of images; apply uniform filters to a group of images; convert movie clips to series of images; and convert a series of images into a movie. You can also imprint a name, date, watermark and catalog numbers on a group of images and create thumbnails.

5.1.13 IMAGING TOOLS

Professional imaging tools include Paint Shop Pro, Adobe PhotoShop and Corel Draw. Shareware and freeware applications for image manipulation include an evaluation version of PaintShop Pro (for Windows; available for download at *http://www.jasc.com*), WWW GIF Animator (for Windows; available for download at *http://stud1. tuwien.ac.at/~e8925005/*); BME (for Macintosh; available for download at *http://www.softlogik.com*); and GraphicConverter (for Macintosh; available for download at *http://www.lemkesoft.de/*).

5.2 Creating Audio for the Web

Adding sound to your Web page is as easy as including an extra line in your HTML code. The time-consuming part is creating sound files for the Web. What kind of sound you integrate into your Web site will depend on the scope and sophistication of your project. To add an audio greeting or a few sound effects is easy. However, to develop a semester's worth of audio support for online language learning will require careful planning and tool selection. In either case, you will need to understand some basic concepts of audio recording, editing and compression.

To record and edit sound files on your computer you can use one of the many good shareware programs available, including Cool Edit for Windows and SoundEffects for Macintosh. In addition to shareware offerings, both Windows and Macintosh computers come with basic sound recorders. While limited in features, these built-in recorders will let you create adequate sound files that can enhance your Web page. The two professional packages that stand out from the current crop of available audio tools are SoundEdit for Macintosh and Sound Forge for Windows. These production tools should satisfy even the most advanced audiophile.

To play sound you will not need the most current computer hardware. All multimedia machines and nearly all other machines equipped with a sound card can play sound files. If you plan to collect sound files from the Internet, you should have a 28.8 kbps modem or better as sound files can download slowly. To record sound files, however, you need a more robust environment, including a good-sized hard drive (at least 2.5 gigabytes), a fast CPU and at least thirty-two megabytes of RAM. In addition to computer hardware, you will also need a good quality microphone to record interviews or for voice narration.

To create raw material you can use a tape recorder or video camera, or you can use your computer's microphone to record directly to your machine. You can also work with existing audiotapes, videotapes and CDs. When you are creating sound for the Web, remember to select sampling rates according to the following criteria:

- For CD-quality sound, use the following setting: 44 kHz 16 bits, mono.
- For radio-quality sound, use the following setting: 22 kHz, 16 bits, mono.
- For acceptable voice recordings of the female voice, use the following setting: 22 kHz, 8 bits, mono.
- For acceptable telephone-quality recordings as well as recordings of the male voice, you will want to use the following setting: 11 kHz, 8 bits, mono.

Once you have selected your source and setting, click the RECORD button on the control panel of your sound application and start recording. While recording, you may use your application's controls to monitor the input levels of your sound. After you have finished recording, use the "normalize" filter to create a distortion-free, richer and fuller sound. Then save the file in a Web-compliant format. (Sound for the Web must conform to specific file types. The acceptable sound file types for the Web are WAV, MIDI, AIFF, AU and QuickTime.) Be sure to play the sound file back and test it for clarity. As with image files, check the byte size and decide whether a given sound file represents an acceptable compromise between quality and download time. As with larger images and animations, your students will have to wait for larger sound files to download before they can hear them.

5.2.1 HOW TO INCORPORATE SOUND ON YOUR WEB PAGE

Just like images, sound files can be added to your Web page as either external links or inline files. To include a sound file in your HTML code as an external file, use the <A HREF="filename"></A> tag. In the following example, the text "My first piece of audio. WAV file - 0.4MB." will link to the sound file called *first.wav*: <A HREF="first.wav">My first piece of audio. WAV file - 0.4MB.</A>. (Note that, as with large image files, it is a courtesy to include the file size in the description. This sound file is almost half a megabyte in size.) When you click on this link, your browsers will load a built-in sound player or plug-in and play the sound.

To include an inline sound in your HTML code, use the EMBED tag. The following code will play the *first.wav* file automatically when your browser finishes loading your Web page: <EMBED SRC="first.wav" AUTOPLAY="TRUE" CONTROLLER="TRUE" WIDTH="140" HEIGHT="60">. Notice the use of two options: the AUTOPLAY= "TRUE" option will start playing the file as the page loads, while the CONTROLLER= "TRUE" option will bring up the sound controller, which in turn will provide START/STOP and VOLUME controls for your students. For this example, we used the AUTOPLAY="TRUE" option. However, in our own work we prefer to use the AUTO-PLAY="FALSE" option, which passes the option to play the file on to the user.

THE MOST COMMON SOUND FORMATS USED ON THE WEB

AU	(UNIX)
AIFF	(Macintosh)
WAV	(Windows)
MIDI	(Universal)
QuickTime	(A format for digital video, however, it can be selectively compressed to deliver audio or video only. In both cases, the file extension will remain the same: *myfile.mov*. QuickTime works on both Macintosh and Windows-based computers.)

DIGITAL AUDIO TERMS

- *DAT or Digital Audio Tape.* Most digital studios use DAT for mixing and archiving sound. At 48 kHz, it has the highest sampling rate available in today's recording media.
- *Digital Transfer.* Digital transfer is employed when going from digital to digital. For instance, DATs and CDs store sound in digital format. In order to edit such sound, you need to transfer it to a computer. Unlike analog-to-digital transfer, there is no quality loss involved in digital-to-digital transfer.
- *Sample Rates.* The sample rate affects the range of your processed sound. It is measured in kilohertz (kHz), usually averaging between 11.025 and 48 kHz, where the higher number means higher quality.

- *Sampling Resolution.* Resolution refers to the number of possible values that a given sample can hold. It can be 8-bit mono, 8-bit stereo, 16-bit mono or 16-bit stereo.
- *Waveform.* Waveform is not a file format, but rather a visual representation of a sound file that allows for easy nonlinear sound editing.
- *MIDI.* MIDI (Music Instrument Device Interface) is both a file format and an interface. MIDI is a departure from traditional sound files in that it does not contain recorded wave-samples of "sound," but rather carries text-based instructions that sound cards can generate and interpret. MIDI files are recorded via musical keyboard input and other triggering devices, rather than through microphones.
- *Normalize.* Normalize is the "autolevel" function of software-based recording and editing systems. In technical terms, this option raises the level of the highest peak to 0 dB, then raises the level of all other samples proportionally. In practical terms, it makes your sound play much richer.

5.2.2 CREATING SOUND FILES FROM CDs USING COOL EDIT

1. Open Cool Edit.
2. Select the "New" item from the "File" menu.
3. Select a CD track, and click the RECORD button.
4. Save the recorded file as a WAV file.

5.2.3 CREATING SOUND FILES OF VOICE NARRATION USING COOL EDIT

1. Find a good microphone and plug it into the computer's "Microphone In" port.
2. Start Cool Edit.
3. On the control panel of Cool Edit, click the RECORD button.
4. Save the recorded file as a WAV file.

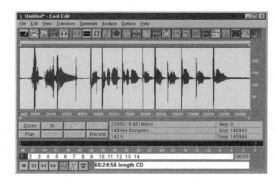

Figure 5.9. Capturing sound from a CD using Cool Edit.

5.2.4 GOOD USES OF AUDIO ON THE WEB

Just like the use of image files, judicious use of voice narration can liven up your pages. Whether you are commenting on images, reading a poem aloud for your students or offering up a short audio sample to round out a course concept, sound always adds

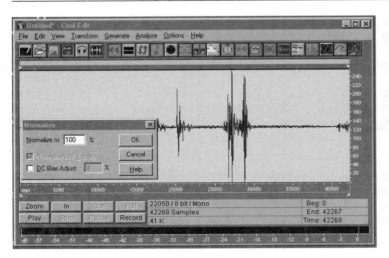

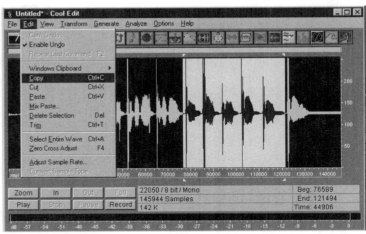

Figure 5.10. *(above)* Using the "normalize" function to enhance a sound file in Cool Edit. Figure 5.11. *(above right)* Editing a waveform file using simple cut-and-paste in Cool Edit.

dimension to your page. There are many good sound sources, archives and language-learning sources on the Internet that offer some form of on-demand playback.

Professional audio tools include: SoundEdit from Macromedia for Macintosh and Sound Forge from Sonic Foundry for Windows. Shareware audio tools include Cool Edit from Syntrillium Software Corporation for Windows and SoundEffects by Alberto Ricci for Macintosh.

5.3 Using Video

Even a few years ago, creating video for the Web was regarded as an arduous task. First you needed specialized hardware to create material, and the available processing power in most cases made for choppy and primitive viewing. While things are far from perfect today, we are definitely a step closer to speedy creation of content, and delivery of video over the Web shows signs of improvement as well.

5.3.1 CREATING CONTENT

A simple, consumer-level video camera will suffice for creating original video footage or raw stock. While filming, work to optimize your conditions, try not to zoom too much, use a tripod when you can and work in good light. When filming for the Web, bear in mind that the video playback frame on a Web page may be as small as two inches square. The farther you are from your subject, the harder it will be to view on a Web page. Try

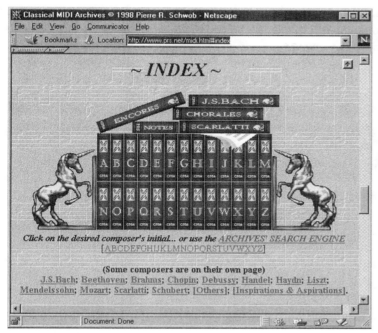

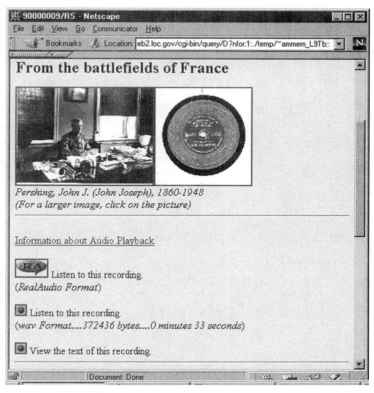

Figure 5.12. *(above)* The Classical MIDI Archives by Pierre R. Schwob at *http://www.prs.net/midi.html#index.* An absolute must for music appreciation, trivia and ambience.

Figure 5.13. *(above right)* A classical model for a historical sound archive is the Motion Picture, Broadcasting and Recorded Sound Division of the Library of Congress at *http://lcweb.loc.gov/rr/record.* This perfectly executed site offers two universal sound formats and also a companion transcript.

for head-and-shoulders set-ups when filming interviews, and try to foreground land-scapes and other dynamic subjects as much as possible. In addition to creating your own content, you can also use existing material from videotapes.

5.3.2 TRANSFERRING VIDEO IMAGES FROM VIDEOTAPE TO COMPUTER

Transferring video from your video camera or VCR to your computer, or the process of moving from an analog format to a digital format, is called sampling or digitizing. To do this you will need a video-capture card. Once the card is installed, connect your VCR or video camera to the proper ports on the back of your computer. Start your video-capture software and then start the tape running on your camera or VCR. The steps for digitizing video are similar to those for working with sound. First you will need to select incoming video and audio sampling rates. Then you will do the actual recording from video camera or VCR to your computer. Once the video is on your computer, you can do any necessary edits. Finally, you will select the outgoing compression rates and save your Web-ready video clip.

5.3.3 VIDEO SOFTWARE TOOLS

The professional video-capturing and editing package used on most university campuses is Adobe's Premiere, which is available for both Macintosh and Windows machines. (As of Premiere version 4.2 there are slight differences in the user interface between Macintosh and Windows versions. In version 5.0—released summer 1998—both are identical.) While difficult to master, Premiere is nonetheless a friendly application to start off with and lends itself to experimentation. If you are working on a strict budget, you should look at the Apple Video Player that comes standard on AV Macintosh computers. This utility will permit you to capture video clips from videotapes or directly from video cameras. Although this is a good tool for a quick video capture, Apple Video player does not provide any video editing functions. To do rudimentary edits, you will have to use MoviePlayer, another standard application on the Macintosh.

5.3.4 VIDEO HARDWARE TOOLS

Unlike sampling sound, sampling or digitizing video is processing intensive. In order to work with video, your computer will have to be equipped with a video-capture card. (Your regular video card is not a video-capture card. Video cards drive your monitors; video-capture cards digitize incoming analog video signals.) In addition to the video-capture card, you will need a speedy CPU and plenty of hard-drive space. How much space will depend on how ambitious your video projects are. A good rule of thumb for uncompressed digitized material is three megabytes of disk space for every second of video. While this number might seem prohibitive, bear in mind that this refers to the pre-processed video file size. Also, you will be creating very small movies for the Web, not feature-length films or even documentary shorts. If you do not have enough hard-drive space, you can supplement by using removable disks such as Iomega ZIP disks.

5.3.5 DIGITIZING VIDEO ON A SHOESTRING BUDGET

You can use the Apple Video Player utility on an AV Macintosh to digitize video clips, capture still images or record a soundtrack from videotapes. To work with Apple Video Player, you will need to connect video and audio cables between computer and VCR and start Apple Video Player.

Figure 5.14. *(right)* Capturing a "small size" video clip using Apple Video Player, a built-in utility on the Macintosh. Image by Joseph Hargitai.

Figure 5.15. *(far right)* Capturing a "full size" (640 x 480) video clip using the Apple Video Player. Image by Joseph Hargitai.

In Apple Video Player

1. Set the movie size from the "Windows" menu option to "Small" (160 x 120).
2. In the "Preferences" option, set compression to "Most."
3. Use the RECORD/STOP button on the Apple Video Player control menu to initiate recording.
4. When you press STOP, you will be prompted to save the file.
5. Apple Video Player will then save your file as a QuickTime movie.

5.3.6 USING ADOBE PREMIERE 4.2 ON THE MACINTOSH

While Apple Video Player will help you create good video clips for the Web, you may eventually want to use a more robust software video editing application such as Adobe Premiere. To work with Adobe Premiere you will need to connect video and audio cables between computer and VCR and start Adobe Premiere. In Adobe Premiere follow these steps:

1. Select the "New Project" item from the "New" submenu of the "File" menu.
2. In the "New Project Presets" window, select 160 x 120.
3. Select the "Movie Capture" item from the "Capture" submenu of the "File" menu.

RECOMMENDED QUICKTIME VIDEO SETTINGS FOR THE WEB

QuickTime is the most popular video plug-in on the Web. When you create video files for your Web pages, keep the following specification in mind:

Movie Size: 160 x 120.

Audio settings: 22 kHz, 8 bits, mono

Video settings: Cinepak Compression/ Thousands of Colors/ Medium Quality/ 15 Frames Per Second

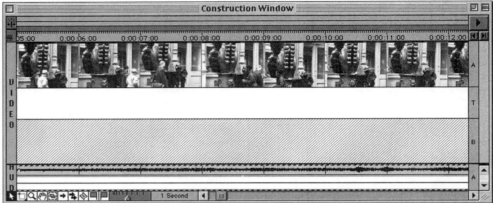

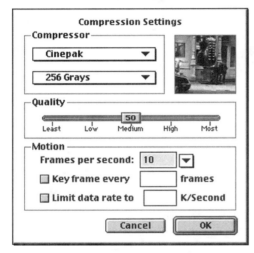

Figure 5.16. *(top right)* Using Adobe Premiere's Construction Window to edit and assemble the final video clip.

Figure 5.17. *(top)* Using Adobe Premiere's Clip Window to monitor incoming video and set up in and out points for editing.

Figure 5.18. *(above)* Selecting compression options using Adobe Premiere's Project Output Option window.

To define capture parameters, select "Record Settings" from the "Movie Capture" menu and set the size to 160 x 120. Next, you will need to define the video settings:

1. Select the "Video Input" item from the "Movie Capture" menu.
2. Select "Compression" and set it to "None."
3. Set "Depth" to "Thousands of Colors" or "256 Grays."
4. Set "Frames Per Second" (FPS) to 10 or 15.

Then define the audio settings:

1. Select the "Sound Input" item from the "Movie Capture" menu.
2. Set "Compression" to "None."
3. Set "Sample Rate" to 22 kHz.
4. Set "Size" to 8- or 16-bit mono.

Now you are ready to start digitizing:

1. Click on the "Record" button in the "Movie Capture" window.
2. Click your mouse to stop recording when you have captured enough footage.
3. Select the "Save As" item from the "File" menu and save your file.

Your raw movie is now ready to be edited or further compressed for your Web page. To do this, drag the movie icon from your "Clip" window to the "Project" window and from your "Project" window to the "Construction" window. To edit your movie, use the "in" and "out" options from the "Clip" window. You can either use the "sliding bar" to mark edits, or you can enter numerical timecode. To compress your movie for the Web, follow these steps:

1. Select the "Output Options" item from the "Movie" submenu of the "Make" menu.
2. Select "Entire Project."
3. Select "QuickTime" movie.
4. Set audio "Rate" to 22 kHz.
5. Set audio "Format" to 8- or 16-bit mono.
6. Set video "Size" to 160 x 120.

The final step to making your movie is to define its compression:

1. Select the "Compression" item from the "Movie" submenu of the "Make" menu.
2. Select "Cinepak."
3. Select "Thousands of Colors" or "256 Grays."
4. Select "Medium Quality."
5. Select "10–15 Frames Per Second."
6. Click "OK."
7. Highlight your movie in the "Construction" window.
8. Select the "Movie" item from the "Make" menu.
9. Name your movie.

5.3.7 INCORPORATING VIDEO FILES IN WEB PAGES

Just as with image and sound files, there are two ways to incorporate video files in a Web page: either as inline files or external links. To include video as an external or linked file, all you need to do is include a line in your HTML file similar to this one: <A HREF="first.mov">My first video file, 1.4MB.</A>. (Again, it is a courtesy to your viewer to include the file size. Note the almost megabyte-and-a-half size of this one— video files are going to be big.) To include a video file as inline, you will need to use the EMBED tag (do not forget to define the controller's HEIGHT and WIDTH options): <EMBED SRC="first.mov" AUTOSTART="FALSE" CONTROLLER= "TRUE"

Figure 5.19. The American Ballet Theatre's online "dictionary" uses video clips to illustrate proper position, movement and delivery of ballet elements. Courtesy American Ballet Theatre at *http://www.abt.org.*

WIDTH="160" HEIGHT="120">. As with audio files, try to avoid setting the AUTOSTART option to TRUE and leave the choice of playing the video file to your students. Despite its current shortcomings, there are some nice examples of video in use as teaching models on the Web. The American Ballet Theatre's *Online Dictionary* (see Figure 5.19) models a particularly effective use of video clips that illustrates proper position, movement and delivery of ballet elements.

COMMON AUDIO-VISUAL TERMS

- *AVI.* Stands for "Audio-Video Interleaved." It is Microsoft's video definition for Windows.
- *Codec.* A general term for compression/decompression standards. While varied in the compression rates they can produce, codecs in general shrink your files to be small enough for multimedia or Web delivery.
- *Cinepak.* Cinepak is a popular codec. Its high compression rates allow creating relatively small video files.
- *FPS.* Stands for "frames per second." Videos played on a regular television set use 30 frames per second. On the Web, most videos use 10–15 frames per second. To the eye, movies containing less than 15 frames per second will look extremely jumpy.
- *QuickTime.* Apple Computer's answer to a one-stop multimedia solution. It offers highly sophisticated video, music and voice compression for both Macintosh and Windows platforms. In version 3.0, QuickTime also offers streaming-like playback for online audio and video as well as image display for file formats traditionally not associated with the Web, such as BMP and PhotoShop.

5.4 Streaming Media

Streaming media applies to delivering time-based media, such as audio and video, over the Internet. For a long time, these media were transferred over the Internet using the same "blind transfer" as images and text. You clicked on an image or a movie and waited until the entire file downloaded to your machine. Once it arrived—a process that could take more than a few minutes—you could finally look at it. Streaming media allows the user to view and listen to a video or sound clip as soon as the transfer is initiated. Streaming media is similar to radio and television in concept, but is much more limited in capacity. If you are coming to this idea with expectations of real-time television or radio broadcast quality video and sound, you will be disappointed. This

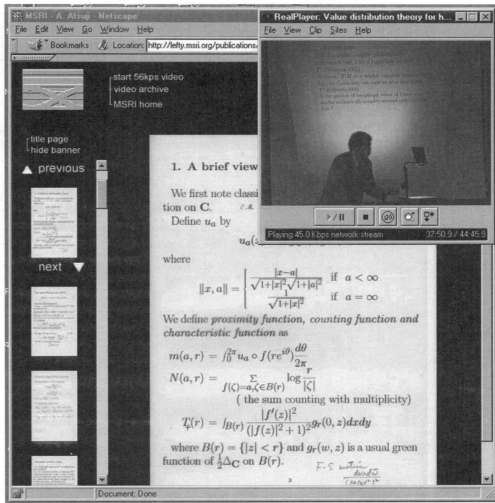

Figure 5.20. *(right)* Lecture notes combined with streaming media delivery. Courtesy of A. Atsuji and the Mathematical Sciences Research Institute at *http://lefty.msri.org/*. Figure 5.21. *(above)* Duna Television's daily RealMedia news broadcast from Budapest at *http://www.dunatv.hu.*

medium is still choppy and, in the case of video, can still only be delivered in a 160 x 120 pixel box (that is, a box approximately two and a half inches wide by two inches high.)

Why is it important to have network-based audio and video delivery instead of using television and radio? There are two compelling reasons: network-based streaming media can be accessed on demand, and can be replayed, fast-forwarded, and in general controlled like a VCR. With fast-growing audio and video archives, you can view and listen to a wide variety of material twenty-four hours a day from any multimedia computer connected to the Internet.

5.4.1 HOW DOES STREAMING MEDIA WORK?

As you saw in chapter 2, the basic idea behind using TCP on IP networks is to deliver data securely from one end of the network to the other. Unfortunately, this also means that larger files are sent over the network in packets or chunks of data, and all these packets must arrive on your computer before they are assembled into a file you can listen to or view. With time-based media, like streaming media, the TCP transmission speed and the order of the data packets is a major issue. Optimally, one would like to have this information delivered in a seamless flow (just like television and radio broadcast).

One company is moving away from the standard TCP protocol. RealNetworks, formerly known as Real Audio, is a leading company in streaming technology and uses a different protocol called UDP (user datagram protocol) to deliver time-based media. UDP is better suited to keep data packets of information steadily flowing through the network. It can deliver motion picture and audio at a good speed. However, this speed comes at the price of occasional data loss, since any data packet that cannot be sent over the Web and arrive on your computer in time is not seen. While this would be unacceptable with e-mail and text files, it is currently an acceptable compromise for sound and video files.

RealNetworks offers a three-part package to deliver streaming media content to Web users:

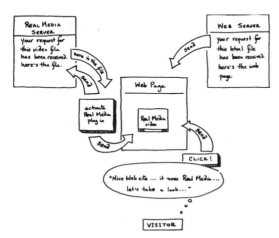

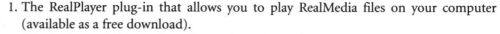

1. The RealPlayer plug-in that allows you to play RealMedia files on your computer (available as a free download).
2. The RealEncoder, a combination audio/video utility that allows for propriety compression and encoding of audio and video files on your computer (also available as a free download).
3. The RealServer, an application that contains and delivers RealMedia-compliant files. This application must be installed and run from a server. If your university is not already running RealServer, then your system administrator or Webmaster will have to install it. For your purposes, you will only need to know the Internet address of the

Figure 5.22. Pencil sketch of RealMedia interaction. Illustration by Anne B. Keating.

server running RealServer so you can transfer any streaming media files you create to this server, and also so you can refer to it in your RealMedia file.

5.4.2 HOW TO CREATE STREAMING MEDIA CONTENT

You can create your sound or video files for streaming delivery using the audio and video tools introduced in the previous two sections. Most of these applications allow you to save your audio or video files as a RealMedia file. If your application does not have that option, you can always use RealEncoder to encode your files.

You can also create your files from scratch, using RealEncoder. You will see immediately that RealEncoder works very much like other audio or video editing utilities. Here, for example, are the steps to create a voice narration file using RealEncoder on a Windows machine:

1. Open RealEncoder.
2. Fill out options such as FILENAME, AUDIO, VIDEO and NETWORKSPEED as prompted.
3. Start and then stop recording.
4. Click on "Encode."

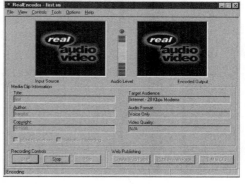

Figure 5.23. Creating a streaming audio file using RealEncoder's control panel (*http://www.realnetworks.com*). Once you select your choice of AUDIO/VIDEO, TARGET AUDIENCE NETWORK SPEED, you are ready to hit the START button to record your first RealMedia narration.

5.4.3 HOW TO INCORPORATE REALMEDIA FILES ON YOUR WEB PAGE

On the surface, including a RealMedia file will seem identical to including an external link in your HTML code. However, RealMedia works a little differently. For one thing, you will be working with two files. The first is your actual RealMedia file containing your audio or video. The second is a META or STUB file, a single line of text that contains the location of your RealMedia file on the Internet. In this example, we have labeled these two files *first.ram* and *first.rm*. Here is how you write the code for your HTML file:

1. Include the following line in your HTML code to call *first.rm* from the RealServer: <A

Since RealPlayer is a stand-alone program, you can call your RealMedia files directly from the player by typing their URLs on the Internet, or their location on your hard drive. In either case, there is no need to use a browser.

HREF="first.ram">here is my first RealMedia file, it is only 500k</A>. (You may have spotted the difference between the extensions: *first.rm* and *first.ram*. This is not a mistake, but an important distinction between the two files.)

2. Create a META file in your text editor and call it *first.ram*. All you need to write in this file is the URL of your RealMedia file, like so: *pnm://www.mycollege.edu/realmediaserver/first.rm*.
3. Upload the text file *first.ram* to your Web server.
4. Upload the RealMedia file *first.rm* to your RealServer.
5. When your browser comes across the *.ram* extension of the *first.ram* text file in your HTML document, it will call up the RealPlayer plug-in on your machine. In turn, the RealPlayer plug-in will read the address contained in the *first.ram* file, which points to your RealMedia file that is stored on the RealServer as *first.rm*. A connection will then be made between RealPlayer and RealServer and the streaming of your actual video or audio file will start immediately.

5.4.4 TRADITIONAL AUTHORING PROGRAMS AND THE WEB

The first authoring tool to revolutionize the creation of distributed courseware was HyperCard, developed by Bill Atkinson in 1987. Its simplified scripting language, user-friendly interface and incorporation of multimedia made HyperCard an instant favorite with users and developers alike. The use of HyperCard cut down on development time and allowed easy portability on the Macintosh computer—the preferred platform of educational institutions during the Apple computer era of the 1980s. From chemistry to language learning to physics to Greek mythology, HyperCard stacks proliferated in all areas of teaching, learning and research.

On a technical level, HyperCard was based on scripting and, like hypertext, provided nonlinear access to a variety of materials including multimedia. In early versions, as with HTML, much of this content had to be created outside of the HyperCard environment; images were made in image editors, movies in movie editors and voice and music assembled in sound applications.

At the height of HyperCard's success, Macromedia's Director took center stage. Director drew from the experience of HyperCard and offered a more seamless incorporation of multimedia, with the downside of a somewhat heavier authoring style. Director was also a cross-platform application, making it a favorite with the business community, which used Director to create in-house "movies" for training and advertising purposes. While development for HyperCard is slowing down, the popularity of Director is increasing. This is in part due to Director's portability to the Web. Director files in the form of a "Shockwave" can be included on a Web page with a single command: <EMBED SRC="myfile.dcr">. However, this relative ease is tempered by a lengthy development time for Director files, concerns over file size and the propagation of updated material. To translate Director's success from the desktop to the Web remains a challenge for developers.

5.5 Virtual Reality (VRML)

VRML, or "virtual reality modeling language," has its roots in engineering and the sciences, but borrows its popularity from science fiction. For several decades, scientists and engineers have been searching for ways to conceptualize massive amounts of data and interaction through dynamic graphic visualization. With the addition of three-dimensional viewing, these models, though not entirely realistic, are rich enough to provide new ways of looking at many different kinds of objects.

VRML, like many of these programs, uses spatial movement, texture rendering, lighting, ray-tracing and object manipulation. In addition to taking hold in the sciences as a modeling language, VRML has also become popular in the arts. Since it breaks with traditional linear and two-dimensional presentations, VRML has become a tool for experimental artists, who are using it to explore asynchronous art on a spatial canvas that combines sculpture and painting yet completely escapes the rules of these classic forms. Science fiction writer William Gibson, in his novel *Neuromancer,* describes cyberspace as the "matrix," a vast network of many levels of computing resources that can actually be seen by the user. The major characters in Gibson's novel "jack in" to the matrix through wiring that connects the user's mind directly to the matrix. The user has a "deck," or computer console, that provides a holographic view of the matrix. VRML aficionados have adopted Gibson's vision of the matrix as the prototype of the ultimate spatial interconnection of individuals with artificially created digitized computer worlds.

Technically, VRML is a three-dimensional modeling concept, designed for real-time client-side rendering and Web transfer. It is text-based and, like HTML, can be linked through hot-spots to other Web documents and multimedia components. The most interesting features of VRML are its spatial representation and interactive user interface. Unlike other programs that try to build three-dimensional interfaces over existing two-dimensional ones, the essence of VRML is working with and in space.

Creating VRML "worlds" can seem quite intimidating. However, VRML is a text-based authoring tool and VRML files are simply text files. VRML files act as "containers" describing objects and behavior, just as HTML files act as containers describing text, formatting and the placement of images. The actual creation of a VRML file is outside the

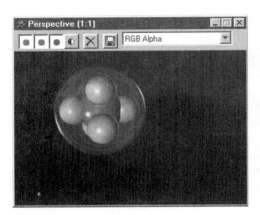

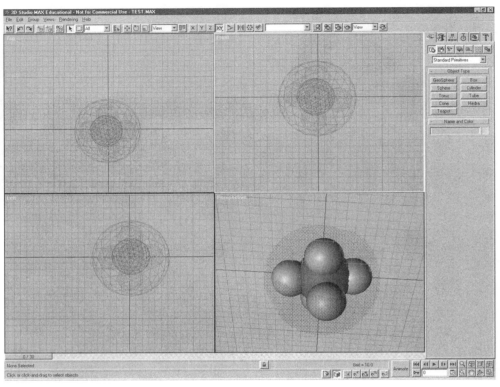

Figure 5.24. *(right)* Creating an animated simulation of a Bohr Nucleus in 3D StudioMax. Courtesy Suprotim Bose.
Figure 5.25. *(above)* Animated simulation of the Bohr Nucleus in 3D StudioMax. Courtesy Suprotim Bose.

scope of this guide. However, at the end of this chapter we have listed a good resource on the Web that should help. To incorporate VRML into your Web site, you would create an "external" file in your HTML using the <A HREF="VRML_filename"></A> tags.

Be aware that, as with animations, sound and video, VRML files can be problematic on the Web and often require your students to install special plug-ins before they can view your work. Also, the size of VRML files can be deceptive. While even complicated projects can be easy to download, the subsequent client-side rendering of shades, textures and forms can take a long time even on the fastest machines.

However, we feel that you should take the opportunity to explore VRML worlds both online and in terms of thinking about your own technology goals. The importance of

Figure 5.26. *(above)* VRML worlds can be created using photographs rendered on objects like a box, cylinder or sphere. Parts of the world, in this case the image, can be hot-spots or buttons that can connect to different URLs. Image by Joseph Hargitai. Figure 5.27. *(right)* Depending on the quality of the image, different resolutions or detail can be obtained through zooming. Image by Joseph Hargitai.

VRML can be explained on two levels. First, you can create extraordinary material for learning. Second, once VRML matures, it will easily create a new paradigm for communication with obvious consequences for education. Even as HTML is currently the universal language of the Web, VRML or some derivative of it may well become the universal language of the post-Web era. For centuries, presentation of information has been two-dimensional. Books, newspapers, paintings, television even the World Wide Web continue to use this two-dimensional framework for presenting information. However, VRML is uniquely positioned not only to better reproduce our multidimensional existence, but also to create an entire world in the space defined by the Internet. Just as Web pages are connected by links to other pages that span the globe, VRML "worlds" could soon be connected in the same space. Perhaps a few years from now we will no longer speak of having home pages. In fact, your location on the Internet may no longer be the address of your home page, but a set of map coordinates that will define where you will be at a given moment so your students can zoom in on you. While this may sound like science fiction now, VRML is situated to radically redefine the Internet and the online communal meeting space. Professional modelling and VRML tools include 3D StudioMax (for Windows), ZWorld (for Macintosh) and CosmoWorld (for Silicon Graphics).

VRML TERMS

- *Avatar.* Whereas text-based virtual communities use nicknames and aliases, visual and three-dimensional gaming worlds use characters, players and avatars to assume your voice, looks and personality on the Web. Typically, avatars are primitive cartoon-like designs either provided by the administrators of the virtual world or created by the participants themselves.
- *Multi-user Environments.* One of VRML's great promises is the potential to create communities in three-dimensional cyberspace. What ties such communities together is multi-user activity. Multi-user environment refers to single environments in which multiple participants communicate with each other.
- *QuickTime VR.* QTVR is Apple Computer's version of VRML. This software allows developers to stitch series of photographs together to create a world that can then be viewed from a single camera point. Unlike VRML, QTVR does not provide a true three-dimensional experience because your views and movements within the environment are limited.
- *Texture Mappping.* VRML, like three-dimensional modeling and rendering programs, uses geometrical shapes to create an object world. To hide this underlying geometry and to add realism to these objects, developers use the technique of texture mapping. The speed of this process is determined by the complexity of the objects as well as the quality and detail of images and textures applied.
- *Virtual Reality.* A projected, artificial or simulated reality most often related to computers or other multimedia devices. In such reality participants can interact with each other using a software interface or with characters or situations created by the program itself.
- *Worlds.* Grandiose as this may sound, VRML developers like to call their creations "worlds," even as you or I would refer to our HTML pages as "home pages."

5.6 CGI/Perl Scripts

If you have been using the Web for any period of time, you surely have encountered a number of examples and implementations of CGI scripts, such as online order forms, access counters, banners, message boards and, of course, the ever-popular guest books. While these examples might seem different on the surface, they all depend on small external programs called "scripts" for interaction. Although referenced within HTML code, these scripts are not part of your HTML code, but reside in a special directory called "cgi-bin" on your Web server. To write CGI scripts, programmers use a variety of programming languages, including C, C++ and Python. However, one of the most popular of these languages is Perl. The reason for Perl's popularity is that it works very well with text-based files—that is, it searches, replaces and extracts text characters with great ease and transparency, which is exactly the level of interactivity that Web designers need to incorporate in their Web pages.

5.6.1 WHAT IS CGI?

CGI stands for "Common Gateway Interface" and is a protocol that allows for information from the client browser to be passed seamlessly to the server and scripts to run on the server, allowing for dynamically created Web pages, database access and so on.

5.6.2 HOW DOES CGI WORK?

In order to have a guest book, bulletin board or online test, you need to analyze and return user input produced in the browser. To do this, your server needs to (1) execute a script that works with the information keyed in by the user and passed to the script via CGI; (2) if necessary, run calculations on the data entered; and (3) if so requested, pass results back in the form of HTML. In order for these programs to run you need to call them from your HTML page. However, while the initial request comes from your HTML page, all the processing takes place on the server. Here, for example, is the behind-the-scenes activity of a typical CGI-based quiz:

1. You have an HTML page containing all the quiz questions.
2. You previously installed a script to interpret the student answers to the quiz questions.
3. Students key in all their answers and then click on the "submit" button.
4. A request is generated from your HTML page to the server to start processing this request. The initial response on the part of the server may include any or all of the following:
   a. The server activates the CGI quiz script that returns with a quick note to your student acknowledging the successful submission of the quiz.

b. The quiz script analyzes the student's answers.

c. The script compares the student's answers to its database of correct answers.

d. The script automatically saves the student's answers in a designated file on the Web server.

e. The script automatically e-mails the student's answers and overall score to the teacher.

5. The script prints a page on the Web with a comparison of the answers the student submitted with the correct answers and provides the overall score. (This page is dynamically generated and lasts only as long as it is viewed by the student.)

5.6.3 RUNNING CGI PROGRAMS

To run CGI programs, you will need at minimum an HTML page that invokes a CGI script that can handle the interaction and a Web server to host both your HTML and CGI files. The HTML page needs a pointer to call the script. In your HTML code, this pointer is called a "method" and is used as part of a form. Typically, this pointer will look like the following: <FORM METHOD="post" ACTION="form.cgi">. (See figure 5.34 for an an example of a form that processes a guest book entry request.)

5.6.4 SCRIPT ARCHIVES

The majority of scripts used in academic Web pages are available in the public domain and can be downloaded from free archives such as Selena Sol's script collection. Whether you will be running your scripts on your university's Web server or your ISP's Web server, your scripts will need to be placed in a directory specified by your Webmaster.

5.6.5 CGI-BIN

CGI scripts need to run from a designated directory on your server. While this could be any directory, traditionally servers are configured to use the directory called *cgi-bin*. You will need proper instructions from your Webmaster to point out where the *cgi-bin* directory is located on your server, or if your account has a link to the *cgi-bin*, how you can link to it. Your Webmaster will also be able to tell you how to write the reference path to your CGI scripts from your HTML document.

5.6.6 PERL BASICS

By now, you know that if you create a Web page, name it *hello.html* to display the following message: "Hello World, Hi There!" the HTML is going to look like this:

Figure 5.28. Selena Sol's Script Archive at *http://www.extropia.com/Scripts*. Courtesy of Selena Sol.

```
<HTML>
<HEAD>
<TITLE>Hello World</TITLE>
</HEAD>
<BODY>
<H1>Hello World</H1>
<P>Hi There!
</BODY>
</HTML>
```

In Perl, a file called *hello.cgi* to generate this Web page would like look like this:

```
#!/usr/local/bin/perl
print "Content-type: text/html\n\n";
print "<HTML>\n";
print "<HEAD>\n";
print "<TITLE>Hello World</TITLE>\n";
print "</HEAD>\n";
print "<BODY>\n";
print "<H1>Hello World</H1>\n";
print "<P>Hi there in perl!\n";
print "</BODY>\n";
print "</HTML>\n";
```

Once you have created this file, saved it and transferred it to your server using FTP, start a Telnet session and go to the directory where you put *hello.cgi* and type *perl -c hello.cgi* at the UNIX prompt. What you hope for is the following message: "syntax o.k." If you get errors, then you will need to edit the script. Especially watch for missing semi-colons and quote marks—Perl is less forgiving than HTML. You should relax, though. With some careful proofreading you will start to spot the errors.

Figure 5.29. Interaction between user, form and server using CGI. Illustration by Anne B. Keating.

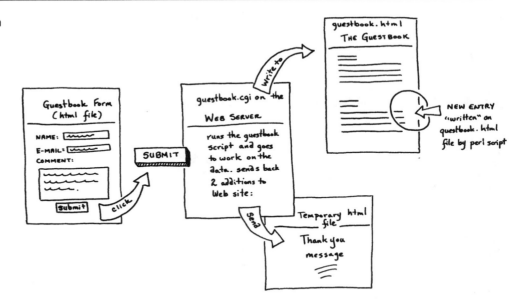

In order to use the scripts on the Web, you will need to set the permissions on the file. You do this at the command prompt in the directory where you have placed *hello.cgi*, by typing: *chmod 755 hello.cgi*. Now you are ready to invoke the script from your browser. Open up your browser and type in the URL for the script. You may discover quickly that if you type the URL *http://www.mycollege.edu/~myname/cgi-bin/hello.cgi* you will just see the Perl script you have written and not an HTML-formatted page that reads "Hello World" and so forth. The address to activate a script may be different from that to view the script. You could, for example, have a URL for your script that reads *http://www.mycollege.edu/cgi-bin/cgiwrap/~myname/hello.cgi*. Once you type this you will see the HTML output from the script.

While "Hello World" is not the most exciting of scripts, it does represent the acquisition of some critical skills that you will need working with CGI- and Perl-generated threaded discussion boards and guest books. While seemingly simple, *hello.cgi* has actually worked the server in an interesting fashion. Figures 5.30 and 5.31 offer a behind-the-scenes look at what happens when a user requests a Web page and types in a URL on his or her computer. In terms of *hello.cgi*, this could be simplified to the exchange shown in Figure 5.31.

Figure 5.30. (*right*) Surfing the Web with HTML. Interaction between user, browser and server. Illustration by Anne B. Keating. 5.31. (*far right*) Surfing the Web with Perl. Interaction between user, browser and server. Illustration by Anne B. Keating.

Forms are an integral part of designing interactive Web pages. A form is part of an HTML document that allows users to enter input. Here is an example form and what the HTML code will look like:

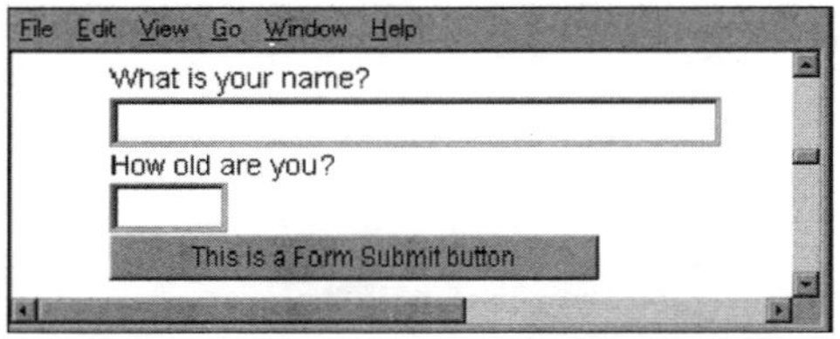

Figure 5.32. This is the form the user fills out.

```
<FORM METHOD="post" ACTION="form.cgi">What is your name?<BR>
<INPUT TYPE="text" size="35" NAME="yourname">
<BR>How old are you?<BR>
<INPUT TYPE="text" SIZE="5" NAME="yourage">
<BR>
<INPUT TYPE="submit" VALUE="Submit this Form">
</FORM>
```

Here is the actual CGI script that takes the data and then prints it as a new Web page:

```
#!/usr/local/bin/perl
#—————————————————————————————————-
# "What's Your Name/Age" script was created by Timothy Metzler and
# is archived at "Tim's CGI Scripts" at http://www.inlink.com/~unity
# Now a subroutine will start that will read the data that was
# submitted.
#—————————————————————————————————-
&ReadParse(*input);
#—————————————————————————————————-
# Now in order to work with the data that was submitted, the
# script will create two variables—one for "name" and one for
# "age."
#—————————————————————————————————-
($yourname=$input{'yourname'});
($yourage=$input{'yourage'});
#—————————————————————————————————-
# Now the script will start creating the HTML file "container"
# for the output of this script.
#—————————————————————————————————-
print "Content-type: text/html\n\n";
```

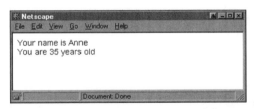

Figure 5.33. This is what the user sees after clicking the submit button.

```
print "<HTML>\n";
print "<HEAD>\n";
print "<TITLE>Personal Information</TITLE>\n;
print "</HEAD>\n";
print "<BODY>\n";
#——————————————————————————————————————————
# Now the script will create the "space" to print the "name" and
# "age" data that will be prepared in the subroutines below.
#——————————————————————————————————————————
print "Your name is $yourname<BR>\n";
print "You are $yourage years old<BR>\n";
print "</BODY>\n";
print "</HTML>\n";
#——————————————————————————————————————————
# Now the script will start to process the data it received for
# "name" and "age." What follows is a modified version of cgi-lib.pl
# by Steven E. Brenner. The original version of cgi-lib.pl is
# available at http://cgi-lib.stanford.edu/cgi-lib/
#——————————————————————————————————————————
sub ReadParse {
local (*in) = @_ if @_;
local ($i, $key, $val);
#——————————————————————————————————————————
# Now the script will read in the text entry for the name.
#——————————————————————————————————————————
if (&MethGet) {
   $in = $ENV{'QUERY_STRING'};
} elsif (&MethPost) {
   read(STDIN,$in,$ENV{'CONTENT_LENGTH'});
}

@in = split(/[&;]/,$in);
```

```
foreach $i (0 .. $#in) {

    $in[$i] =~ s/\+/ /g;

    # Split into key and value.
    ($key, $val) = split(/=/,$in[$i],2); # splits on the first =.
#————————————————————————————————————
# Now the script will read in the data that was submitted for
# age.
#————————————————————————————————————
$key =~ s/%(..)/pack("c",hex($1))/ge;
$val =~ s/%(..)/pack("c",hex($1))/ge;
$in{$key} .= "\0" if (defined($in{$key})); # \0 is the multiple separator
$in{$key} .= $val;
#————————————————————————————————————
# Now the script will perform some basic maintenance on the data
# it received removing any odd characters. Then the script will
# return the data to the two variables listed above in the first
# lines of the script and print out the Web page with this new
# entry.
#————————————————————————————————————
$in{$key} =~ s/\*|\$|\<|\>|\#|\%//gi;
    }

return scalar(@in);
}

sub MethGet {
return ($ENV{'REQUEST_METHOD'} eq "GET");
}

sub MethPost {
return ($ENV{'REQUEST_METHOD'} eq "POST");
```

```
}

exit;
#————————————————————————————————————————————————
# This is the end of the script.
#————————————————————————————————————————————————
```

5.6.7 SELENA SOL'S GUEST BOOK

Guest books and modified guest books have found a niche "market" between Usenet newsgroups and today's threaded CGI-based bulletin boards. Easy to set up and maintain, these makeshift "discussion boards" have generated many memorable topical discussions. Here is how you would install one of these on your Web site:

1. Find Selena Sol's script at *http://www.extropia.com*.
2. Even if you know how to install the script, read the README file here, just in case there is an update or bug report.
3. Download the "tar" version of the file to your UNIX account. If you are working on a Macintosh or Windows machine, download and save the file to your hard drive and then upload it, intact in its "tar" form, to your Web server using FTP.
4. Move the file to the cgi-bin directory of your Web server.
5. Recreate the file from its "tar" archive by issuing the following command at the UNIX command prompt: "tar xvf guestbook.tar."

This will result in the creation of the following directories and files:
Guestbook Root Directory
|____Html
  |____guestbook.html
|____cgi-lib.pl
|____cgi-lib.sol
|____guestbook.cgi
|____guestbook_admin.cgi
|____guestbook.setup
|____mail-lib.pl

"tar" is a popular UNIX archival utility with the command structure of *tar flag filename.tar*. The tar "flags" or options are as follows:

x (extract)—extract files from the tar file

f (file)—use a file instead of a tape (very common)

v (verbose)—output information on what files are being manipulated

The most common combination would be *tar xvf filename.tar*, which expands the archive and generates a report on any errors or inconsistencies in the unpacked files.

6. Set permissions using the "chmod" command from the UNIX prompt as follows: For the Guestbook directory: *chmod 755 Guestbook.* For the files, change permissions as follows:

chmod 666 guestbook.html
chmod 644 cgi-lib.pl
chmod 644 cgi-lib.sol
chmod 755 guestbook.cgi
chmod 755 guestbook_admin.cgi
chmod 644 guestbook.setup
chmod 644 mail-lib.pl

Configuration of the Guest Book Script

Selena Sol uses a special "setup" file to allow for easy configuration and modification of the script. Here is the basic order of the modifications that you will need to do in this *guestbook.setup* script file:

1. $guestbookurl = "http://www.nyu.edu/acf/usg/hargitai/guestbook.html";
2. $guestbookreal = "/cwis/providers/acf/usg/hargitai/guestbook.html";
3. $cgiurl = "http://www.nyu.edu/cgi-bin/cgiwrap/~hargitai/Guestbook/guestbook.cgi";
4. $cgi_lib_location = "cgi-lib.pl";
5. $mail_lib_location = "mail-lib.pl";
6. @bad_words = ("rain", "fog", "taxman");
7. $mail = 1;
8. $recipient = 'jh2@acf3.nyu.edu';
9. $email_subject = "Entry to Guestbook";
10. $linkmail = 0;
11. $separator = 1;
12. $remote_mail = 0;
13. $allow_html = 0;
14. @required_fields = ("realname", "comments");

Figure 5.34. This is the submission form the Guestbook script generates. Script courtesy of Selena Sol at *http://www.extropia.com.*

Following the numbered steps above, here is a running explanation of what just happened.

1. We typed in the URL or location of our guest book (guestbook.html) on the Web.
2. We typed in the location of our guest book (guestbook.html) file. This is where we

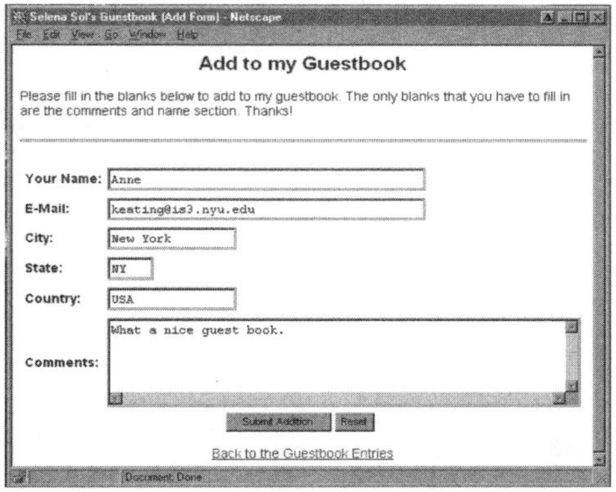

Figure 5.35. A sample entry on the Guestbook form. Script courtesy of Selena Sol at *http://www.extropia.com.*

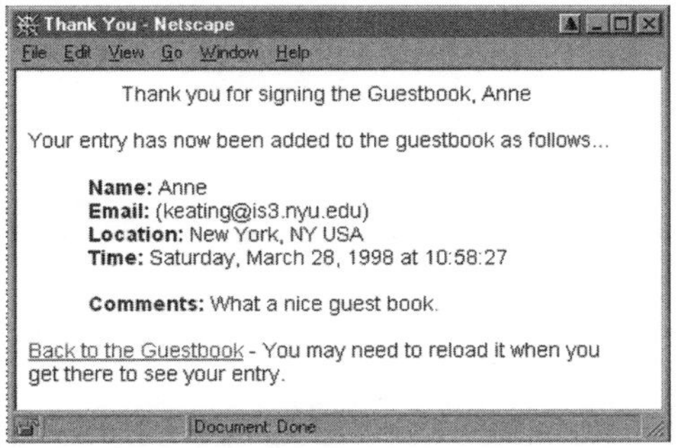

Figure 5.36. A "thank you" note is generated by the script upon submission of your comments. Script courtesy of Selena Sol at *http://www.extropia.com.*

placed the *guestbook.html* file on our server (in most cases, where your other HTML files are). If you are unsure what this location is, type the UNIX command "pwd," which stands for "print working directory," in the directory where the *guestbook.html* file is and use that information.

3. We typed in the location of our *guestbook.cgi* script on the Web server.
4. We added the location of an important auxiliary file on the server called *cgi-lib.pl,* which should be in the same directory as the *guestbook.cgi* script.
5. We added the location of Selena Sol's *mail-lib.pl* script, which should be in the same directory as the *guestbook.cgi script.*
6. Here we created a short list of words we are uncomfortable seeing posted in our guest book. These will be filtered out automatically from postings.(Remember the commas and quotation marks.)
7. If we want to be e-mailed every time there is a new entry, we can specify this here: Yes = 1 and No = 0.
8. We were prompted for our e-mail address so that the script knows how to address the automatic e-mail described in 7.
9. We defined the text of subject line in the e-mail to be sent.
10. We determined whether e-mail addresses submitted by our guests would be printed as hypertext links: Yes = 1 and No = 0.
11. The separator draws a neat horizontal line between guest book entries. This is a nice design feature: Yes = 1 and No = 0.
12. This option sends an automatic "thank you" note to people who have posted to our guest book: Yes = 1 and No = 0.
13. We have the option of disallowing any HTML code to be included in guest book postings. An unclosed tag or inline image could throw our guest book off or render it unusable. We recommend turning this option off: Yes = 1 and No = 0.
14. In order for the guest book to be usable by everyone, we will want to set certain fields as "required" before the entry is processed by the script. Typically, the name of the poster and the comments are set as required.

While the rest of the script will appear intimidating, the material we entered above is all we actually need to modify in order to run the guest book script. However, in order to customize the look of our guest book, we may want to modify the HTML code embedded in the *guestbook.html* file. (If you do modify the HTML code it is critical that you not

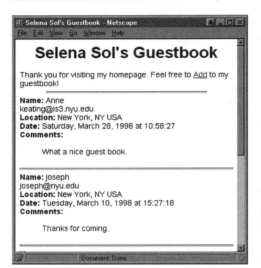

Figure 5.37. At last, here are the entries to the Guestbook. Script courtesy of Selena Sol at *http://www.extropia.com.*

delete the <!—begin—> line and that you click on your "ENTER" or carriage-return key at least twice to create two spaces below this code.)

```
<HTML>
<HEAD>
<TITLE>Selena Sol's Guestbook</TITLE>
</HEAD>
<BODY BGCOLOR = "FFFFFF" TEXT = "000000">
<CENTER><H1>Selena Sol's Guestbook</H1></CENTER>
Thank you for visiting my home page. Feel free to
<A  HREF="http://www.nyu.edu/cgi-bin/cgiwrap/~hargitai/Guestbook/guest-
    book.cgi">Add</A>to my guestbook!
<HR WIDTH = "75%">
<!—begin—>


<!—end of guest book entries—>
</BODY>
</HTML>
```

Here is what the HTML code for the *guestbook.html* file looks like before a new entry is submitted (you will note that there is already one entry on this page):

```
<HTML>
<HEAD>
<TITLE>Selena Sol's Guestbook</TITLE>
</HEAD>
<BODY BGCOLOR="FFFFFF" TEXT="000000">
<CENTER><H1>Selena Sol's Guestbook</H1>
</CENTER>
Thank you for visiting my home page. Feel free to
```

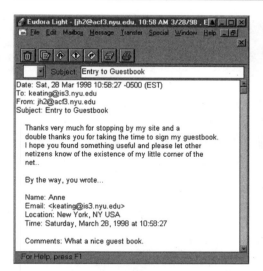

Figure 5.38. An "optional" e-mail message can also be generated by the script. You may send this message to any user-defined address. Script courtesy of Selena Sol by *http://www.extropia.com/Scripts/*.

```
<A  HREF="http://www.nyu.edu/cgi-bin/cgiwrap/~hargitai/Guestbook/guest-
    book.cgi">Add</A> to my guestbook!
<HR WIDTH = "75%">
<!—begin—>
<B>Name:</B>joseph<BR>
joseph@nyu.edu<BR>
<B>Location:</B> New York, NY USA<BR>
<B>Date:</B>Tuesday, March 10, 1998 at 15:27:18<BR>
<B>Comments:</B><BLOCKQUOTE>Thanks for coming.</BLOCKQUOTE><HR>
</BODY>
</HTML>
```

Here is what the HTML code for the *guestbook.html* file looks like after the new entry is submitted (the script has written the entry directly into this HTML file):

```
<HTML>
<HEAD>
<TITLE>Selena Sol's Guestbook</TITLE>
</HEAD>
<BODY BGCOLOR="FFFFFF" TEXT="000000">
<CENTER><H1>Selena Sol's Guestbook</H1>
</CENTER>
Thank you for visiting my home page. Feel free to
<A  HREF="http://www.nyu.edu/cgi-bin/cgiwrap/~hargitai/Guestbook/guest-
    book.cgi">Add</A> to my guestbook!
<HR WIDTH = "75%">
<!—begin—>
<B>Name:</B> Anne<BR>
keating@is3.nyu.edu<BR>
<B>Location:</B> New York, NY USA<BR>
<B>Date:</B> Saturday, March 28, 1998 at 10:58:27<BR>
```

```
<B>Comments:</B><BLOCKQUOTE>What a nice guest book.
  </BLOCKQUOTE><HR>
<B>Name:</B> joseph<BR>
joseph@nyu.edu<BR>
<B>Location:</B> New York, NY USA<BR>
<B>Date:</B> Tuesday, March 10, 1998 at 15:27:18<BR>
<B>Comments:</B>
<BLOCKQUOTE>Thanks for coming. </BLOCKQUOTE>
<HR>
</BODY>
</HTML>
```

Once you have mastered the process of installing your first script, you can download more scripts to experiment with. Our first recommendation would be to set up Selena Sol's Bulletin Board Script. Like a Usenet newsgroup, this CGI-based bulletin board Perl script allows for threaded discussions that will permit your students to move easily between topics and also between postings and replies. (See figure 3.22 for an example of a bulletin board that Anne set up for her Politics of Cyberspace class.) The bulletin board script is more complex than the guest book script, but the modifications follow the same principles described above. Bulletin boards also require more maintenance. However, once set up, you will find this script to be a powerful addition to your course Web site and an invaluable communication tool for your students.

5.7 Administrative Issues

You will be working with a new administrative division on campus that resembles a traditional administrative unit. University computing services units, however have their own unique culture. It is important to have a sense of how such units identify and serve faculty Web-based computing requests.

5.7.1 Obtaining Student and Class Accounts

While it may vary from university to university, account creation is usually done through a central computer accounts office. There is a good chance that this office will be linked to the registrar database, in which case your class number will bring up all the students in your class and create the necessary accounts automatically. If the registrar at your uni-

SOME GENERAL CGI-RELATED TIPS

• FTP single CGI/Perl scripts as "ASCII text" and an archived script (tar file) as "binary."

• chmod sets the permissions on the CGI/Perl scripts and directories. In most cases, all you need to do is the following:

chmod 775 (drwx rwx-r-x)   for the directory the script resides in
chmod 755 (-rwxr-xr-x)   for the scripts that do the action
chmod 777 (drwx rwx rwx)   for any subdirectories that the script has to write to
(this is relevant if you have one script printing results to a number of directories (bulletin boards typically do this).

• Checking to see if your permissions have been set requires only typing the *ls -l* command at your UNIX prompt.

• Make sure you are not overwriting placeholders in the HTML part of scripts. Remember that the line <!—begin—> in guest books is critical.

• Whenever you need the script to write to an HTML file you have created, make sure the file permissions are set to permit an online visitor to write to your file. Otherwise, the script will not be able to write the new entry in your HTML file. Typing the following command at the UNIX prompt typically sets this permission: *chmod 755 filename.* For example: *chmod 755 my_guestbook.html.*

• If you get a "server configuration error," first make sure your permissions are set correctly, then make sure the directions for the location of the pertinent files being called and being written to are correct. If there is still a problem, make sure the correct HTTP header is being printed. This is usually as follows:
print "Content-type: text/html\n\n";

versity is not linked to the computer accounts database, you may have to submit a list of your students by e-mail or interoffice mail to the accounts office. Be mindful of the semester system, create the accounts as early as possible, and notify students of the expiration date of their accounts.

It is a good idea to add yourself to the class list, using your preferred e-mail account. Verify that the accounts have been created before the first class meets and make sure that all your students have working accounts and that they can use them properly. If you are planning to run a class newsgroup, you should request it with the accounts. It may not be the computer accounts manager who will do this, but his or her department will be able to pass on the request.

5.7.2 Showing Web Pages in the Classroom

Like most "wired professors," you will want to bring the Web and your course Web site into your classroom, much as you currently incorporate video and overhead transparencies. If this is the case, make sure that your classroom has a proper modem or Ethernet connection. (As we mentioned in chapter 3, classrooms are being redesigned to be Internet-ready, but many older classrooms are not set up for this.) You will also need to verify that the computer you are using—whether it is your own laptop or a computer loaned from the university media services department—is fully set up with PPP software, an appropriate Web browser, Telnet and FTP clients. You should also check what kind of network connection you will need to make. In some cases, you will be using a standard modem, which will need to be configured properly; in other cases, you will be connecting to the school's network, in which case you will need an Ethernet card. If the classroom does have a network connection, you will need a network card, network cable, network software and your client software. Most importantly, your network card needs to be registered with your network administrator, often referred to as "hostmaster." If you do not register your machine's network card, you may not be able to connect to the Internet. Your hostmaster will most likely be found via email at *hostmaster@yourcollege.edu*. Should there be no such e-mail address, you may need to make a few phone calls to your campus computer support department regarding network-card registration.

5.7.3 Requesting Computer Rooms and Equipment

Your university most likely will have general computing facilities. Since these are busy places, make arrangements for class use at the beginning of the semester. If you decide to use equipment other than your own in the classroom, you should do the same. Make provisions early and familiarize yourself with the equipment, LCD screens, projectors, cable hook-ups, and any related software well before your class time.

5.7.4 ACCESS TO YOUR SITE

Should my Web site be accessible to everyone?
While academic work in general is treated with liberal openness, there are times when you might prefer your material to be available only to students registered for the class. In this case, you can ask your Webmaster to implement password protection for the directory containing your Web site files.

What should I do with the course page after the semester is over?
You will probably want to archive your course page. Simply deactivating the starting page by renaming it to something in context, for example, *f99chem.html,* can do this. If you have not done so already, we recommend that you set up a directory structure in your account. Using this option, you would create a directory called *f99chem* and then move all the relevant course files into this new directory. (However, if you do this, check to make sure that you do not disrupt the integrity of your links.)

What should I do with student material posted during the semester?
Start by offering your students the electronic copy of all their materials. They can either move the files to their accounts or to a disk. Newsgroup and bulletin board material should also be offered to them as a courtesy (use the same rationale here that you already use in returning traditional student materials: papers, lab notebooks and projects). To close a semester, archive all class material on a high-capacity removable disk, as it may be of interest down the line.

What should I do about expiring student accounts?
If your students have sensitive data on class accounts that are due to expire at the end of the term, advise them to do a careful backup or ask for an official account extension at the computer accounts office. This request is usually granted.

5.7.5 WORKING WITH ASSISTANTS

At some point you may find that you will need help creating and extending your Web-based presentations. Your online work may also require a level of sophistication that takes more time than you can spare. In this case, delegating time-consuming work such as image scanning, sound digitizing and extended data entry will be a big help. While many of these tasks can be accomplished through service bureaus, enlisting the help of a Web-savvy student assistant is often a better choice. If your assistants are updating your files on the Web, make sure they have and are working from their own accounts. To do that, you need to ask your Webmaster to make your Web directory accessible to them. As a general rule, do not share your password with your assistant.

Conclusion As this technology becomes increasingly commonplace, how you use it will become more and more transparent. E-mail, home pages, videophones and network-delivered audio and video will become a natural part of your life, just as the telephone, radio and television have. Education, whether it is conducted in a traditional form in a classroom or over the Web and at distance, is becoming increasingly technology-dependent. How your pedagogical values will shift as a result of the introduction of these high-tech tools is hard to predict. However, it is clear that technology has moved from being solely an experimental platform and is becoming a part of our classes and universities. The issue of distance learning by now is a familiar theme to most of us. A natural extension of advanced instructional design, Web-based distance learning offers opportunities that were nonexistent just a few years ago. In the next chapter, we will examine the implications of distance learning and how technology will influence learning beyond and away from the classroom.

Research Links and Resources

1. Darrell Sano, *Designing Large-Scale Web Sites: A Visual Design Methodology* (John Wiley and Sons, 1996). The major benefit of this book is that it focuses on the design of the entire site as opposed to simply designing individual, disconnected pages. Despite the title, the book is also useful if you are building medium-sized or even small sites.

2. David Siegal, *Creating Killer Web Sites: The Art of Third-Generation Site Design* (Indianapolis, IN: Hayden Books, 1997). This design book for the Web, lavishly illustrated and beautifully designed, is targeted at designers but is accessible to just about anyone interested in creating stunning Web pages.

3. Lynda Weinman, *Deconstructing Web Graphics* (New Riders, 1996). A behind-the-scenes look at how some of the best Web sites today are created. The author worked with designers to create a walk-through of how top Web sites were created.

4. Robert Bringhurst, *The Elements of Typographic Style* (Hartley and Marks, 1997). Bringhurst writes about designing with the correct typeface; striving for rhythm, proportion and harmony; choosing and combining type; designing pages; using section heads, subheads, footnotes and tables; applying kerning and other type adjustments to improve legibility; and adding special characters, including punctuation and diacritical marks. Packed with useful information and written in a clear, flowing style. Despite its professional focus, it is perfect for those approaching typography for the first time.

5. *Edward Johnston [1872–1944]* at *http://www.umich.edu/~umsoais/ejweb/* is a Web site devoted to the life and work of Edward Johnston, calligrapher and designer of the London Underground typeface. Modern calligraphy begins with Johnston, who was able to emulate the skill of late medieval professional scribes and could write in a variety of hands. However, his work is of interest not just to calligraphers, but to anyone involved in designing with type or translating text to the Web. This University of Michigan Web site is worth a visit, not just for its rich ideas on design, but also for the site's own rich design. See especially "The Qualities of Good Writing" at *http://www.umich.edu/~umsoais/ejweb/goodwriting.html.*

6. *Type and Typography* at *http://bsuvc.bsu.edu/prn/type.html* contains information and ideas for Web site design. The creators of the site argue that good typographical design is as critical on the Web as in traditional print media. "Typography is very similar whether delivered on paper or on a computer screen. The most significant difference at present is the fact that when we consider the World Wide Web, we must design in such a way that the result will remain attractive regardless of the user's choice of operating system, browser, window size, font, set of installed fonts, graphics hardware, or any of the many other variables involved."[2]

7. *Type Books: For the Well-Read Typographer* at *http://www.typebooks.org/* is the online version of *Type Books*, which is published six times per year. This Web site is especially useful if you are looking for up-to-date reviews of current books on typography. Type Books has extensive reviews and a top-ten rating list that makes this Web site like having a typography expert on call.

8. Jerry Isdale, *What Is Virtual Reality? A Homebrew Introduction and Information Resource List,* at *http://www.cms.dmu.ac.uk/People/cph/VR/whatisvr.html,* offers a lengthy but readable introduc-

tion to virtual reality. The site also has an extensive collection of links to Web sites as well as Internet sources and print resources with more information on virtual reality.

9. Steven E. Brenner and Edwin Aoki, *Introduction to CGI/PERL: Getting Started with Web Scripts* (New York: M and T Books, 1996). Nice, short book with an emphasis on guiding the novice through the basics of setting up Perl scripts.

10. Selena Sol's *Public Domain Script Archive and Resource Library* at *http://www.extropia.com/* mainly documents the CGI work that Selena Sol and Gunther Birznieks have done so that other programmers can learn from their example. The site includes working examples of Perl scripts, as well as the text of the code and helpful FAQs and directions on how to set up the scripts for your Web site. See also Selena Sol and Gunther Birznieks, *Instant Web Scripts with CGI Perl* (New York: M and T Books, 1996).

## CHAPTER 6

Visions for a Virtual University

> Lack of criticism and cultural perspectives have lead to an illusion of the power of technology in changing pedagogy. Instead of highlighting the technological solutions, we should focus on the goals and methods of education and establish after that the role which we wish to give to technology.[1]

THIRD-stage design in higher education is increasingly taken to mean a push toward distance learning. This is neither a fair nor an accurate assumption. However, because the connection between instructors with Web pages and distance learning has inevitably come up in conversations with administrators and faculty (outside of our small die-hard band of "professors with Web pages" co-conspirators), we realize that it is important to address this subject. However, it is important to stress that this is not a book about distance education, nor is distance learning the only logical outcome of adopting the Web as a teaching platform. As you will see in this chapter, depending on whom you talk to, distance learning is either seen as the next great educational tool or the ultimate technological evil about to be forced on vulnerable faculty by administration. In this chapter, we will do several things. First, we will show the current controversy over the use of Web pages in university courses and how this has become intertwined with distance learning in many people's minds. Then we will define what distance learning is and place it briefly in context of other recent remote-learning experiments. Finally, we will summarize the current pedagogy of Web-aided instruction. While we may not agree with the lumping together of course Web pages with distance learning, we do believe that the experiences of educators working with distance learning are a valuable resource for advanced instructional design.

Make no mistake about it—distance learning is a hot topic in higher education. Critics are alarmed at what they view as the coopting and commercialization of higher education. David F. Noble, in his essay "Digital Diploma Mills: The Automation of Higher Education" (1998), gives voice to some of these anxieties. He argues that by integrating technology and exploring distance learning, "universities are not simply undergoing a technological transformation. Beneath that change, and camouflaged by it, lies another: the commercialization of higher education. For here as elsewhere technology is but a vehicle and a disarming disguise."[2] Noble blames administrators, who wave vague and romantic ideals of reaching geographically distant or disadvantaged students with distance learning courses in front of unsuspecting faculty. In fact, Noble believes that administrators are focusing far closer to home and are eager to make money on the growing technology market while simultaneously looking to cut costs by replacing faculty and classrooms with computers and educational software. "It is important to emphasize that, for all the democratic rhetoric about extending educational access to those unable to get to the campus, the campus remains the real market for these products, where students outnumber their distance learning counterparts six-to-one." Noble blames as well "the ubiquitous technozealots who simply view computers as the panacea for everything, because they like to play with them." He argues that these zealots have received support and encouragement from the private sector and university patrons "without support for their pedagogical claims about the alleged enhancement of education, without any real evidence of productivity improvement, and without any effective demand from either students or teachers."

The ambivalence over the arrival of course Web pages on campus and distance learning is not limited to critics such as Noble. At York University, where Noble teaches, a recent faculty strike demonstrated how technology can become a focal point of a firestorm of controversy over university policy. In the spring of 1997, the faculty of York University in Toronto went out on strike for eight weeks. Among their reasons for doing so was a concern about the possible loss of quality of education at York. The faculty zeroed in on what they viewed as the administration's fascination with technology. In their contract negotiation they demanded that a provision be included "to protect departments and individual instructors against imposition of course and programme restructuring and of alternate modes of delivery."[3] In a strike pamphlet titled "The Real Issue Is the Classroom against the Boardroom," strike organizers explained:

> Our working conditions are your learning conditions. If we win, you win. Over the last ten years, we've watched our teaching situation deteriorate. Many of our classes have doubled and even quadrupled in size. Now we hear we could have even bigger classes some run by correspondence or on the Internet so that students will have little contact with professors.[4]

In their new contract, York faculty have the right to veto "any course conversion to a new technology."[5]

What is particularly interesting is that the technology provisions in the new faculty contract at York were a reaction to a perceived threat rather than an actual university policy. While faculty expressed their concerns about being forced to integrate technology and accept distance learning, the administration at York stated that it had "no intention of forcing faculty members to use the technology."[6] In fact, one faculty member at York pointed to a policy adopted at UCLA as reason enough for faculty to "take a fresh look at their contracts."[7]

At UCLA, the College of Letters and Science launched an Instructional Enhancement Initiative in 1997. Not content with simply providing support for faculty who wanted to experiment with Web pages, UCLA's goal is to have "a Web site for every undergraduate non-tutorial course offered in the College of Letters & Science, the largest academic unit in the University of California system (about 3,000 courses per year)."[8] At York and elsewhere, the UCLA policy is viewed with apprehension. Some faculty are concerned about a possible loss of academic freedom implied by such a demand. One professor argued:

> The U.C.L.A. mandate may be defended as an extension of existing format requirements governing course materials. These must be typed or word processed, must be handed out by a certain date, must clearly state certain department, college, university policies, etc. But the mandate goes beyond the issue of format: it impacts the way that instruction is delivered, and that is an academic-freedom issue. Academic freedom means not merely having the right to take an extreme position in the pursuit of knowledge, but also having the right to adopt the instructional method of choice in that pursuit. The U.C.L.A. mandate, while not debarring other methods, does impose one.[9]

Another professor opined that "Web pages may prove to be the 'Sesame Street' of higher education, a useful attention-getter, but no substitute for a rigorous and engaging classroom environment."[10] Another professor argued that Web pages were a sop to the "video generation" and would further pull instructors and students away from the printed word:

> I think we all know how strongly our students are influenced as a "video generation." If they don't get sound bites, light shows (whoops! "slide lectures") and every-

thing neatly packaged like a news anchor, they just do the academic equivalent of changing the channel. Having W.W.W. pages can play to these worst instincts. Worse still, the faculty who do utilize them can immediately get a privileged status in student eyes—meaning more enrollments, better course evaluations, and the like.[11]

At the heart of the controversy is a fear that as the shift of course content to the Web continues and increasingly includes integrating external resources and even educational software, college instructors will lose their autonomy in the classroom. George Sadowsky argues that even more important than this perceived loss of autonomy "is the perennial question of the extent to which instruction can be delivered effectively in a pre-packaged form, as a commodity, across potentially large distances. The traditional western model of education is, at the least, skeptical of this view, stressing the relationship and interplay between professor and students as an essential part of the learning process."[12]

While professors should be concerned about the commercialization of their courses, we would argue against the outright dismissal of this technology. If experimenting with Web pages in classes, or even requiring a Web page for every course, enriches the students' experience with the course material and enhances classroom instruction—and even, in some cases, goes as far as to revitalize an instructor's teaching method—then there is much to learn from this technology and, by extension, from experiments in distance learning as well. Sadowsky argues that "experimentation in distance learning can help us learn what this new medium can add to the increasingly diverse set of opportunities for education and training available throughout the world."[13]

What Is Distance Learning?

Few things pedagogic sound more dubious than that vintage phrase "correspondence course." But maybe it's time to rehabilitate this unfortunate term. The Internet offers a broad range of online learning experiences, including regular classes that do seem to be correspondence courses, more or less, but many of them are offered by major universities charging tuition and even offering credit toward a degree.[14]

In chapter 3, we briefly discussed the role that media innovations played in educational experiments earlier in this century. Radio and television in particular were thought to present exciting possibilities for extending the reach of the traditional classroom. A variety of educational schemes, from correspondence courses to televised extension courses, fall under the definition of distance learning. The term in fact simply refers to "a variety of educational models that have in common the physical separation of the faculty member and some or all of the students."[15] In distance education, as in the traditional classroom, instructors and students come together to study a body of knowledge and to assess and apply what has been learned. The principle difference between traditional education and distance learning is that the latter uses "technology to either enhance or serve as delivery medium for one or all of these activities."[16]

Correspondence courses, developed in Britain along with the introduction of the modern postal service, were the earliest form of distance education. Each discovery and advance in communications technology has resulted in developments in distance education. In 1921, with introduction of radio broadcasting, the federal government gave the Latter Day Saints' University of Salt Lake the first educational radio license. The University of Wisconsin and the University of Minnesota followed quickly and received their radio licenses the following year. In 1945, with the advent of television, Iowa State applied for the first educational television (ETV) license and started broadcasting in 1950.[17] The launching of Sputnik in 1957 stirred national interest in educational reform, along with an awareness that children would have to be educated for a new type of society in part molded by "modern communications such as radio, film, television and computers [that] had created an information-rich society. Schools were no longer the only center of information, but had to compete for student attention."[18]

One of the earliest implementations of educational computing was a research and development program on computer-assisted instruction in mathematics and reading, established by Patrick Suppes and Richard Atkinson at Stanford in 1963. They sought to free students from the lock-step process of group-paced instruction and developed individualized instructional strategies that allowed the learner to correct his or her responses through rapid feedback. The self-paced programs allowed a student to take an active role in the learning process. Mastery was obtained through drill and practice.[19]

In the late 1960s, in order to make access to computers widely available, the National Science Foundation (NSF) supported the development of thirty regional computing networks, which included three hundred institutions of higher education and some secondary schools. By 1974, over two million students used computers in their classes. In 1963, only 1 percent of U.S. secondary schools used computers for instructional purposes. By 1975, 55 percent of the schools had access and 23 percent were using computers primarily for instruction.[20]

The Web as a Distance Learning Platform

The World Wide Web is an interesting and potentially rich platform for distance learning ventures. In fact, early on in the workshops we conducted with faculty, there was often a misconception that posting any course materials on the Web constituted distance learning. While a course Web page will give a student access to course materials after class meeting times and outside of the instructor's office hours, this Web presence is heavily dependent on the work going on in the traditional classroom. (If this constitutes distance learning, then one could argue that sending students to the library to conduct research is also engaging in distance learning.)

While having a course Web page up is not itself distance learning, it is possible that, especially if you add interactivity (for example, Perl-based bulletin boards) to your Web site, you may come to a point where developing an online course becomes a very real interest. A course Web page can bridge the distance between the physical classroom and the metaphysical classroom that teachers and students create together each semester and can provide continuity from week to week. The online course can bridge geographic limits and the fixed nature of scheduled class meeting times, reaching students who because of physical, work-related or other obstacles will otherwise go unserved by the university.

Linda Wolcott argues that the introduction of the Web as a new distance education medium has come at the same time as two other equally important developments:

> Distance education is experiencing a convergence of technologies and a pendulum swing back to asynchronous delivery—but this time using computers rather than print or broadcast delivery. At the same time, among the trends that we are witnessing is a greater acceptance and integration of distance learning into the mainstream of education so that the lines are blurring between traditional education and what we have been calling distance education. In fact it is becoming common now to talk about distributed learning rather than distance learning.[21]

To understand Web-delivered distance education and to project its growth, it is important to examine the demographics of Internet users and current distance education students. As we saw above, the current controversy surrounding the adoption of technology on campus for the delivery of educational materials is a heated one. Some of the controversy has to do with the fact that the technology is still foreign to many teachers. However, there is a dramatic demographic shift underway in the number of people using the Internet that lends credence to the argument that as comfort levels with the technology increase and the Internet and Web become as ubiquitous as video and television, Internet-based distributed learning will become an accepted educational method.

For all the controversy surrounding the use of Web in the classroom, the number of people using the Internet has continued to grow dramatically both in academia and among the general public. A 1997 poll determined that more than sixty-two million Americans, or 30 percent of the U.S. population, were using the Internet. That represents a 32 percent increase in the Internet population from 1996, and it was estimated that in 1998 another seven million people would log onto the Internet as new users. (Among those polled, 46 percent reported that they were using the Internet at work, which indicates that by 1997, the Web had evolved from being a mainstream fad and new form of entertainment to a workplace tool.)[22] In a survey of Internet use among faculty, the demographic profile was similar. T. Matthew Ciolek reports that

> it appears that in 1997 an average respondent spent roughly: 10% (4.6 hrs) of that time adding information to the Internet (or maintaining/repairing existing resources); 9% (4.1 hrs) dedicated to online communication with other people (via personal email and the mailing lists); and 24% (11.0 hrs) on surfing, browsing, reading and querying the Net. This means that, on average, during 1997, scholars who participated in our online survey spent approximately 43% of their office hours on working on the Net, and 57% on paper-based and face-to-face activities.[23]

Within this Internet population are two critical groups who are either currently being served by distance education or will shortly become influential in terms of how elements of distance education are integrated into traditional classroom practice. The current generation of K–12 students, as well as students who are now applying to colleges, are part of a generation in which computers, the Internet and the Web have been a regular part of instruction. Where a few years ago, prospective college students were interested in buying computers to help them with their course work, now applicants are interested in knowing whether their dorm rooms are wired for the Internet. While it would be inaccurate to suggest that these students want distance education courses piped into their dormitory rooms, many are coming to college with educational experiences that have included distance education components. In K–8 education, many teachers have successfully been integrating distance education as an extension of the classroom. (It should be noted here that while the debate over distance learning in higher education has focused on the value of synchronous learning and seat time, distance learning in grammar schools has focused on bringing educational resources from outside the school into the classroom.) Wolcott explains that K–8 distance education "has a different flavor. K–8 teachers are not turning the instruction of their students over to distant teachers. Rather they are collaborating with them! . . . They partner with the distant teacher; together, and as a result of the instructional design of the program, they provide the interaction and feedback."[24] An example of such collaboration is the Web-based MayaQuest project, which "allowed students to be present on an archeological dig. Through this electronic or virtual field trip, the students not only received information from a distant 'teacher,' they also interacted with persons on the dig, influenced the activities of the exploration, and interacted with other students."[25] This example "illustrates uses of distance education that are different from those we typically see in secondary and higher education."[26]

Down the line, distance education may evolve into a variety of distributed learning ventures, but the current thrust of distance education is to serve a different student population. The average distance education student is older, has a job and is responsible for a family. In order to take courses, these students must coordinate their study with other demands. Many are motivated by the need to add skills or to obtain a degree to qualify for a better job, though some do enroll in distance education courses to broaden their education and are not interested in completing a degree.[27]

In short, the current distance learning student population comes from the ranks of adult continuing education or extension students. On many campuses, these students are viewed as inferior to traditional-age students. This unfortunate and ill-deserved stereotype, coupled with the stigma of "correspondence course," is at the heart of many arguments about the dubious value of distance education courses. When viewed in this light, it no wonder that many college faculty are concerned about the watering down or commercialization of their courses. While we should all be concerned about the unscrupulous use of our course materials and generally about "diploma mills," distance education has been unfairly singled out. While colleges and universities will continue to educate young people, we must be aware of a growing constituency of prospective adult students who bring with them new educational needs: the need to upgrade skills and the need for learning on demand. As "job content changes rapidly in the new science-based information world, new pedagogies are needed to upgrade one's knowledge and to develop skills that answer current and immediate problems on the job."[28]

The Pedagogy of Distance Education

Typically, the distance educator faces several challenges. Key among these is the isolation of the student and the fact that teachers and students often will have little in common in terms of background and daily experiences. These factors add new challenges for the distance educator, who starts a course knowing that the motivational factors that develop naturally in a classroom from contact and competition with classmates will be absent in a distance education course. Meeting the instructional needs of students is the cornerstone of every effective distance education program, and the test by which all efforts in the field are judged. Regardless of the educational context, the primary role of the student is to learn. This is a daunting task under the best of circumstances, requiring motivation, planning, and an ability to analyze and apply the instructional content being taught.

The success of any distance education effort rests squarely on the shoulders of the faculty, who must adapt teaching styles taking into consideration the needs and expectations of multiple, often diverse, audiences. Furthermore, faculty must develop a working understanding of the technology they are using while remaining focused on their teaching role. Last but not least, faculty teaching distance learning courses must balance their traditional role with that of a skilled facilitator.[29]

Along with the traditional grouping of faculty and students, there is an additional and essential cast of characters in successful distance education ventures. There should be a site facilitator who can act as a bridge between the students and the instructor. In some instances, the site facilitator will act like the traditional teaching assistant—that is, by understanding the needs of the students as well as mediating the instructor's expectations. In other instances, the site facilitator will act more as an instructional designer who is able to mediate among the needs of the instructor, the course content, the distance education students and the technology or technologies that will be pulled together to support the course. There should also be a support person who can deal with issues ranging from the securing of copyright clearances to managing technical resources, scanning and converting print resources into Web-ready form.

Administrators can play an influential role in planning an institution's distance education program. However, in order for a distance education program to be effective, administrators need to take a more hands-on approach to project management. "Effective distance education administrators are more than idea people. They are consensus builders, decision makers, and referees. They work closely with technical and support service personnel, ensuring that technological resources are effectively deployed to further the institution's academic mission. Most importantly, they maintain an academic focus, realizing that meeting the instructional needs of distant students is their ultimate responsibility."[30]

**A Look at Four
Distance Learning Ventures**

There are several models for distance education worldwide. Many distance education courses are offered as extension courses by major universities; others have emerged as new academic enterprises. To give you a sense of the variety of distance learning projects, we examine four projects that demonstrate some of the challenges and expectations of distance educators. Among the newest academic enterprises are two projects, the University of Phoenix and Western Governors University.

John Sperling, who views education as a service business, founded the "Online Campus" in San Francisco in 1989. He believes that online "computer-mediated education was an outgrowth of the technological transformation of the work place and a response to the increasing use of computers and modems for communication."[31] The "Online Campus" grew into the University of Phoenix and currently serves 2,600 students who log-in to Phoenix's virtual classrooms via modem. At the University of Phoenix Web site, Phoenix's designers explain that

> we could more accurately be called the "Center for Accessible Education" since our aim is to make distance an imperceptible part of your educational experience. In an age when time and efficiency are at a premium—when it's often more practical to e-mail or call a co-worker down the hall than to locate them—we bring "distance" education as close to working students as their colleagues.[32]

They argue that they offer a unique service to working students and that Phoenix students

> cite many advantages over traditional—and even other non-traditional—campus programs, including more direct access to faculty, superior time management, and freedom from scheduling and location conflicts. Administrative transactions which are time-consuming in a physical setting: meeting with your counselor, registering for class, and buying books, are conveniently and efficiently handled by telephone, e-mail, or fax.[33]

There is no doubt that the University of Phoenix is working on a for-profit model of education. In an article on Phoenix, *Forbes* compared this school's operating costs with those of Arizona State University:

> It costs Phoenix on-line $237 to provide one credit hour of cybereducation, against $486 per hour for conventional education at Arizona State. The big difference: teach-

ing salaries and benefits—$247 per credit hour for Arizona State against only $46 for Phoenix. Arizona State professors get an average of $67,000 a year. The typical University of Phoenix on-line faculty member is part time and earns only $2,000 a course, teaching from a standardized curriculum.[34]

Western Governors University (WGU) is another experiment in creating new educational enterprises. In design, WGU is a radical departure from the classic definition of a university. It has neither a campus nor lecturers of its own, but rather acts as a course broker, getting its courses from participating universities, community colleges and commercial suppliers. However, "students will enroll directly with WGU and get their degrees from it rather enrolling in a participating institution."[35]

The justification for this radical departure is that WGU will lower costs of higher education. As can be expected, WGU has drawn fire from critics, including one who argues that while attempting to make the prospect of lowered college tuition an attractive draw for WGU, the motives behind the plan are sinister:

> The corporate and legislative backers of WGU hope to do more while finding a way to lower the costs of education, make quick use of new technology, and absorb booming enrollments. They want to change the definition of a college education. Seat time and credit hours will mean less than what students can show they're able to do by taking tests. The initiative will focus on the needs of students and employers.[36]

However, not all distance education ventures fit into the model of the University of Phoenix and Western Governors University. The Monterrey Institute of Technology and Advanced Studies in Mexico offers an "Information Technology Strategic Planning" course as part of a master's degree program. This course is the subject of a case study by Hartwig Stein that offers an interesting look at the internal workings of distance education. The thirteen-week course ran from April to June 1997 and started out with a roster of forty-four students located at twelve different campuses. The Monterrey campus was selected for the videotaped portion of the course, and thirteen students acted as the live audience for these taped sessions. During the course of the semester, seven students dropped out and two failed. The students were initially put together into fourteen groups, which became eleven groups by the end of the semester. There were a total of twelve days of satellite classes, each lasting about an hour. The estimates for the amount of time students were expected to spend on the course were as follows: a total of twelve hours devoted to learning activities for each of the twelve modules, including one hour of the satellite class (group work session) and a prerecorded video of ninety minutes, for a total of 144 hours of learning activities. One class was devoted to the presentation of team projects.[37]

Most of the students had taken distance education courses before enrolling in "Information Technology." Stein, who taught the course, had eight years of experience in distance education prior to teaching this course, and his academic assistant had two and a half years of experience. The administrators were also experienced in this field. The course itself was delivered using a variety of new media, including twelve videotapes, twelve satellite classes, the Internet, newsgroups, IRC chat, and e-mail as well as telephone and fax.

His case study emphasizes the significant time outlay required to launch a distance education course. The creation of the course involved several critical production specialists as well as many hours of work. Thirty-three hours per person were devoted to the overall course design, including the production of the videotapes and graphics for the course. Additionally, the teacher and academic assistant on the project logged fifteen hours each on the academic design. During the course of the online semester, both the teacher and the academic assistant spent 430 hours facilitating the online learning process. "This averaged to fifteen hours per person per week spent in reading and writing . . . electronic mail, revision of newsgroups, structuring of groups, individual feedback, answering questions and administrative issues."[38] Despite the initial estimates of how much time students would spend on the course, "some students reported that they invested between 8 and 14 hours every week in the course and that they did their activities throughout the week."[39] Stein concludes that a successful distance learning course "must have clearly defined objectives whose accomplishment is easy to validate, such as seen in successful training courses in the business sector."[40] He emphasizes that it is critical for teachers contemplating teaching distance education courses to understand that

the model of transmission of information from teacher to student practiced by both conventional institutions and the large, autonomous distance teaching universities is no longer sufficient in a society where knowledge is changing rapidly, and the skills needed both at work and in our social lives are becoming increasingly complex. People need to know how to communicate effectively, work in teams, search out and analyze new knowledge, participate actively in society, and generate as well as assimilate knowledge.[41]

It is clear that in order to be effective, distance education courses need to focus on student activities. Activities that demand reading, analysis, synthesis and evaluation are likely to involve students in worthwhile learning experiences. A top-down teaching style will not work in this teaching medium. Students must have guidance throughout the entire course to maintain their motivation.[42]

The UNIWORLD virtual university project is a Hungarian distance education venture launched in 1997 by the Institute of Philosophy of the Hungarian Academy of Sciences. The aim of UNIWORLD is to organize and manage a wide range of Internet-based distance education activities. The most important of these activities is the launch of master's degree courses in September 1998 in cooperation with the University of California, Santa Barbara. Students of the pilot courses are regular undergraduates at Eötvös Lóránd University in Budapest and Janus Pannonius University in Pécs, Hungary. Both universities have agreed to accept these courses as equivalent to traditional courses. UNIWORLD will provide university courses leading to an American master's degree. As with any university, participation in a UNIWORLD program will require an application, enrollment, payment of tuition and examinations.

The master's degree programs offered by UNIWORLD include the following: cross cultural communications, which combines technical and humanistic studies as well as theoretical and practical approaches; international migration studies, which focuses on international population movements, labor migration, refugee problems and legal and illegal immigration; and internet studies in religion, which will combine traditional studies in religion and the history of religion with electronic communication and particularly networked communication. Of the latter course, the designers explain: "this subject is warranted by the ever-growing presence of religion in the various newsgroups, discussion groups and Websites on Internet. The new religious environment requires a new group of practical experts."[43] A master's program in environmental management studies will address issues that have become increasingly global in scope, such as hazardous waste, the threat of nuclear catastrophes, pollution, deterioration of soil and deforestation.

In each case, UNIWORLD's designers have given some thought to the Internet not just as a means of delivery, but also as a critical teaching platform with global reach. The programs in international migration studies and environmental management, for example, attest to the uniqueness of this platform for their subject matter. In the case of degree programs in cross-cultural communications and internet studies in religion, there is an implied rationale that the Internet is a place where a specific discourse is yielding topics worthy of examination.

László Turi of the Institute of Philosophy, Hungarian Academy of Sciences, and editor of *Internetto Webzine,* helped launch UNIWORLD's pilot program of two courses in communication philosophy in 1997. We asked him to describe some of the challenges of setting up this ambitious project. One question was whether new faculty would have to be hired to teach the courses, or whether UNIWORLD organizers were going to hire faculty who were trained in traditional classroom teaching. Turi explained: "UNIWORLD was initiated outside the university, because Hungarian higher education is fairly conservative. So far, these universities have not offered any financial support for the project. However, despite this obstacle, UNIWORLD organizers are trying to attract high quality teachers and lecturers who have experience in traditional forms of education."[44] Turi explained the educational model that the UNIWORLD designers had in mind for the delivery of online content:

> We have studied and are still studying a number of existing virtual universities that can be accessed on the Web. On this basis we set up a simple communication system that attempts to model traditional classroom communication channels. Separate communication channels (i.e. Web pages) were provided for teacher-to-students communication (i.e. for lectures), for discussions of the lectures and for the recommended readings and also for student-to-teacher communication, that is for the paper assignments. This system proved to be functional in Prof. Nyíri's online philosophy classes, however, it is clear that it needs further refinement and development for disciplines that are more practical than philosophy.[45]

We also asked Turi to comment on the unexpected problems UNIWORLD designers encountered during the pilot phase of the project and what strategies they developed for problem solving on the project. Turi explained that one unanticipated problem was that it quickly became clear to the designers that a face-to-face meeting needed to take place during the course:

> It had to be realized that face-to-face meetings must be organized at least once a term. Since some of the students are not Budapest residents, we are trying to set up an online videoconference system for the occasions of the meetings. Otherwise UNI-WORLD is based on asynchronous communication methods. We have made an

attempt to create a Web-software for the purposes of class-management but the attempt failed. It is a recurring problem that students' Internet access is limited due to the lack of proper infrastructure.[46]

Distance learning ventures of the scale envisioned by UNIWORLD's designers typically require a significant investment of start-up capital. We asked Turi to talk about the financial aspect of the project and to give us a sense of when UNIWORLD's designers expected to see a "profit" with the on-line courses. Turi responded that UNIWORLD's designers anticipated that it would be at least four to five years before they saw a profit. However, he made it clear that the start-up capital for the project was modest: "A commercial bank . . . provided us some modest support to cover basic organizational costs for about a year. However, this support does not cover the actual costs of education."[47]

Vision for a Virtual University Historically, innovations in communications technology have fueled significant cultural and intellectual change, as well as contributed to social upheavals. At each point, the products of these technologies or the technologies themselves—whether printed books or radio broadcasts or now Web pages—have led directly to an intellectual revolution. The Internet only heightens and highlights the problem that whoever owns information is in a position of power. As teachers, we have a duty to be cautious about technology. In our own century, we have the discoveries of atomic energy and radio as examples of technologies that were used for sinister ends. The atom bomb is a cautionary tale about the seductive power of technological innovation. Radio in the hands of the Nazis was a powerful demonstration of the power of communications technology as a propaganda tool. Joseph Goebbels, the Nazi propaganda minister, explained that while the press was an "exponent of the liberal spirit, the product and instrument of the French revolution," radio was "essentially authoritarian" and, therefore, a suitable "spiritual weapon of the totalitarian state."[48] As the critics of distance learning warn, the danger of the Internet for us as teachers is not the technology itself, but the cooptation and commercialization of our profession.

We live in a complex time educationally. The challenge of the incorporating new technology into our teaching practice is not limited to the effects of this technology on our craft. We are also witnessing a change in the nature of education itself. Technology has brought some of this change. Margaret Mead observed in *Culture and Commitment* that there were three cultural systems that could be defined in terms of who was learning from whom. In post-figurative cultures, or what we would think of as the traditional educational model, children learned from their parents. In co-figurative cultures, children and parents learned from their peers. In pre-figurative cultures, parents learned from their children. We are now entering a pre-figurative phase, "when a father can go up to his son and ask how does this computer work."[49]

Coupled with this expanding definition is a change in the way information is presented and preserved. While the traditional university revolves around the building that houses its library, the virtual university will revolve around building electronic information resources—which are electronic libraries, but also new ways of shaping information and distributing it. Not just the physical structures, but also the actual concepts and foundations are changing as we move into this electronic sphere. Libraries traditionally have focused on collecting books in one place and universities on facilitating research. However, more and more material is being digitized and is going directly to the Internet. For example, in physics and chemistry more and more documents are available only in online form. In addition, materials that previously were published in only one medium (print, video or sound recordings) are now being combined as multimedia on the Web. This means that some content on the Web that now incorporates animations, video and sound cannot be "printed out." The trend toward fuller multimedia Web sites means that in time this medium will escape the two-dimensional realm and linear representation.

Critics of distance learning aside, whereas before students went to the university, now the universities must prepare to come to the students. It should be noted that the exclusivity of American universities (implied in the separation of "town and gown") is not universal, nor is the model of the American and English university practical everywhere. In other countries, places of higher learning are more intertwined with the life of the communities in which they are located. It may well be that these universities will make the transition to the Web more easily. David Lodge's academic novel *Nice Work* (1988) takes as its major theme the separation of the university and the local community. Early in *Nice Work*, Lodge writes the following description of the British university: "With its massive architecture and landscaped grounds, guarded at every entrance by a watchful security staff, the University seems . . . rather like a small city-state, an academic Vatican."[50] However, toward the end of the novel, Lodge writes the following vision of a different kind of university:

Universities are the cathedrals of the modern age. They shouldn't have to justify their existence by utilitarian criteria. The trouble is, ordinary people don't understand what they're about, and the universities don't really bother to explain themselves to the community. . . . It seemed that the university was an ideal type of human community, where work and play, culture and nature were in perfect harmony, where . . . people were free to pursue excellence and self-fulfillment, each according to her own rhythm and inclination.[51]

However, even beyond a greater involvement in community life, virtual universities can reach into areas around the world where setting up and maintaining places of higher learning is financially restrictive. (In the debate on distance learning, it is easy to forget that extension programs in the United States have often served rural communities.) In the West, and particularly in the United States, universities are part of the educational landscape. Thus, we can afford to argue about the evolutionary step that we will take by establishing virtual universities. However, in the third world, the virtual university offers the possibility of a great leap forward. In Africa, where higher education facilities are limited, as well as in geographically isolated communities in the United States, the virtual university can provide a critical source for higher education and help revitalize these communities. The virtual university provides an opportunity for those at the periphery of the academic community to come closer to the center. In many third world countries, higher education is in a crisis because of a "brain drain" of teachers and scholars who have gone to the colleges and universities in the West. The virtual university can help revitalize higher education in these countries.

Lifelong learning is almost a necessity in the United States. No longer restricted to retraining workers or updating skills, the concept of lifelong learning centers on the fact that we are becoming increasingly an information-centered culture. Finishing college is no longer the end of education, but simply enough to get you started. To meet this need, we must now adjust our educational model. This is a convergence of necessity and technology.

The information explosion has greatly increased our understanding of the world about us. However, the growth and exploitation of information rests not only upon the ability of scientists to produce new knowledge, but also upon society's capacity to absorb and use it. . . . Research shows that educational technology, when properly applied, can provide an effective means for learning. However, the new intellectual technologies offer new and better ways to expand human capacity, multiply human reasoning, and compensate for human limitations. . . . The world of education has changed from an orderly world of disciplines and courses to an infosphere in which communication technologies are increasingly important. . . . It is clear that in the future we will see a major restructuring of our social, industrial and educational institutions, and an increased reliance on computers and telecommunications for work and education.[52]

The "Wired Professor"   In our conversations over the course of the year that we researched and wrote this book, we used to talk about the persona of the "wired professor"—the alter ego we created who was the composite of the instructors we spoke to and corresponded with. Sometimes we would play with the pun in "wired" to describe professors who were tired after many hours of crunching HTML code on top of their other scholarly and teaching work. This term also described the instructors who would dash into the Innovation Center with some last-minute coding or hardware disaster, as well as friends and colleagues who would work themselves into such a state of creative obsession with their Web-page experiments that they would ask questions in a rapid volley, even as their fingers flew over their keyboards and the answers appeared on their screens as variations in Web design neither of us had ever seen before.

So pervasive has the theme of creativity been at the Innovation Center that George Sadowsky, the director of NYU's Academic Computing Facility, where the Innovation Center is housed, explained that the name "innovation" is misleading. Typically, innovation in computer technology refers to the creation of new software or the development of new computers. Instead, Sadowsky thinks of the importance of the Innovation Center in the following terms:

> If you're going be on the frontier . . . there ought to be some place where people can go and experiment, and furthermore, we see it as part of our mandate to understand what the frontier looks like as best we can. We can't do that without playing with these things.[53]

This concept of creative play has become a part of our conception of the "wired professor." Added to this is the final and most important element of all—a true appreciation for the medium. Before the term "hacker" became synonymous with individuals cracking security on computer systems with malicious or criminal intent, it used to be the highest compliment you could pay a truly creative programmer. In our own way, we have combined that definition with the description of a gifted teacher who uses the Web in ways that enhance it as a creative medium.

The term "wired professor" also describes an older teacher I met at an all-day workshop for faculty interested in learning how to write their first Web pages. She told me that she had resisted learning how to use e-mail and the Internet and had only written her first e-mail a month earlier. She had recently spent a month in South Africa and made a number of friends there with whom she wanted to keep in touch. Her South African friends told her that they could use e-mail, and this is when she began reconsidering her views on using the Internet. Now, with e-mail, she has been able to stay in contact with her South African friends. However, what she wanted to explain to me was how thrilled she was about making Web pages for her classes. She explained that she was going to go home and spend the rest of the evening making Web pages. She added that her excitement made her remember how exciting it had been when she first learned how to use the darkroom and how, in her initial excitement and in the first flourishing of creativity with that tool, she completely lost track of time. This teacher, as much as those who can code without having to stop and refer to a manual, fits our definition of a "wired professor." Each in their own way has been overtaken by the creative possibilities of this medium. Carpenters and other craftspeople often speak of the pleasure of working with their hands. We feel that creating materials for the Web offers the same pleasure—the delight in being able to see what one has imagined take form. With this in mind, we invite you to join us in the wonderful adventure of writing for the World Wide Web.

Distance Learning Links and Resources

1. *Distance Learning* at *http://www.memex-press.com/cc/askcc280797.html* offers a basic but thorough overview of distance education.

2. *Distance Learning News Group* at *alt.education.distance* is an online discussion group.

3. *The Official alt.education.distance FAQ* at *http://pages.prodigy.com/PAUM88A/* offers answers to the most frequently asked questions regarding distance learning.

*4. *Distance Education Clearinghouse* at *http://www.uwex.edu/disted/home.html* lists many distance learning sites.

5. *International Center for Distance Learning* at *http://www-icdl.open.ac.uk/* serves as an international repository of information on distance education worldwide.

6. *Internet University* at *http://www.caso.com/* is one of the more complete indexes of online college courses by accredited providers. This site has more than 2,430 pages of online education.

7. *Distance Learning—Colleges and Universities* at *http://www.yahoo.com/Education/Distance_Learning/Colleges_and_Universities/* provides a regularly updated list of links to distance education sites.

8. *The American Center for the Study of Distance Education (ACSDE)* at *http://www.outreach.psu.edu/ACSDE/Default.html* is an interinstitutional, multidisciplinary center that aims to facilitate collaboration among individuals and institutions in the United States and overseas.

9. *Distance Education Report* at *http://www.distance-educator.com/* reports the latest news, trends and developments in distance education, presents strategies and techniques to develop a successful distance education program and reviews hundreds of distance learning resources.

10. *Distance Education at a Glance Guides* at *http://www.uidaho.edu/evo/* presents a series of thorough and well-designed guides to all aspects of distance education created by the University of Idaho Engineering Outreach staff.

Appendix: Useful HTML Tips and Tricks

WE have discovered that there is a set of basic HTML tricks and tools we refer to so often that we have this information pinned to our bulletin boards over our computers. There are also special character sets and hexadecimal color equivalents that we need less often, but are equally important to have nearby. (For additional information and dynamic examples of the techniques in this chapter go to the companion site for this book at *http://www.nyuupress.nyu.edu/professor.html.*)

In addition to the HTML tags and tactics that have already been introduced, here are some others you may find helpful.

A.1 Commenting Files

Now and then, you might want to include comments in your HTML files. Such comments might be the name of the person updating a file, the software and version used in creating a file, or the date that an edit was made. The browser does not interpret the text you enter within the "comment tag." It is only visible when you edit your HTML file. Comments are indicated by the symbol <!— and are closed by the symbol —>. Here is an example of a comment line:

```
<!—this site has been updated by ABK and JH on 3/23/98.—>
```

COMMENTING OUT LINES

Another use of the "comment tag" is to temporarily disable parts of the HTML code. For example, you added three new images to your page and suddenly the page is unusually slow to load. You can find out which item is causing the delay by "commenting out" the files one after the other.

```
<!—<IMG SRC="offender.gif">—>
<IMG SRC="goodguy.gif">
<IMG SRC="lazy.gif">
```

A.2 "Frames Are Lovely, But . . .": Escape Tags

If you use frames, sooner or later a colleague or student will come up to you and tell you that they are having a hard time bookmarking interesting sites they find as a result of exploring your set of links. Chances are that you have set your list of links within a framed set of pages. Every time your visitor tries to bookmark the wonderful site they have found, they keep getting a bookmarked link for your framed page. Luckily, there are solutions that enable you to continue using frames, but do not trap your visitors in them. Here are some of these tags:

1. <TARGET="_top"> removes the frame and takes you to the intended Web page in a clean browser window.
2. <TARGET="_blank"> opens a clean browser window over top of the old one.
3. <TARGET="_self"> makes the link load in its own window.
4. <TARGET="_parent"> makes the link load in the full body of the window and removes the frame.

A.3 "View Source": Learning by Example

During the early days of the Web, when flashy style manuals were nonexistent and even straightforward manuals for programmers were rare, people learned HTML by copying parts of the code of other HTML documents. This is still a valid way to create pages, and a great way to learn HTML. If you see a page that you like on the Web,

1. Go to the "View Source" option on your browser's menu.
2. Copy or save the source to your hard disk.
3. Replace the text and images with your own text and images.
4. Replace the title in <TITLE></TITLE> with your own.
5. Save the file.
6. Publish your page.

While this approach still works to a certain extent, be aware that with the arrival of tables, frames and advanced scripting, Web pages have grown in complexity to the point where they often only reveal their workings to advanced HTML writers.

A.4 Perfect Background Images

Here is a tip on making a background image that will work every time. In your paint program, create an image 25 x 1200 pixels wide. This will load fast and will fill the screen width on even larger monitors without repeating. A standard use of this 1,200 pixel–wide ribbon is as a template for a background image consisting of a decorative left-hand border for a Web page. The way to create this border is to create a second highly decorative image with the same height dimensions as the template—25 pixels—and to set the width of this new image to 120 pixels. Once you have finished creating this smaller image, it is a simple process to copy and paste this into your ribbon template image.

A.5 Background Colors by Name and Hexadecimal Value (Asterisk Indicates Standard Colors):

The color names and RGB values defined in the HTML standard are:

AQUA	#00FFFF	NAVY	#000080
BLACK	#000000	OLIVE	#808000
BLUE	#0000FF	PURPLE	#800080
FUCHSIA	#FF00FF	RED	#FF0000
GRAY	#808080	SILVER	#C0C0C0
GREEN	#008000	TEAL	#008080
LIME	#00FF00	YELLOW	#FFFF00
MAROON	#800000	WHITE	#FFFFFF

The color names and RGB values defined in Netscape are:

AQUA*	#00FFFF	DARKMAGENTA	#8B008B
AQUAMARINE	#7FFFD4	DARKOLIVEGREEN	#556B2F
AZURE	#F0FFFF	DARKORANGE	#FF8C00
BEIGE	#F5F5DC	DARKRED	#8B0000
BLACK*	#000000	DARKSLATEBLUE	#483D8B
BLUE*	#0000FF	DARKSLATEGRAY	#2F4F4F
BROWN	#A52A2A	DARKTURQUOISE	#00CED1
CHARTREUSE	#7FFF00	DARKVIOLET	#9400D3
CRIMSON	#DC143C	FORESTGREEN	#228B22
CYAN	#00FFFF	FUCHSIA*	#FF00FF
DARKBLUE	#00008B	GOLD	#FFD700
DARKCYAN	#008B8B	GRAY*	#808080
DARKGRAY	#A9A9A9	GREEN*	#008000
DARKGREEN	#006400	INDIGO	#4B0082
DARKKHAKI	#BDB76B	KHAKI	#F0E68C

LAVENDER	#E6E6FA	NAVY*	#000080
LIGHTBLUE	#ADD8E6	OLIVE*	#808000
LIGHTCYAN	#E0FFFF	ORANGE	#FFA500
LIGHTGREEN	#90EE90	PALEGREEN	#98FB98
LIGHTGREY	#D3D3D3	PALETURQUOISE	#AFEEEE
LIGHTPINK	#FFB6C1	PINK	#FFC0CB
LIGHTSLATEGRAY	#778899	PURPLE*	#800080
LIGHTSTEELBLUE	#B0C4DE	RED*	#FF0000
LIGHTYELLOW	#FFFFE0	SIENNA	#A0522D
LIME*	#00FF00	SILVER*	#C0C0C0
MAGENTA	#FF00FF	SLATEBLUE	6A5ACD
MAROON*	#800000	SLATEGRAY	#708090
MEDIUMAQUAMARINE		STEELBLUE	#4682B4
#66CDAA		TAN	#D2B48C
MEDIUMBLUE	#0000CD	TEAL*	#008080
MEDIUMPURPLE	#9370DB	TURQUOISE	#40E0D0
MEDIUMSLATEBLUE	#7B68EE	VIOLET	#EE82EE
MEDIUMTURQUOISE	#48D1CC	WHITE	#FFFFFF
MIDNIGHTBLUE	#191970	YELLOW*	#FFFF00

A.6 FTP on Two Platforms

When you start WS_FTP or Fetch, a dialog box automatically opens to create a connection. You will need to use your mouse or the tab key to move among fields as you fill in the following information:

1. In the "Host" or "Host Name" field, enter the name of the anonymous FTP server.
2. In the "User ID" field, enter your user ID.
3. In the "Password" field, enter your user password. This will be displayed as a series of asterisks or bullets.
4. In the "Directory or Remote Host" field, enter the directory that contains the files you want.
5. Click on the "OK" button. A connection with the FTP server is established and the session window opens.

Figure A.1. *(near right)* The WS_FTP log-in dialogue box. Image by Keating/Hargitai. Figure A.2. *(far right)* The FETCH log-in dialogue box. Image by Keating/Hargitai.

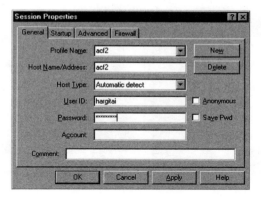

INSTRUCTIONS FOR USING "WS_FTP" ON THE WINDOWS PLATFORM

Once connected, the WS_FTP window contains information about the local and remote computers. Files and directories on your local computer appear in the left-hand box. Files and directories on the remote computer appear in the right-hand box. To navigate among directories, double-click on a directory name. To move up a level in the directory structure, double-click on the two dots (..). The current directory appears at the top of the screen. To move a file select a name from the pop-up menu. Remember that image files need to load as binary, text files as ASCII.

When uploading entire directories make sure to go to the "Options" button and make the changes shown in Figure A.6. For more information on WS_FTP, see John Junod's Web site at *http://www.ipswitch.com/junodj*.

INSTRUCTIONS FOR USING "FETCH" ON THE MACINTOSH PLATFORM

Once connected, the Fetch window displays file and directory information on the remote computer much in the same way as WS_FTP above. To navigate among directories, double-click on a directory name. To move up in the directory structure, select a name from the pop-up menu.

Remember that image files need to load as binary, text files as ASCII. Set your FTP software accordingly. Fetch, your Macintosh FTP software, will have two options for "Binary" upload: "Raw" and "MacBinary." You must select "Raw."

For more information on Fetch, select "Fetch Help" or see the Dartmouth Fetch Web site at *http://www.dartmouth.edu/pages/softdev*.

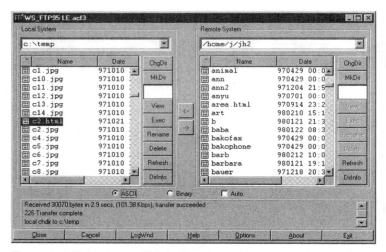

Figure A.3. Uploading an HTML file using ASCII encoding in WS_FTP.

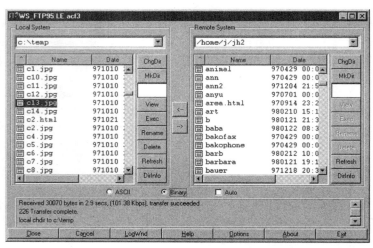

Figure A.4. Uploading a JPEG file using binary encoding in WS_FTP.

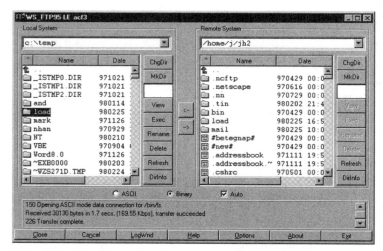

Figure A.5. When uploading directories, WS_FTP uses binary encoding.

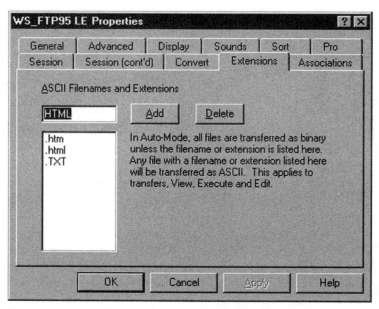

Figure A.6. In the "Options" box, add the html, HTML, htm and HTM extensions to force ASCII upload all of your HTML files in WS_FTP.

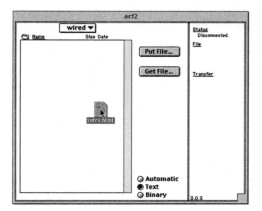

Figure A.7. Uploading an HTML file as "Text," using "drag and drop" in Fetch.

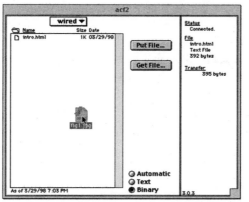

Figure A.8. Uploading a JPEG file as "Binary," using "drag and drop" in Fetch.

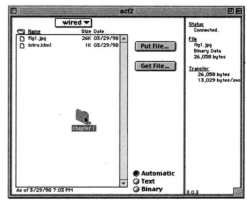

Figure A.9. Uploading a directory as "Automatic," using "drag and drop" in Fetch.

A.7 Are All Web Servers UNIX-Based?

Not at all. Server software packages can run on any platform that uses TCP/IP as its network protocol. This means you can run a Web server from a Macintosh or a Windows-based machine just as well.

A.8 Top UNIX Commands

ls	lists your directory
mv	moves or renames your files
cd	changes directories
cd ~/	returns you to your parent directory
cp	copies files
pwd	shows you which directory you are in
man cp	shows you help on the command "cp"
man mv	shows you help on the command "mv"

A.9 Changing File Permissions in UNIX

To change file permissions in UNIX, type *chmod* plus the change (see list of possible changes below) and then the name of the file. Briefly, there are three different permissions that you can set at three different levels: (1) you, the creator of the file and owner of the account; (2) the group (if more than one person can have access to work with your files on the server); and (3) your visitors on the Web. You can set three different permissions: (1) *read permission* means you can look at a file's contents; (2) *write permission* means you can change or delete the file; and (3) *execute permission* means you can run the file as a program. Permissions can be set by number or by text. (Setting by number is easier, though a long file listing generated by ls -l will show the results in text form.) For example, if you type *chmod 755 thisfile* at the UNIX prompt and then check the permission on that file by typing *ls -l thisfile* you will get the following information: *-rwxr-xr-x thisfile.* Here are the number and text values for files:

0	=	---	=	no access
1	=	--x	=	execute
2	=	-w-	=	write
3	=	-wx	=	write and execute
4	=	r--	=	read
5	=	r-x	=	read and execute
6	=	rw-	=	read and write
7	=	rwx	=	read write execute (full access)

WHAT PERMISSIONS SHOULD I SET? Text Files and Images (gifs, jpgs) should be set to read, write and execute by owner and read=only by group and others. For example: *chmod 744 filename*

```
rwx r--r-- thispicture.gif
rwx r--r-- index.html
```

Directories in general should be set to read, write and execute by owner and read and execute by group and others. For example: *chmod 755 directory*

```
drwxr-xr-x my_course_files
```

CGI Scripts in general should be set to read, write and execute by owner and read and execute by group and others. For example: *chmod 755 myscript.cgi*

-rwxr-xr-x guestbook.cgi

A.10 Reserved and Special Characters in HTML

Occasionally, your text will call for characters that are not available in straight HTML form. In this case, the chart of special characters below should provide the additional code that you need. For example, here is how to insert one of these characters in your code: <i> Künstlerroman </i>, which will appear on your Web page as *Künstlerroman*.

To See This	Write This in Your HTML Code	Description
<	&#60;	less than
>	&#62;	greater than
×	&#215;	multiply sign
÷	&#247;	division sign
@	&#64;	commercial at
		nonbreaking space
¢	&#162;	cent sign
£	&#163;	pound sterling
¤	&#164;	general currency sign
¥	&#165;	yen sign
§	&#167;	section sign
©	&#169;	copyright
®	&#174;	registered trademark
¯	&#175;	macron accent
°	&#176;	degree sign
±	&#177;	plus or minus
µ	&#181;	micro sign
¶	&#182;	paragraph sign
·	&#183;	middle dot
1/4	&#188;	fraction one-fourth
1/2	&#189;	fraction one-half
3/4	&#190;	fraction three-fourths

To See This	Write This in Your HTML Code	Description
&	&#38;	ampersand
¡	&#161;	inverted exclamation
¿	&#191;	inverted question mark
À	&#192;	capital A, grave accent
Á	&#193;	capital A, acute accent
Â	&#194;	capital A, circumflex accent
Ã	&#195;	capital A, tilde
Ä	&#196;	capital A, umlaut
Æ	&#198;	capital AE diphthong
Ç	&#199;	capital C, cedilla
È	&#200;	capital E, grave accent
É	&#201;	capital E, acute accent
Ê	&#202;	capital E, circumflex accent
Ë	&#203;	capital E, umlaut
Ì	&#204;	capital I, grave accent
Í	&#205;	capital I, acute accent
Î	&#206;	capital I, circumflex accent
Ï	&#207;	capital I, umlaut
Ñ	&#209;	capital N, tilde
Ò	&#210;	capital O, grave accent
Ó	&#211;	capital O, acute accent
Ô	&#212;	capital O, circumflex accent
Õ	&#213;	capital O, tilde
Ö	&#214;	capital O, umlaut
Ù	&#217;	capital U, grave accent
Ú	&#218;	capital U, acute accent
Û	&#219;	capital U, circumflex accent
Ü	&#220;	capital U, umlaut
Ý	&#221;	capital Y, acute accent
ß	&#223;	lowercase sharp s, German
à	&#224;	lowercase a, grave accent
á	&#225;	lowercase a, acute accent

To See This	Write This in Your HTML Code	Description
â	&#226;	lowercase a, circumflex accent
ã	&#227;	lowercase a, tilde
ä	&#228;	lowercase a, umlaut
æ	&#230;	lowercase ae diphthong
ç	&#231;	lowercase c, cedilla
è	&#232;	lowercase e, grave accent
é	&#233;	lowercase e, acute accent
ê	&#234;	lowercase e, circumflex accent
ë	&#235;	lowercase e, umlaut
ì	&#236;	lowercase i, grave accent
í	&#237;	lowercase i, acute accent
î	&#238;	lowercase i, circumflex accent
ï	&#239;	lowercase i, umlaut mark
ñ	&#241;	lowercase n, tilde
ò	&#242;	lowercase o, grave accent
ó	&#243;	lowercase o, acute accent
ô	&#244;	lowercase o, circumflex accent
õ	&#245;	lowercase o, tilde
ö	&#246;	lowercase o, umlaut mark
ù	&#249;	lowercase u, grave accent
ú	&#250;	lowercase u, acute accent
û	&#251;	lowercase u, circumflex accent
ü	&#252;	lowercase u, umlaut
ý	&#253;	lowercase y, acute accent
ÿ	&#255;	lowercase y, umlaut

A.11 Skeleton Key to HTML Tags
BASIC HTML DOCUMENT ELEMENTS

<HTML>...</HTML>	Starts and ends an HTML document
<HEAD>...</HEAD>	Starts and Ends a Text Heading
<TITLE>...</TITLE>	Document running title (not part of the text); recommended maximum length is sixty-four characters
<BODY>...</BODY>	Container for the information to be presented on the Web page

SECTION HEADINGS	<H#>...</H#>	Section headings; six levels available, <H1> to <H6>

BACKGROUNDS AND COLORS

<BODY BACKGROUND="this_image.gif"> Tiled background image
<BODY BGCOLOR="#010101"> Solid background color (see hexadecimal colors above)
<BODY TEXT="#010101"> Text color (see hexadecimal colors above)
<BODY LINK="#010101"> Link color (see hexadecimal colors above)
<BODY VLINK="#010101"> Visited link color (see hexadecimal colors above)
<BODY ALINK="#010101"> Active link color (see hexadecimal colors above)

GENERAL LAYOUT ELEMENTS

<P>...</P>	Paragraphs of regular text
 	Forced line break
<ADDRESS>...</ADDRESS>	Postal address information
<BLOCKQUOTE>...</BLOCKQUOTE>	Block quotations
<PRE>...</PRE>	Preformatted text
<HR>	Horizontal rule

LISTS

<OL>...</OL>	Ordered lists; listed entries items will be numbered consecutively
<UL>...</UL>	Unordered lists; listed entries will be bulleted
<MENU>...</MENU>	Menu lists
<DIR>...</DIR>	Directory lists
<LI>...</LI>	Used to list entries within ordered, unordered, menu, and directory lists. (<LI> may be used alone without </LI>)
<DL>...</DL>	Definition lists
<DT>...</DT>	Definition term in a definition list
<DD>...</DD>	Definition discussion in a definition list; may contain other block-oriented elements

Note: All lists may be nested.

FONTS

<BLINK></BLINK>	Blinking
<FONT SIZE="#"></FONT>	Font size; ranges from 1 to 7
<FONT SIZE="+#"></FONT>	Change font size up or down a size
<FONT COLOR="#010101"></FONT>	Set font color (see hexadecimal colors above)

VISUAL MARKUP

<B>...</B>	Bold type
<I>...</I>	Italic type

<TT>...</TT>   Typewriter type
<U>...</U>   Underlined

HYPERTEXT LINKS   <A HREF="url">...</A>   Link to another document or resource
<A HREF="url#anchor">...</A> Link to a specific destination in another document
<A HREF="#anchor">...</A> Link to a specific destination in the same document
<A NAME="anchor"></A> Points to the target destination
Note: An <A> element may contain both HREF and NAME attributes.

TABLES   <TABLE>...</TABLE>   Defines a table
<CAPTION>...</CAPTION> Supplies a caption
<TR>...</TR>   Encloses a table row
<TH>...</TH>   Encloses a column or row header inside a row
<TD>...</TD>   Encloses table data (a cell value)
Note: The <TH> and <TD> elements can have ALIGN and SPAN attributes.

FRAMES   <FRAMESET></FRAMESET> Frame document
<FRAMESET ROWS="#,#,#,"></FRAMESET> Row heights (# set as either pixels or a percentage of the window size)
<FRAMESET ROWS="*"></FRAMESET> Row heights (* = relative size, or simply: "fill the rest of the browser window with this HTML file")
<FRAMESET COLS="#,#,#"></FRAMESET> Column widths (# equals either width in pixels or percents)
<FRAMESET COLS="*"></FRAMESET> Column widths (* = relative size, or simply: "fill the rest of the browser window with this HTML file")
<FRAMESET FRAMEBORDER="yes|no"> Borders
<FRAMESET BORDER="#"> Border width
<FRAMESET BORDERCOLOR="#010101"> Border color (see hexadecimal colors above)
<FRAME>   Define frame (contents of an individual frame)
<FRAME SRC="URL">   Display document
<FRAME NAME="main"|_blank|_self|_parent|_top> Frame name; "content" is often used to designate the main framed window
<FRAME MARGINWIDTH="#"> Margin width (left and right margins)
<FRAME MARGINHEIGHT="#"> Margin height (top and bottom margins)

<FRAME SCROLLING="YES|NO|AUTO"> Include the scrollbar?

<FRAME NORESIZE>   Do not let visitors resize your frame

<FRAME FRAMEBORDER="yes|no"> Border

<FRAME BORDERCOLOR="#010101"> Color the frame border? (see hexadecimal colors above)

<NOFRAMES></NOFRAMES> Unframed content; text for an unframed HTML courtesy page for visitors using non-frames capable Web browsers.

FORMS   Generally, you will need a script running on your server to effectively use forms. However, here is the basic guide to writing the form to collect and send data to the script running on the server. (See chapter 5, section 5.6, for information on setting up scripts on the server.)

<FORM ACTION="URL" METHOD="GET|POST">...</FORM> Define form

<INPUT TYPE="TEXT|PASSWORD|CHECKBOX|RADIO| IMAGE|HIDDEN|SUBMIT|RESET"> Input field

<INPUT NAME="yourname">   Field name

<INPUT VALUE="submit">   Field value

<INPUT CHECKED>   Checked? (checkboxes and radio boxes)

<INPUT SIZE="#">   Field size (in characters)

<INPUT MAXLENGTH="#"> Maximum length (in characters)

<SELECT>...</SELECT> Selection list

<SELECT NAME="item1">...</SELECT> Name of list

<SELECT SIZE="#">...</SELECT> Number of options

<SELECT MULTIPLE>   Multiple choice (can select more than one)

<OPTION>   Option (items that can be selected)

<OPTION SELECTED>   Default option

<TEXTAREA ROWS="#" COLS="#">...</TEXTAREA> Input box size

<TEXTAREA NAME="yourname">...</TEXTAREA> Name of box—for example, "your name"

<TEXTAREA WRAP="OFF|VIRTUAL|PHYSICAL"> ...</TEXTAREA>   Wrap the text a visitor enters?

Notes

For easy use throughout the book all URLs are italicized. URLs never end in periods, but for clarity's sake periods have been inserted at the end of sentences.

Note to the Preface

1. Robert M. Pirsig, *Zen and the Art of Motorcycle Maintenance* (New York: Bantam, 1981), 132.

Notes to Chapter 1

1. Ithiel de la Sola Pool et al., *Communications Flows: A Census in the United States and Japan* (Amsterdam: University of Tokyo Press, 1984), 33.

2. "FA (from ARPANet) groups are 'from the arpanet' and are mostly copies of mailing lists or 'digests' distributed on that network. (A digest is a collection of mail put together by an editor and sent out every so often. It is much like a newsletter.)" Ronda Hauben, "On the Early Days of Usenet: The Roots of Cooperative Online Culture," in Michael Hauben and Ronda Hauben, eds., *Netizens: On the History and Impact of Usenet and the Internet* (Piscataway, NJ: IEEE Computer Society Press, 1997), archived at *http://www.columbia.edu/~hauben/netbook/*.

3. Ibid.

4. E-mail communication from Tom Truscott quoted in Hauben, "On the Early Days of Usenet."

5. Will Durant, *The Life of Greece* (New York: Simon and Schuster, 1939), 273.

6. Homer, "Armour for Achilles," Book XVIII in *The Iliad*, trans. E.V. Rieu (Harmondsworth, Eng.: Penguin, 1950), 342.

7. Aeschylus, *Agamemnon*, 8–10, as quoted in *The Continental Edition of World Masterpieces*, vol. 1, ed. Maynard Mack (New York: W. W. Norton, 1966), 239.

8. *Grolier's Academic American Encyclopedia* (1992), s.v. "Postal Services."

9. Jeremiah 51:31 (King James Version).

10. Xenophon, *Cyropaedia*, Book VIII, 6.17–18, quoted in Gerard J. Holzmann and Björn Pehrson, "The Early History of Data Networks," archived at *http://www.it.kth.se/docs/early_net/*.

11. Herodotus quoted in Lionel Casson, *Travel in the Ancient World* (Baltimore: Johns Hopkins University Press, 1994), 53–54.

12. Casson, *Travel in the Ancient World*, 182.

13. Cicero quoted in Casson, *Travel in the Ancient World*, 220–21.

14. Casson, *Travel in the Ancient World*, 221.

15. Will Durant, *Caesar and Christ* (New York: Simon and Schuster, 1944), 324.

16. Ibid.

17. Logan Thompson, "Roman Roads," *History Today* (February 1997), Northern Lights ID: PC19970926120003678 archived at *http://www.northernlight.com/*.

18. Durant, *Caesar and Christ*, 324.

19. The *quipu* consisted of a long rope from

which hung forty-eight secondary cords and various tertiary cords attached to the secondary ones. Knots were made in the cords to represent units, tens, and hundreds. In imperial accounting, the cords were differently colored to designate the different concerns of government—such as tribute, lands, economic productivity, ceremonies and matters relating to war and peace.

20. There is a striking parallel in modern history. During World War II, the U.S. military employed Navajos to transmit sensitive information by radio. The Navajo language has no linguistic connections to any Asian or European language and no written form or alphabet. In addition, only a few thousand people spoke the language, which is so linguistically complex that only a handful of non-Navajos spoke it. This made the Navajo "codetalkers" a force to be reckoned with. The communications system thus created was so secure that it was never broken. The Japanese, prepared to break codes that would reveal messages in English, were completely baffled by what they saw as a new code. The Navajo codetalkers completely bypassed the need for encryption simply by talking to one another in their own language. See Kenji Kawano, *Warriors: Navajo Code Talkers* (Flagstaff, AZ: Northland Publishing Co., 1990).

21. *QuipuNet* is located online at *http://www.quipu.net/English/information.html.*

22. Tim O'Connor, e-mail to Anne B. Keating and Joseph Hargitai, 16 February 1998.

23. Ibid.

24. Ibid.

25. Ibid.

26. Herodotus quoted in Gerard J. Holzmann, "The Ties That Bound," *Inc. Technology* 2 (1995), archived at *http://www.inc.com/incmagazine/archives/169506 61.html.*

27. Ibid.

28. "Chappe—Innovation and Politics in 1793 and 1794," *Proceedings of a Symposium on the Optical Telegraph*, Telemuseum, Stockholm, 21–23 June 1994), archived at *http://www.telemu-seum.se/historia/optel/otsymp/Frankrike.html.*

29. Holzmann, "The Ties That Bound."

30. Ibid.

31. J. Munro, "Heroes of the Telegraph," archived at *http://www.cdrom.com/pub/guten-berg/etext97/htgrf10.txt.*

32. Joanna Buick and Zoran Jevtic, *Introducing Cyberspace* (New York: Totem Books, 1995), 48.

33. Nathaniel Hawthorne, "The Flight of the Two Owls," in *The House of the Seven Gables* (1851), archived at *http://www.tiac.net/users/eldred/nh/sg.html.*

34. Quoted in Maimark and Barba, Inc., "Folio 12 Abet Innovation (Embrace a New Concept Today.)" (1997), archived at *http://www.boot-strap.org/augment-133217.htm.*

35. "Brief History of Networking," archived at *http://www.silkroad.com/net-history.html.*

36. "A Brief History of the Morse Telegraph," archived at *http://www.cris.com/~Gsraven/histo-ry.html.*

37. Buick and Jevtic, *Introducing Cyberspace*, 48.

38. "The Telecommunications Quiz," archived at *http://www.e-media.com/telecom/q6.html.*

39. Norbert Weiner, *Cybernetics, or Control and Communication in the Animal and the Machine* (Cambridge, MA: MIT Press, 1961), 176–77. In the story, the apprentice is left by his master to fetch water. The apprentice is lazy and so repeats words of magic he has heard the master use. The process backfires on him, as the bucket fetches water without stopping. The master has to bail out the apprentice.

40. Genesis 11:1–9 (King James Version).

41. *Catholic Encyclopedia*, s.v. "Babel, Tower of," archived at *http://www.knight.org/advent/cathen/02177b.htm.*

42. Umberto Eco, *The Search for the Perfect Language*, trans. James Fentress (Cambridge, MA: Blackwell, 1995).

43. Jacques Vallee, *The Network Revolution: Confessions of a Computer Scientist* (Berkeley, CA: And/or Press, 1982).

44. Stephen Braich, "The Tower of Babel Project," archived at *http://www.cs.pdx.edu/~stephen/babel/.*

45. Norma Levarie, *The Art and History of Books* (New Castle, DE: Oak Knoll Press, 1995), i. "Estimates place the contents of Ashurbanipal's library at the time of his death at 1,200 tablets containing over 2,000 verses in several languages." Barbara B. Moran, "Libraries," *Collier's Encyclopedia* (1998), Northern Lights ID: ZZ19971121030084834, archived at *http://www.northernlight.com/.*

46. "While speaking is a universal human competence that has been characteristic of the species from the beginning and that is acquired by all normal human beings without systematic instruction, writing is a technology of relatively recent history that must be taught to each generation of children." "The Nature and Origin of Writing," *Encyclopedia Britannica On-Line*, at *http://www.eb.com/.*

47. Beatrice Andre-Salvini, "The Birth of Writing," *UNESCO Courier* (April 1995), Northern Lights ID: SL19970923020121208, archived at *http://www.northernlight.com/.*

48. Gaston Wiet, Vadime Elisseef, Phillipe Wolff and Jean Nandou, *The Great Medieval Civilizations*, History of Mankind Cultural and Scientific Development Series, vol. 3 (New York: Harper and Row, 1975), 295.

49. Thomas W. Eland, "Orality, Literacy, and

Textual Communities in the Middle Ages" (1996), archived at *http://sites.goshen.net/LibraryOfGod/eland3.html*.

50. Michael T. Clanchy, *From Memory to Written Record: England 1066–1307* (London: Edward Arnold, 1979), 185, quoted in Eland, "Orality, Literacy, and Textual Communities in the Middle Ages."

51. James J. O'Donnell, "The Pragmatics of the New: Trithemius, McLuhan, Cassiodorus," archived at *http://ccat.sas.upenn.edu/jod/sanmarino.html*. See also James O'Donnell, "The Virtual Library: An Idea Whose Time Has Passed," archived at *http://ccat.sas.upenn.edu/jod/virtual.html*.

52. Richard de Bury also chided the abbots of monasteries who had turned their attention to more worldy matters and had "neglected the notable clause of Augustine's rule, in which we are commended to his clergy in these words: Let books be asked for each day at a given hour. . . . Scarcely anyone observes this devout rule of study after saying the prayers of the Church." Richard de Bury, *The Philobiblon*, ed. Ernest C. Thomas (London: Kegan Paul, Trench, and Co., 1888), archived at *ftp://uiarchive.cso.uiuc.edu/pub/etext/gutenberg/etext96/phlbb10.txt*.

53. Will Durant, *The Age of Faith* (New York: Simon and Schuster, 1950), 907.

54. St. Jerome, "De Viris illustribus," quoted in *The Scriptorium* at *http://www.christdesert.org/noframes/script/history.html*.

55. "The available evidence suggests that from the middle of the fourteenth century at least, the university owned and kept in chests in its treasury a small collection of books which began to be expanded and was formally established as the Common Library of the University during the second decade of the fifteenth century." The "earliest surviving catalogue . . . entitled *A register of the books given by various benefactors to the Common Library of the University of Cambridge*, lists 122 volumes in nine subject divisions. . . . More than half of [the books] were works of theology and religion, and there were twenty-three volumes of canon law. The writers of ancient Rome were represented by Lucan alone, and the early Christian poets and the English chroniclers were entirely absent." J. C. T. Oates, *Cambridge University Library: A Historical Sketch* (1975), archived at *http://www.lib.cam.ac.uk/History/index.html*.

56. "The new secular book trade became a licensed appendage of the university, consisting of stationers, scribes, parchment makers, paper makers, bookbinders, and all those associated with making books. . . . Books tended to be sold and resold through many generations and it was the stationer's responsibility to sell a book and buy it back and sell it again, and so forth. . . . In order to produce the large numbers of textbooks required by students and maintain their textual accuracy, the pecia system of copying was instituted. . . . The stationer held one or more exact copies (the exemplar) of a text in pieces (hence pecia). . . . Each exemplar was examined to ensure it was correct, and any exemplar found to be incorrect resulted in a fine for the stationer. Each part was rented out for a specific time (a week at Bologna) so that students, or scribes, could copy them. This way a number of students could be copying parts of the same book at the same time." Richard W. Clement, "Books and Universities: Medieval and Renaissance Book Production—Manuscript Books," *ORB Online Encyclopedia—Manuscript Books*, archived at *http://orb.rhodes.edu/encyclop/culture/books/medbook1.html*.

57. Levarie, *The Art and History of Books*, 80. *Catholicon* (also known as the *Summa Grammaticalis*) by John of Genoa, a large theological grammar and dictionary, is the last major printed work attributed to Gutenberg. Other developments followed soon after. In 1501, Aldus Manutius produced a book in a new type of edition called the *octavo*, which was "light inexpensive, [and] compact. The octavo was designed "to be carried about, slipped into the pocket or saddlebag. . . . Before long this new kind of book was being printed everywhere" (ibid.). Aldus is credited as the inventor of the modern book.

58. Alberto Manguel, "How Those Plastic Stones Speak: The Renewed Struggle between the Codex and the Scroll," *Times Literary Supplement*, 4 July 1997, 8.

59. Richard Polt, "Typology: A Phenomenology of Early Typewriters," archived at *http://xavier.xu.edu/~polt/typology.html*.

60. Johannes Trithemius, *In Praise of Scribes* (1494), quoted in O'Donnell, "The Pragmatics of the New."

61. Ibid.

62. Quoted in S. H. Steinberg, *Five Hundred Years of Printing* (Harmondsworth, Eng.: Penguin, 1955), 44.

63. O'Donnell, "The Pragmatics of the New."

64. Ibid.

65. Anne Lyon Haight, and Chandler B. Grannis, *Banned Books 387 B.C. to 1978 A.D.* (New Providence, NJ: R. R. Bowker, 1978). The first such index included, among other works, Copernicus's *De Revolutionibus Orbium Coelestium* and Galileo's *Dialoga*.

66. Quoted in A. Minnis and A. B. Scott, *Medieval Literary Theory and Criticism c. 1100–c. 1375* (New York: Oxford University Press, 1988), 269. Minnis and Scott refer to the work of Mary and Richard Rouse, who showed at length how

the application of print to the organization of knowledge was anticipated by the handwritten indexes and concordances in medieval manuscripts. These indexes needed print for the full realization of their potential. One could argue that hypertext extends this potential.

67. Walter Ong, "Print, Space, and Closure," in *Communication in History: Technology, Culture, Society*, ed. David Crowley and Paul Heyer (White Plains, NY: Longman, 1995), 116.

68. O'Donnell, "The Pragmatics of the New."

69. Marc Demarest, "Controlling Dissemination Mechanisms: The Unstamped Press and the 'Net" (August 1995), archived at *http://www.hevanet.com/demarest/marc/unstamped.html*. In an interesting parallel to the illegal press, Demarest describes the ways in which people got around the Stamp Acts, which levied a tax on printed materials from 1770 to 1819. He writes that the Stamp Acts were an attempt "to take printed materials out of the hands of the working class by making the paper used in books so expensive that the "cover price" of a book or journal would be far beyond the means of an average individual. There were a variety of responses to this: coffee houses, where one could go, have a drink and read a journal or magazine subscribed to 'by the house' for a fee smaller than the cover price of the journal, reading societies and subscription societies, in which a group of individuals pooled economic resources to purchase a book or journal in common, and frequently read it aloud to one another, and alternate media: radical tracts were published on all sorts of material, including muslin and other cloth, which was not taxed, and some publishers sold other objects (like straw, matches and rocks), and gave away the printed material as a 'bonus' to people buying the other item, thus evading the letter of the law entirely."

70. George Saunders, foreword to *Samizdat: Voices of the Soviet Opposition* (New York: Pathfinder, 1974), quoted in Fred Wright, "The History and Characteristics of Zines," archived at *http://thetransom.com/chip/zines/resource/wright2.html*.

71. Josef Kroutvor, "Prague Report: Literature Remains Alive and Well," *TriQuarterly* (fall 1995), Northern Lights ID: LW19970923040129876, archived at *http://www.northernlight.com/*.

72. Ibid. See also H. Gordon Skilling, *Samizdat and an Independent Society in Central and Eastern Europe* (Oxford: Macmillan, 1989).

73. Fred Wright, "The History and Characteristics of Zines," archived at *http://thetransom.com/chip/zines/resource/wright1.html*.

74. For more on 'zines, see "alt.culture: zines," available at *http://www.pathfinder.com/altculture/aentries/z/zines.html*.

75. Howard Rheingold, "Democracy Is about Communication" (1996), archived at *http://www.well.com/user/hlr/texts/democracy.html*.

76. Jay David Bolter, *Writing Space: The Computer, Hypertext and the History of Writing* (Hillsdale, NJ: Lawrence Erlbaum, 1991), 46.

77. Jesse Weissman, "A Brief History of Clocks: From Thales to Ptolemy," archived at *http://www.perseus.tufts.edu/GreekScience/Students/Jesse/CLOCK1A.html*.

78. Michelle Gomes, "A History of Clocks," archived at *http://library.scar.utoronto.ca/ClassicsC42/Gomes/wat.html*. "Today, virtually every advance in modern technology demands a highly accurate, stable and reliable time standard. Atomic clocks are at the top of the timekeeping 'food chain,' setting the standard by which all other precision instruments are calibrated. These instruments, in turn, are used to design, manufacture and operate virtually all modern technologies. . . . The demand for clocks with ever greater levels of precision is now being driven by the needs of high technology. Crafted by physicists and electrical engineers, atomic clocks play a vital role in modern communications, synchronizing the rapid movement of information through telephone systems and computer networks." Quoted from the "The Criticality of Time," archived at *http://www.haas.com/doc/time-use.htm*.

79. Mark Twain, Letter, Villa Quarto, Florence, January 1904, published in *Harper's Weekly*, 18 March 1905.

80. Polt, "Typology."

81. David G. Stork, "Computers, Science and Extraterrestials," in *HAL's Legacy: 2001's Computer as Dream and Reality*, ed. David G. Stork (Cambridge, MA: MIT Press, 1997), 338.

82. David G. Stork, "The End of an Era, the Beginning of Another? HAL, Deep Blue and Kasparov," archived at *http://www.chess.ibm.com/learn/html/e.8.1d.html*.

83. Joel Shurkin, *Engines of the Mind* (New York: W. W. Norton, 1996), 31.

84. Ibid.

85. Ibid., 35.

86. Ibid., 37.

87. Ibid., 42.

88. "Computers: History and Development," archived at *http://www.digitalcentury.com/encyclo/update/comp_hd.html*.

89. Shurkin, *Engines of the Mind*, 46.

90. Ibid., 47.

91. Ibid., 53–56.

92. Ibid., 61.

93. "Computers: History and Development."

94. Shurkin, *Engines of the Mind*, 47.

95. Ibid., 69.

96. Ibid., 82.

97. Ibid., 92.

98. Andrew Hodges, "The Alan Turing Internet Scrapbook: Who Invented the Computer?" archived at *http://www.turing.com/turing/scrapcomputer.html.*

99. Shurkin, *Engines of the Mind*, 197.

100. Mike Muuss, "History of Computing Information" archived at *http://ftp.arl.mil:80/~mike/comphist/.*

101. Quoted in Robert Strauss, "When Computers Were Born; Technology: They Began Humbly Enough—The War Department Needed to Be Able to Calculate Numbers Quickly. Who Knew the Impact of the Revolution?" (1996), archived at The Ada Project Web site at *http://www.cs.yale.edu/homes/tap/past-women-cs.html.*

102. Andrew Hodges, "The Turing Machine," archived at *http://www.turing.com/turing/T-machine.html.*

103. "The Turing Machine," archived at *http://mathserv.math.sfu.ca./History_of_Math/Europe/20thCenturyAD/Turingmachine.html.*

104. Amy Hagen, "Grace Murray Hopper" (18 September 1995), archived at *http://www.texas.net/~wayne/grace3.html.*

105. A *compiler* is a program that is written in human-readable programming language that translates statements into machine-readable executable programs.

106. Hopper not only helped program the first commercial large-scale electronic computer, but she also coined the term *computer bug* when she discovered a moth had crawled into one of the computers and caused an electrical short.

107. Description of "Rome Reborn: The Vatican Library and Renaissance Culture" exhibit at *http://sunsite.unc.edu/expo/EXPO.*

108. Preface to *A Hundred Highlights from the Koninklijke Bibliotheek*, available online at *http://www.konbib.nl/100hoogte/menu-welcome-en.html.*

Notes to Chapter 2

1. "The Effortless Internet" *Yahoo!* August 1997, 60.

2. John Harlow, "The Queen Goes Surfing with Chums in High Places," *Sunday Times*, 20 July 1997, archived at *http://www.the-times.co.uk/news/pages/sti/97/07/20/.* It is interesting to note that the Queen also sent one of the early e-mails in 1976.

3. "The Queen's Speech at the Banqueting House Luncheon Thursday 20th November 1997," Buckingham Palace Press Releases archived at *http://www.coi.gov.uk/coi/depts/GQB/coi4810d.ok.*

4. Katie Hafner and Matthew Lyon, *Where Wizards Stay Up Late: The Origins of the Internet* (New York: Simon and Schuster, 1996), 24.

5. F. J. Corbató and V. A. Vyssotsky, "Introduction and Overview of the Multics System," paper presented at the Fall Joint Computer Conference, 1965, archived at *Multics Papers Online, http://www.lilli.com/fjcc1.html.*

6. Michael Buckland, "Emanuel Goldberg and His Statistical Machine, 1927" (1995), archived at *http://www.sims.berkeley.edu/~buckland/statistical.html.*

7. Vannevar Bush, "As We May Think," *Atlantic Monthly* 176, no. 1 (July 1945), archived at *http://www.theAtlantic.com/atlantic/atlweb/flash-bks/computer/bushf.htm.*

8. Ibid.

9. Ibid.

10. J. C. R. Licklider, "Man-Computer Symbiosis," in *In Memorium: J. C. R. Licklider, 1915–1990* (Digital Equipment Corporation, 1990), archived at *ftp://ftp.digital.com/pub/DEC/SRC/research-reports/SRC-061.pdf.* This is a reprint of an article in *IRE Transactions on Human Factors in Electronics*, vol. HFE-1 (March 1960): 4–11.

11. Ibid.

12. Ibid.

13. Barry M. Leiner et al., "The Past and Future History of the Internet," *CACM* 40, no. 2 (1997): 102–8.

14. J. C. R. Licklider, "Some Reflections on Early History," in *A History of Personal Workstations*, ed. Adele Goldberg (Reading, MA: Addison-Wesley, 1988), 118.

15. J. C. R. Licklider, "The Computer as a Communication Device" (1968), in *In Memorium: J. C. R. Licklider, 1915–1990* (Digital Equipment Corporation, 1990), archived at *ftp://ftp.digital.com/pub/DEC/SRC/research-reports/SRC-061.pdf.* This is a reprint of an article from *Science and Technology*, April 1968.

16. Ibid.

17. "I might add that this article of yours has probably influenced me quite basically. I remember finding it and avidly reading it in a Red Cross library on the edge of the jungle on Leyte, one of the Phillipine Islands, in the Fall of 1945." Douglas Engelbart, letter to Vannevar Bush, 24 May 1962, archived at *http://www.histech.rwth-aachen.de/www/quellen/engelbart/Engelbart2Bush.html.*

18. Christina Engelbart, "Biographical Sketch: Douglas C. Engelbart," at *http://www2.bootstrap.org/dce-bio.htm.*

19. Ibid.

20. Douglas C. Engelbart, "Augmenting Human Intellect: A Conceptual Framework," Summary Report AFOSR-3223 under Contract AF 49(638)-1024, SRI Project 3578 for Air Force Office of Scientific Research, Stanford Research Institute,

Menlo Park, California (October 1962), archived at *http://www.histech.rwth-aachen.de/www/quellen/engelbart/ahi62index.html*.

21. Ibid.

22. Ibid.

23. "Ted Nelson Cites Him as a Major Influence: Douglas Engelbart," archived at *http://jefferson.village.virginia.edu/elab/hfl0035.html*.

24. Ted Nelson, "The Story So Far," *Interesting Times—The Ted Nelson News Letter* 3 (October 1994), archived at *http://sensemedia.net/993*.

25. Ted Nelson, "World Enough: Ted Nelson's Autobiography" (1993), archived at *http://www.obs-uropa.de/obs/english/papers/ted/tedbio11.htm*.

26. Thierry Bardini, "Bridging the Gulfs: From Hypertext to Cyberspace," archived at *http://www.ascusc.org/jcmc/vol3/issue2/bardini.html*.

27. Ted Nelson, in his self-published *Literary Machines*.

28. "In Xanadu did Kubla Khan/A stately pleasure-dome decree." Samuel Taylor Coleridge, "Kubla Khan: Or, A Vision in a Dream."

29. Ted Nelson, "What Is Literature?" from *Literary Machines* (1987), archived at *http://www.bit.ac.at/philosophie/vw/literat.htm*.

30. Bruce Sterling, "A Short History of the Internet," *Magazine of Fantasy and Science Fiction*, February 1993, archived at *http://www.forthnet.gr/forthnet/isoc/short.history.of.Internet*. The reference is to Paul Baran, "Introduction to Distributed Communications Network," Part I of On *Distributed Communications*, Rand Corporation Memorandum RM-3420-PR, August 1964, archived at *http://www.rand.org/publications/RM/RM3420/*.

31. Hafner and Lyon, *Where Wizards Stay Up Late*, 55.

32. Ibid., 57.

33. Baran, "Introduction to Distributed Communications Network."

34. Ibid.

35. Hafner and Lyon, *Where Wizards Stay Up Late*, 62.

36. Ibid., 64.

37. Lawrence G. Roberts, "Connection Oriented," archived at *http://www.data.com/25years/lawerence_g_roberts.html*.

38. How many computers are connected to the Internet? In January 1998 the number of hosts was 29,670,000. Hosts are defined as the domain name that has an IP address record associated with it—for example, *any.university.edu*—and could be any computer connected to the Internet. We can only estimate the actual number of computers connected to the Internet. However, the number of domains has doubled every twelve to fifteen months. The following figures show the dramatic growth in the number of hosts: August 1981: 213; January 1991: 376,000; October 1992: 1,136,000; October 1993: 2,056,000; October 1994: 3,864,000; January 1995: 4,852,000; July 1995: 6,642,000; January 1996: 9,472,000; January 1997: 16,146,000; July 1997: 19,540,000; and January 1998: 29,670,000. Source: "Network Wizards Internet Domain Survey," archived at *http://www.nw.com/zone/WWW/*.

39. "Internet/NSFNET Overview and Introduction," archived at *http://www.eff.org/pub/Net_info/Introductory/net-intro.article*.

40. Ibid.

41. David G. Stork, "The Best Informed Dream," in *HAL's Legacy: 2001's Computer as Dream and Reality*, ed. David G. Stork (Cambridge, MA: MIT Press, 1997), 11.

42. Ibid.

43. Leonard Kleinrock, "Packet Man," archived at *http://www.data.com/25years/leonard_kleinrock.html*.

44. Ibid.

45. Vinton Cerf, "Requiem for the ARPANET," archived at *http://www.mci.com/mcisearch/aboutyou/interests/technology/ontech/requiem.shtml*.

46. Steve Crocker, "RFC 1-Host Software," Network Working Group 4689 (7 April 1969), archived at *http://info.internet.isi.edu:80/in-notes/rfc/files/rfc1.txt*.

47. Steve Crocker, "RFC-3: Documentation Conventions," Network Working Group 4689 (April 1969), archived at *http://info.internet.isi.edu:80/in-notes/rfc/files/rfc3.txt*. "The Network Working Group seems to consists of Steve Carr of Utah, Jeff Rulifson and Bill Duvall at SRI, and Steve Crocker and Gerard Deloche at UCLA. Membership is not closed. The Network Working Group (NWG) is concerned with the HOST software, the strategies for using the network, and initial experiments with the network. Documentation of the NWG's effort is through notes such as this. Notes may be produced at any site by anybody and included in this series."

48. Ibid.

49. Ibid.

50. *PC Webopedia*, s.v. "TCP/IP," at *http://www.pcwebopedia.com/TCP_IP.htm*.

51. Ibid.

52. *PC Webopedia*, s.v. "IP," at *http://www.pcwebopedia.com/TCP_IP.htm*.

53. Ibid.

54. Vinton Cerf, "How the Internet Really Works—A Modest Analogy," archived at *http://www.mci.com/mcisearch/aboutyou/interests/technology/ontech/hownetworks.shtml*.

55. Nathaniel Wice, "Videogames," at *http://www.pathfinder.com/altculture/aentries_ew/v/videogames.html*. However, Gibson says he abstains from using the Internet himself: "I'm not a techie. I don't know how these things work. But I like what they do, and the new human processes that they generate." Quoted in Michaela Drapes, Michael Hayden and Alex Peguero, "William Gibson (1948–)" (1996), archived at *http://www.levity.com/corduroy/gibson.htm*.

56. Dan Josefsson, "An Interview with William Gibson" (23 November 1994), archived at *http://www.algonet.se/~danj/gibson1.html*.

57. John Lions, "Source Code and Commentary on UNIX level 6." The two parts of this book contained (1) the entire source listing of the UNIX Version 6 kernel, and (2) a commentary on the source discussing the algorithms. These were circulated internally at the University of New South Wales beginning 1976–77 and were, for years after, the only detailed kernel documentation available to anyone outside Bell Labs. Because Western Electric wished to maintain trade secret status on the kernel, the "Lions Book" was only supposed to be distributed to affiliates of source licensees. "In spite of this, it soon spread by samizdat to a good many of the early UNIX hackers." The Jargon Dictionary, at s.v. "Lions Book," *http://www.netmeg.net/jargon/terms/l/lions_book.html*.

58. For a definitive history of UNIX, see Peter H. Salus, *A Quarter Century of UNIX* (Reading, MA: Addison-Wesley, 1994).

59. "Using Telnet," at *http://www.ee.mcgill.ca/~yoontr/telnet.html*.

60. Ian Hardy, "The Evolution of ARPANET email" (13 May 1996), archived at *http://server.berkeley.edu/virtual-berkeley/email_history*.

61. Ibid.

62. "Applications of Information Network," *Proceedings of the IEEE* 66, no. 11 (November 1978): 44.

63. Ibid.

64. "Life on the Internet-Electric Mail," *PBS Life on the Internet series* Web site at *http://www.pbs.org/internet/stories/email/index.html*.

65. Quoted in Ronda Hauben, "The Evolution of Usenet News: The Poor Man's Arpanet," archived at *http://studentweb.tulane.edu/~rwoods/netbook/ch.1_poorman_arpa.html*.

66. Life on the Internet—Internetworking," *PBS Life on the Internet series* Web site at *http://www.pbs.org/internet/stories/newsgroups/index.html*.

67. Sterling, "A Short History of the Internet."

68. LISTSERV mailing list at INFO@BITNIC.

69. David Burrell, "Negotiating Book Reviews: A Study of Technology, H-Net, and the Emergent Status of a Contemporary Print Form" (May 1996), archived at *http://h-net2.msu.edu/~burrell/book.html*.

70. Ibid.

71. David Burrell, "A Virtual Community of Scholars: Frontiers, Networks, and Continuing Limitations in Academic Listservs," paper given at the conference From Microchip to Mass Media: Culture and the Technological Age, DePaul University, 3 May 1996.

72. Internet Forum Internet Relay Chat, at *http://www.nku.edu/~ogorman/irc.html*.

73. Jarkko Oikarinen, "IRC History," archived at *http://www.the-project.org/history.html*.

74. Charles A. Gimon, "IRC: The Net in Realtime" (1996), archived at *http://www.skypoint.com/members/gimonca/irc2.html*.

75. Bunyip information at

http://www.bunyip.com/corpinfo/corpinfo.html.

76. *Whatis.com*, s.v. "gopher," at *http://www.whatis.com/*.

77. Ibid.

78. *Whatis.com*, s.v. "Veronica," at *http://www.whatis.com/*.

79. *Whatis.com*, s.v. "Jughead," at *http://www.whatis.com/gopher.htm*.

80. Ben Segal, "A Short History of Internet Protocols at CERN" (April 1995), archived at *http://wwwcn.cern.ch/pdp/ns/ben/TCPHIST.html*.

81. David Bank, "Father of the Web," archived at *http://203.158.3.66/news/berners.htm*.

82. Robert Cailliau, "A Little History of the World Wide Web," archived at *http://www.w3.org/History.html*.

83. Tim Berners-Lee, "Longer Bio," at *http://www.w3.org/People/Berners-Lee-Bio.html/Longer.html*.

84. Carol Levin, "Web Inventor Berners-Lee Reflects on the Web's Origins and Future," *PC Magazine*, 30 May 1996, archived at *http://www8.zdnet.com/pcmag/news/trends/t960530b.htm*.

85. Tim Berners-Lee, "Information Management: A Proposal" (March 1989), archived at *http://www.w3.org/History/1989/proposal.html*.

86. Ibid.

87. Tim Berners-Lee, "Intended Uses" (1990), archived at *http://www.w3.org/DesignIssues/Uses.html*.

88. Berners-Lee, "Longer Bio."

89. Including Viola and Cello, the applications that inspired Marc Andreessen and Eric Bina to write Mosaic. "Spinning the Web" (17 October 1997), archived at *http://www.data.com/25years/tim_berners-lee.html*.

90. Gary Wolf, "The (Second Phase of the)

Revolution Has Begun," archived at *http://www.hotwired.net/wired/2.10/features/mosaic.html*.

91. Ibid.

92. Marc Andreessen, "Assembling Mosaic" (21 October 1997), archived at *http://www.data.com/25years/marc_andreessen.html*.

93. Ibid.

94. Ibid.

95. Tim Berners-Lee, "About the World Wide Web Consortium" (5 February 1998), at *http://www.w3.org/Consortium*.

96. *An Atlas of Cyberspaces* Web site at *http://www.cybergeography.org/atlas/atlas.html*, maintained by Martin Dodge, Cyber-Geography Research, Centre for Advanced Spatial Analysis (CASA), University College, London.

Notes to Chapter 3

1. Victor Keegan, "The Wired and the Unwired," *Times Literary Supplement*, 4 July 1997, 6.

2. Ibid.

3. The phrase is borrowed from the *X-Files*.

4. Archie is covered in chapter 2.

5. "Life on the Internet—Finding Things," *PBS Life on the Internet Series* Web site at *http://www.pbs.org/internet/stories/findingthings/index.html*.

6. Troy Corley, "Internet Is Reducing Need for Information Specialists," *Los Angeles Times*, 16 December 1997, archived at *http://www.cnn.com/TECH/9712/16/internet.searchers.lat/*.

7. "Rumor vs. Fact: The Internet's Role in TWA Crash Probe," *CNN Interactive*, 8 December 1997, archived at *http://www.cnn.com/TECH/9712/08/twa.800.internet/index.html*.

8. Larry Chiagouris, executive vice president and managing director of CDB Research and Consulting, Inc., Comments on findings of CDB Research and Consulting, Inc., Survey, May 1997 (47 percent fear that information on the Internet is not reliable versus 53 percent who believe it is), archived at *http://www.cdbresearch.com/Internet.html*.

9. Quoted in Monica Ertel, "Brave New World: What a Working Librarian Should Know about Living on the Internet," *Searcher* 3 (March 1995): 28–30. BSN is accessible as individual subject files via anonymous FTP to k*suvxa.kent.edu* or on Gopher using Veronica and its full name.

10. Ibid.

11. For more on search engines, go to *CNN Plus Web Kit: Web Basics* at *http://cnnplus.cnn.com/resources/Webkit/Web.faq/*.

12. "Boolean Searching on the Internet," archived at *http://www.albany.edu/library/internet/boolean.html*.

13. Christopher Mele, "Using the Internet for Undergraduate Training in Applied Social Research," *Effective Teaching* 1, no. 1 (12 June 1996), archived at *http://cte.uncwil.edu/et/articles/mele/index.htm*.

14. Jeffrey Lane, "Can the Medium Help the Message? NYU Faculty Members Integrate Internet and Courses," *Connect* (spring 1996), archived at *http://www.nyu.edu/acf/pubs/connect/spring96/InstrLaneMedMesSp96.html*.

15. Joseph Hargitai, working notes, September 1997.

16. Ibid.

17. Robin Nagle, E-mail to Joseph Hargitai, 3 October 1997.

18. Ibid.

19. Robin Nagle, "Teaching with the Internet: Lessons Taught, Lessons Learned," *Connect* (spring 1996), archived at *http://www.nyu.edu/*

acf/pubs/connect/spring96/InstrNagleLessonSp96.html. See also Robin Nagle, "Garbage in Gotham: Enter(ing) the Trashless Classrom," *Connect* (fall 1995), archived at *http://www.nyu.edu/acf/pubs/connect/fall95/InstrNagleF95.html*.

20. Nagle, "Teaching with the Internet."

21. Ibid.

22. Ibid.

23. Ibid.

24. Barbara Kirshenblatt-Gimblett, E-mail to Joseph Hargitai, 21 January 1998.

25. Ibid.

26. Hargitai, working notes.

27. Barbara Kirshenblatt-Gimblett, E-mail to Hargitai.

28. Ibid.

29. Ibid.

30. Ibid.

31. Ibid.

32. Ibid.

33. Ibid.

34. Ibid.

35. Michelle Adelman, E-mail to Joseph Hargitai, 20 February 1998.

36. Ibid.

37. Ibid.

38. Ibid.

39. Ibid.

40. "New York a.m.," at *http://www.nyu.edu/classes/adelman/NY/am.html*.

41. "11pm," at *http://www.nyu.edu/classes/adelman/NY/Hanley/11pm.html*.

42. Adelman, E-mail to Hargitai.

43. Professor Gans's home page at *http://scholar.chem.nyu.edu/~gans/gans.html* and Medieval Technology and Everyday Life course Web page at *http://scholar.chem.nyu.edu/~medtech/medtech97.html*.

44. Jonathan J. Vafai, E-mail to Joseph Hargitai, 17 February 1998.

45. Ibid.
46. Ibid.
47. Ibid.
48. Ibid.
49. Ibid.
50. Ibid.
51. Ibid.
52. Ibid.
53. Julia L. Keefer, E-mail to Joseph Hargitai, 26 February 1998.
54. Ibid.
55. Julia Keefer, "The Role of the Organic Professor on the Inorganic Net," at *http://www.nyu.edu/pages/classes/keefer/body/prof.html*.
56. Ibid.
57. Keefer, E-mail to Hargitai.
58. Ibid.
59. Ibid.
60. Ibid.
61. Jon McKenzie, "Performing Art Online," *Connect* (fall 1996), at *http://www.nyu.edu:80/acf/pubs/connect/spring97/InstrMcKPerfArtSp97.html*.
62. Jon McKenzie, "StudioLab: Thought," at *http://www.nyu.edu/classes/mckenzie/thoughtF2.html*.
63. Jon McKenzie, E-mail to Joseph Hargitai, 3 October 1998.
64. McKenzie, "StudioLab: Thought."
65. Ibid.
66. Ibid.
67. Ibid.
68. Lance Rose, "Net Perceptions," *Silicon Alley Reporter* 11 (February 1998): 43.
69. Alberto Manguel, "How Those Plastic Stones Speak: The Renewed Struggle between the Codex and the Scroll," *Times Literary Supplement* (4 July 1997): 9.

Notes to Chapter 4

1. Julia L. Keefer, "Higher Education on the Internet," archived at *http://www.nyu.edu:80/classes/keefer/net.html*.
2. A list of sites where you can download Fetch and WS_FTP appears in the appendix.
3. *Type and Typography* Web site at *http://bsuvc.bsu.edu/prn/type.html*.

Notes to Chapter 5

1. Brian Murfin, "The Student Genome Project, A Glimpse of the Future of Genetics Education," *Connect* (fall 1997), archived at *http://www.nyu.edu/acf/pubs/connect/fall97/InstructSGPFall97.html*.
2. *Type and Typography* Web site at *http://bsuvc.bsu.edu/prn/type.html*.

Notes to Chapter 6

1. "Technology Changing the Pedagogical Culture," paper presented at the Thirteenth International Conference on Technology and Education, New Orleans, LA, March 17–20, 1996, in *Proceedings, Vol. 1: Technology and Education: Catalyst for Educational Change* (New Orleans: International Conference on Technology and Education, Inc., 1996), 103, 105.
2. David F. Noble, "Digital Diploma Mills: The Automation of Higher Education" (1998), archived at *http://www.firstmonday.dk/issues/issue3_1/noble/index.html*.
3. YUFA, "Summary of Outstanding Issues" (5 April 1997), archived at *http://www.yorku.ca/org/yufa/strike/summary3.htm*.
4. YUFA, "The Real Issue Is the Classroom against the Boardroom" (1 April 1997), archived at *http://www.yorku.ca/org/yufa/strike/student3.htm*.
5. "Lessons from York University: Structure and Anatomy of a Faculty Strike," CAUT Bulletin On-Line 44, no. 6 (June 1997), archived at *http://www.caut.ca/English/Bulletin/97_jun/lessons.htm*.
6. George Sadowsky, "The Appropriate Role of Information Technology in Instruction," *Connect*, 20 January 1998), archived at *http://www.nyu.edu/acf/pubs/connect/spring98/FromDirSp98.html*.
7. Quoted in ibid.
8. Jeffrey R. Young, "UCLA's Requirement of a Web Page for Every Class Spurs Debate," *Chronicle of Higher Education*, 8 August 1997, archived at *http://chronicle.com/colloquy/97/webclass/47a02101.htm*.
9. Stuart Peterfreund, professor of English, Northeastern University, posted to *The Chronicle: Colloquy: Weaving the Web:* "Should colleges require professors to create a Web page, and to use the Web, for every class they teach?" (31 July 1997), archived at *http://www.chronicle.com/colloquy/97/webclass/31.htm*.
10. Daniel W. Ross, acting chair, Department of Language and Literature, Columbus State University, posted to *The Chronicle: Colloquy: Weaving the Web:* "Should colleges require professors to create a Web page, and to use the Web, for every class they teach?" (20 August 1997), archived at *http://www.chronicle.com/colloquy/97/webclass/36.htm*.
11. C. Robert Phillips III, professor of classics, Lehigh University, posted to *The Chronicle: Colloquy: Weaving the Web:* "Should colleges require professors to create a Web page, and to use the Web, for every class they teach?" (29 July 1997), archived at *http://www.chronicle.com/colloquy/97/Webclass/20.htm*.

12. Sadowsky, "The Appropriate Role of Information Technology in Instruction."

13. Ibid.

14. Daniel Akst, "Postcard from Cyberspace: Your Humble Correspondent Finds a Storehouse of Syllabuses," *Los Angeles Times*, 26 August 1996, archived at *http://www.isop.ucla.edu/teachers/Articles/la_time_on-line_classroom.html*.

15. "Models of Distance Education," Institute for Distance Education, University System of Maryland, at *http://www.umuc.edu/ide/modl-menu.html*.

16. Ibid.

17. Farhad Saba, "Introduction to Distance Education," archived at *http://www.distance-educator.com/intro.htm*.

18. Andrew R. Molnar, "Computers in Education: A Brief History," T.H.E. Journal Online (June 1997), archived at *http://www.the-journal.com/SPECIAL/25thani/0697feat02.html*.

19. Ibid. See also Robert P. Taylor, *The Computer in the School: Tutor, Tool, Tutee* (New York: Teachers College Press, 1980), 213–60.

20. Ibid. See also Andrew R. Molnar, "Viable Goals for New Educational Technology Efforts: Science Education and the New Technological Revolution," *Educational Technology* 15, no. 9 (September 1975).

21. Linda Wolcott, "On the Definition of Distance Education, or 'If I Get a Videotape in the Mail from Chicago, Is It Distance Education.'" *Distance Education Report*, March 1998, 6.

22. "US Online Population Grows to 62M," IntelliQuest Information Group, Inc., poll.

23. T. Matthew Ciolek, "The Scholarly Uses of the Internet: 1998 Online Survey," *Asia Web Watch: A Register of Statistical Data*, 15 March 1998, at *http://www.ciolek.com/PAPERS/InternetSurvey-98.html*.

24. Wolcott, "On the Definition of Distance Education."

25. Ibid.

26. Ibid.

27. "Strategies for Learning at a Distance," *Distance Education at a Glance Guides* (October 1995), at *http://www.uidaho.edu/evo/dist9.html*.

28. Molnar, "Computers in Education."

29. "Distance Education: An Overview," *Distance Education at a Glance Guides* (October 1995), at *http://www.uidaho.edu/evo/dist1.html*.

30. Ibid.

31. University of Phoenix Web site at *http://www.uophx.edu/online/*.

32. University of Phoenix-Center for Distance Education Web site at *http://www.uophx.edu/center/*.

33. Ibid.

34. Lisa Gubernick and Ashlea Ebeling, "I Got My Degree through E-mail," *Forbes*, 19 June 1997, archived at *http://207.87.27.10/forbes/97/0616/5912084a.htm*.

35. "Laptop Learning," *CNN Interactive*, 11 March 1998, at *http://www.cnn.com/TECH/computing/9803/11/laptop_learning.ap/*.

36. Ibid.

37. Hartwig Stein, "Redesign of a Distance Education Course at the Monterrey Institute of Technology and Advanced Studies (I.T.E.S.M.) / Mexico" (September 1997), archived at *http://www.caso.com/iu/articles/stein01.html*. Stein is assistant professor and instructional designer at the Institute of Technology and Advanced Studies of Monterrey. Between 1996 and 1997, Stein designed and implemented graduate-level interactive distance education courses that were distributed from twenty-six sites throughout Mexico.

38. Ibid.

39. Ibid.

40. Hartwig Stein, "An Approximation to Virtual University," archived at *http://home-pages.mty.itesm.mx/~hstein/Approx.htm*.

41. Ibid.

42. Stein, "Redesign of a Distance Education Course."

43. UNIWORLD Web site at *http://www.idg.hu/uniworld/*.

44. László Turi, E-mail to Joseph Hargitai, 17 February 1998.

45. Ibid.

46. Ibid.

47. Ibid.

48. Quoted in Sebastian Turullols, "New Media: Nazi Takeover of German Radio," *Stanford University Program in BerlinNazi/Weimar Cultural Reconstructions*, at *http://www-osp.stanford.edu/drama258/SebWeb/naziradio.html*.

49. Nyíri Kristóf, "Van, Akit Vonszol a Sors, Van, Aki Magformálja a Sorsát: Beszélgetés Nyíri Kristóffal a Virtuális Egyetemrol" (Some Are Dragged along by Their Destiny, and There Are the Ones Who Shape Their Own: Discussion with Nyíri Kristóf about the Virtual University), Népszabadsag, 18 April 1997, archived at *http://www.nepszabadsag.hu/Redakcio/Doc.asp?SID=1&IID=461&CID=40&AID=11045*. Quote translated by Joseph Hargitai.

50. David Lodge, *Nice Work* (New York: Viking, 1988), 14.

51. Ibid., 270.

52. Molnar, "Computers in Education."

53. George Sadowsky, interview with authors, New York City, 19 February 1998.

Bibliography

Adelman, Michelle. E-mail to Joseph Hargitai, 20 February 1998.

Aeschylus. *Agamemnon*. In *The Continental Edition of World Masterpieces*, vol. 1, ed. Maynard Mack. New York: W. W. Norton, 1966.

Akst, Daniel. "Postcard from Cyberspace: Your Humble Correspondent Finds a Storehouse of Syllabuses." *Los Angeles Times*, 26 August 1996. Archived at *http://www.isop.ucla.edu/teachers/Articles/la_time_on-line_classroom.html*.

Andreessen, Marc. "Assembling Mosaic" (21 October 1997). Archived at *http://www.data.com/25years/marc_andreessen.html*.

Andre-Salvini, Beatrice. "The Birth of Writing." *UNESCO Courier*, April 1995. Northern Lights ID: SL19970923020121208. Archived at *http://www.northernlight.com/*.

Bank, David. "Father of the Web." Archived at *http://203.158.3.66/news/berners.htm*.

Baran, Paul. "Introduction to Distributed Communications Network." Part I of *On Distributed Communications*. Rand Corporation Memorandum RM-3420-PR (August 1964). Archived at *http://www.rand.org/publications/RM/RM3420/*.

Bardini, Thierry. "Bridging the Gulfs: From Hypertext to Cyberspace." Archived at *http://www.ascusc.org/jcmc/vol3/issue2/bardini.html*.

Berners-Lee, Tim. "About the World Wide Web Consortium" (5 February 1998). Archived at *http://www.w3.org/Consortium*.

———. "Information Management: A Proposal." *CERN*, March 1989. Archived at *http://www.w3.org/History/1989/proposal.html*.

———. "Intended Uses" (1990). Archived at *http://www.w3.org/DesignIssues/Uses.html*.

———. "Longer Bio." Archived at *http://www.w3.org/People/Berners-Lee-Bio.html/Longer.html*.

Bolter, Jay David. *Writing Space: The Computer, Hypertext and the History of Writing*. Hillsdale, NJ: Lawrence Erlbaum, 1991.

"Boolean Searching on the Internet." Archived at *http://www.albany.edu/library/internet/boolean.html*.

Braich, Stephen. "The Tower of Babel Project." Archived at *http://www.cs.pdx.edu/~stephen/babel/*.

"Brief History of Networking." Archived at *http://www.silkroad.com/net-history.html*.

"A Brief History of the Morse Telegraph." Archived at *http://www.cris.com/~Gsraven/history.html*.

Buckland, Michael. "Emanuel Goldberg and His Statistical Machine, 1927" (1995). Archived at *http://www.sims.berkeley.edu/~buckland/statistical.html*.

Buick, Joanna, and Zoran Jevtic. *Introducing Cyberspace*. New York: Totem Books, 1995.

Burrell, David. "Negotiating Book Reviews: A

Study of Technology, H-Net, and the Emergent Status of a Contemporary Print Form" (May 1996). Archived at *http://h-net2.msu.edu/~burrell/book.html*.

Bush, Vannevar. "As We May Think." *Atlantic Monthly* 176, no. 1 (July 1945). Archived at *http://www.theAtlantic.com/atlantic/atlweb/flashbks/computer/bushf.htm*.

Cailliau, Robert. "A Little History of the World Wide Web." Archived at *http://www.w3.org/History.html*.

Casson, Lionel. *Travel in the Ancient World*. Baltimore: Johns Hopkins University Press, 1994.

Cerf, Vinton. "How the Internet Really Works—A Modest Analogy." Archived at *http://www.mci.com/mcisearch/aboutyou/interests/technology/ontech/hownetworks.shtml*.

———. "Requiem for the ARPANET." Archived at *http://www.mci.com/mcisearch/aboutyou/interests/technology/ontech/requiem.shtml*.

"Chappe—Innovation and Politics in 1793 and 1794." In *Proceedings of a Symposium on the Optical Telegraph*. Telemuseum, Stockholm, 21–23 June 1994. Archived at *http://www.telemuseum.se/historia/optel/otsymp/Frankrike.html*.

Ciolek, T. Matthew. "The Scholarly Uses of the Internet: 1998 Online Survey." *Asia Web Watch: A Register of Statistical Data*, 15 March 1998. Archived at *http://www.ciolek.com/PAPERS/InternetSurvey-98.html*.

Clement, Richard W. "Books and Universities: Medieval and Renaissance Book Production—Manuscript Books." In *ORB Online Encyclopedia—Manuscript Books*. Archived at *http://orb.rhodes.edu/encyclop/culture/books/medbook1.html*.

"Computers: History and Development." Archived at *http://www.digitalcentury.com/encyclo/update/comp_hd.html*.

Corbató, F. J., and V. A. Vyssotsky. "Introduction and Overview of the Multics System." Paper presented at the Fall Joint Computer Conference, 1965. Archived at *Multics Papers Online*, *http://www.lilli.com/fjcc1.html*.

Corley, Troy. "Internet Is Reducing Need for Information Specialists." *Los Angeles Times*, 16 December 1997. Archived at *http://www.cnn.com/TECH/9712/16/internet.searchers.lat/*.

"The Criticality of Time." Archived at *http://www.haas.com/doc/time-use.htm*.

Crocker, Steve. "RFC 1-Host Software." Network Working Group 4689, 7 April 1969. Archived at *http://info.internet.isi.edu:80/in-notes/rfc/files/rfc1.txt*.

———. "RFC-3: Documentation Conventions." Network Working Group 4689, April 1969. Archived at *http://info.internet.isi.edu:80/in-notes/rfc/files/rfc3.txt*.

de Bury, Richard. *The Philobiblon*, ed. Ernest C. Thomas. London: Kegan Paul, Trench, and Co., 1888. Archived at *ftp://uiarchive.cso.uiuc.edu/pub/etext/gutenberg/etext96/phlbb10.txt*.

de Sola Pool, Ithiel, et al. *Communications Flows: A Census in the United States and Japan*. North-Holland, Amsterdam: University of Tokyo Press, 1984.

Demarest, Marc. "Controlling Dissemination Mechanisms: The Unstamped Press and the 'Net" (August 1995). Archived at *http://www.hevanet.com/demarest/marc/unstamped.html*.

"Distance Education: An Overview." *Distance Education at a Glance Guides* (October 1995). Archived at *http://www.uidaho.edu/evo/dist1.html*.

Drapes, Michaela, Michael Hayden and Alex Peguero. "William Gibson (1948–)" (1996). Archived at *http://www.levity.com/corduroy/gibson.htm*.

Durant, Will. *The Age of Faith*. New York: Simon and Schuster, 1950.

———. *Caesar and Christ*. New York: Simon and Schuster, 1944.

———. *The Life of Greece*. New York: Simon and Schuster, 1939.

Eco, Umberto. *The Search for the Perfect Language*, trans. James Fentress. Cambridge, MA: Blackwell, 1995.

Eland, Thomas W. "Orality, Literacy, and Textual Communities in the Middle Ages" (1996). Archived at *http://sites.goshen.net/LibraryOfGod/eland3.html*.

Engelbart, Christina. "Biographical Sketch: Douglas C. Engelbart." Archived at *http://www2.bootstrap.org/dce-bio.htm*.

Engelbart, Douglas C. "Augmenting Human Intellect: A Conceptual Framework." Summary Report AFOSR-3223 under Contract AF 49(638)-1024, SRI Project 3578 for Air Force Office of Scientific Research, Stanford Research Institute, Menlo Park, California (October 1962). Archived at *http://www.histech.rwth-aachen.de/www/quellen/engelbart/ahi62index.html*.

———. Letter to Vannevar Bush, 24 May 1962. Archived at *http://www.histech.rwth-aachen.de/www/quellen/engelbart/Engelbart2Bush.html*.

Ertel, Monica. "Brave New World: What a

Working Librarian Should Know about Living on the Internet." *Searcher* 3 (March 1995): 28–30.

Gimon, Charles A. "IRC: The Net in Realtime" (1996). Archived at *http://www.skypoint.com/members/gimonca/irc2.html.*

Goldberg, Adele, ed. *A History of Personal Workstations.* Reading, MA: Addison-Wesley, 1988.

Gomes, Michelle. "A History of Clocks." Archived at *http://library.scar.utoronto.ca/ClassicsC42/Gomes/wat.html.*

Gubernick, Lisa, and Ashlea Ebeling. "I Got My Degree through E-mail." *Forbes*, 19 June 1997. Archived at *http://207.87.27.10/forbes/97/0616/5912084a.htm.*

Hafner, Katie, and Matthew Lyon. *Where Wizards Stay Up Late: The Origins of the Internet.* New York: Simon and Schuster, 1996.

Hagen, Amy. "Grace Murray Hopper" (18 September 1995). Archived at *http://www.texas.net/~wayne/grace3.html.*

Haight, Anne Lyon and Chandler B. Grannis. *Banned Books 387 B.C. to 1978 A.D.* New Providence, NJ: R. R. Bowker, 1978.

Hardy, Ian. "The Evolution of ARPANET Email" (13 May 1996). Archived at *http://server.berkeley.edu/virtual-berkeley/email_history.*

Harlow, John. "The Queen Goes Surfing with Chums in High Places." *Sunday Times*, 20 July 1997. Archived at *http://www.the-times.co.uk/news/pages/sti/97/07/20.*

Hauben, Ronda. "The Evolution of Usenet News: The Poor Man's Arpanet." Archived at *http://studentweb.tulane.edu/~rwoods/netbook/ch.1_poorman_arpa.html.*

———. "On the Early Days of Usenet: The Roots of Cooperative Online Culture." In *Netizens: On the History and Impact of Usenet and the Internet,* ed. Michael Hauben and Ronda Hauben. Piscataway, NJ: IEEE Computer Society Press, 1997. Archived at *http://www.columbia.edu/~hauben/netbook/.*

Hawthorne, Nathaniel. "The Flight of the Two Owls." In *The House of the Seven Gables* (1851). Archived at *http://www.tiac.net/users/eldred/nh/sg.html.*

Hodges, Andrew. *Alan Turing: The Enigma.* New York: Simon and Schuster, 1983.

———. "The Alan Turing Internet Scrapbook: Who Invented the Computer?" Archived at *http://www.turing.com/turing/scrapcomputer.html.*

———. "The Turing Machine." Archived at *http://www.turing.com/turing/T-machine.html.*

Holzmann, Gerard J. "The Ties That Bound." *Inc. Technology* 2 (1995). Archived at *http://www.inc.com/incmagazine/archives/16950661.html.*

Holzmann, Gerard J., and Björn Pehrson. "The Early History of Data Networks." Archived at *http://www.it.kth.se/docs/early_net/.*

Homer. *The Illiad,* trans. E. V. Rieu. Harmondsworth, Eng.: Penguin, 1950.

"Internet/NSFNET Overview and Introduction." Archived at *http://www.eff.org/pub/Net_info/Introductory/netintro.article.*

Josefsson, Dan. "An Interview with William Gibson" (November 23, 1994). Archived at *http://www.algonet.se/~danj/gibson1.html.*

Kawano, Kenji. *Warriors: Navajo Code Talkers.* Flagstaff, AZ: Northland Publishing Co., 1990.

Keefer, Julia L. E-mail to Joseph Hargitai, 26 February 1998.

Keegan, Victor. "The Wired and the Unwired." *Times Literary Supplement,* 4 July 1997, 6.

Kirshenblatt-Gimblett, Barbara. E-mail to Joseph Hargitai, 21 January 1998.

Kleinrock, Leonard. "Packet Man." Archived at *http://www.data.com/25years/leonard_kleinrock.html.*

Kristóf, Nyíri. "Van, Akit Vonszol a Sors, Van, Aki Magformálja a Sorsát: Beszélgetés Nyíri Kristóffal a Virtuális Egyetemrol." ("Some are Dragged Along by Their Destiny, and There Are the Ones Who Shape Their Own: Discussion with Nyíri Kristóf About the Virtual University") *Népszabadsag,* 18 April 1997. Archived at *http://www.nepszabadsag.hu/Redakcio/Doc.asp?SID=1&IID=461&CID=40&AID=11045.*

Kroutvor, Josef. "Prague Report: Literature Remains Alive and Well." *TriQuarterly* (fall 1995). Northern Lights ID: LW19970923040129876. Archived at *http://www.northernlight.com/.*

Lane, Jeffrey. "Can the Medium Help the Message? NYU Faculty Members Integrate Internet and Courses." *Connect* (spring 1996). Archived at *http://www.nyu.edu/acf/pubs/connect/spring96/InstrLaneMedMesSp96.html.*

"Laptop Learning." *CNN Interactive,* 11 March 1998. Archived at *http://www.cnn.com/TECH/computing/9803/11/laptop_learning.ap/.*

Leiner, Barry M., et al. "The Past and Future History of the Internet." *CACM* 40, no. 2 (1997): 102–8.

"Lessons from York University: Structure and Anatomy of a Faculty Strike." *CAUT*

Bulletin On-Line 44, no. 6 (June 1997). Archived at *http://www.caut.ca/ English/Bulletin/97_jun/lessons.htm*.

Levarie, Norma. *The Art and History of Books*. New Castle, DE: Oak Knoll Press, 1995.

Levin, Carol. "Web Inventor Berners-Lee Reflects on the Web's Origins and Future." *PC Magazine*, 30 May 1996. Archived at *http://www8.zdnet.com/pcmag/news/trends/t 960530b.htm*.

Licklider, J. C. R. "The Computer as a Communication Device" (1968). In *In Memorium: J. C. R. Licklider, 1915-1990*. Digital Equipment Corporation, 1990. Archived at *ftp://ftp.digital.com/pub/ DEC/SRC/research-reports/SRC-061.pdf*.

———. "Man-Computer Symbiosis." In *In Memorium: J. C. R. Licklider, 1915–1990*. Digital Equipment Corporation, 1990. Archived at *ftp://ftp.digital.com/pub/ DEC/SRC/research-reports/SRC-061.pdf*.

"Life on the Internet—Electric Mail." *PBS Life on the Internet series* Web site at *http://www.pbs.org/internet/stories/email/ index.html*.

"Life on the Internet—Finding Things." *PBS Life on the Internet Series* Web site at *http://www.pbs.org/internet/stories/findingth-ings/index.html*.

"Life on the Internet—Internetworking." *PBS Life on the Internet series Web site* at *http://www.pbs.org/internet/stories/news-groups/index.html*.

Lodge, David. *Nice Work*. New York: Viking, 1988.

Maimark and Barba, Inc. "Folio 12 Abet Innovation (Embrace a New Concept Today.)" (1997). Archived at *http://www.bootstrap.org/augment-133217.htm*.

Manguel, Alberto. "How Those Plastic Stones Speak: The Renewed Struggle between the Codex and the Scroll." *Times Literary Supplement*, 4 July 1997, 8, 9.

McKenzie, Jon. E-mail to Joseph Hargitai, 3 October 1998.

———. "Performing Art Online." *Connect* (fall 1996). Archived at *http://www.nyu.edu:80/acf/pubs/connect/spri ng97/InstrMcKPerfArtSp97.html*.

Mele, Christopher. "Using the Internet for Undergraduate Training in Applied Social Research." *Effective Teaching (Online)* 1, no. 1 (12 June 1996). Archived at *http://cte.uncwil.edu/et/articles/mele/ index.htm*.

Minnis, A., and A. B. Scott. *Medieval Literary Theory and Criticism c. 1100—c. 1375*. New York: Oxford University Press, 1988.

Molnar, Andrew R. "Computers in Education: A Brief History." *T.H.E. Journal Online*, June 1997. Archived at *http://www.thejournal.com/SPECIAL/25than i/0697feat02.html*.

Munro, J. "Heroes of the Telegraph." Archived at *http://www.cdrom.com/pub/gutenberg/etext9 7/htgrf10.txt*.

Murfin, Brian. "The Student Genome Project, A Glimpse of the Future of Genetics Education." *Connect* (fall 1997). Archived at *http://www.nyu.edu/acf/pubs/connect/fall97/I nstructSGPFall97.html*.

Muuss, Mike. "History of Computing Information." Archived at *http://ftp.arl.mil:80/~mike/comphist/*.

Nagle, Robin. E-mail to Joseph Hargitai, 3 October 1997.

———. "Garbage in Gotham: Enter(ing) the Trashless Classroom." *Connect* (fall 1995).

Archived at *http://www.nyu.edu/acf/ pubs/connect/fall95/InstrNagleF95.html*.

———. "Teaching with the Internet: Lessons Taught, Lessons Learned." *Connect* (spring 1996). Archived at *http://www.nyu.edu/ acf/pubs/connect/spring96/InstrNagleLessonS p96.html*.

Nelson, Ted. "The Story So Far." *Interesting Times—The Ted Nelson News Letter* 3 (October 1994). Archived at *http://senseme-dia.net/993*.

———. "What Is Literature?" from *Literary Machines* (1987). Archived at *http://www.bit.ac.at/philosophie/vw/l iterat.htm*.

———. "World Enough: Ted Nelson's Autobiography" (1993). Archived at *http://www.obs-uropa.de/obs/english/ papers/ted/tedbio11.htm*.

Noble, David F. "Digital Diploma Mills: The Automation of Higher Education." (1998). Archived at *http://www.firstmonday.dk/ issues/issue3_1/noble/index.html*.

Oates, J. C. T. *Cambridge University Library: A Historical Sketch* (1975). Archived at *http://www.lib.cam.ac.uk/History/index.html*.

O'Connor, Tim. E-mail to Anne Keating and Joseph Hargitai, 16 February 1998.

O'Donnell, James J. "The Pragmatics of the New: Trithemius, McLuhan, Cassiodorus." Archived at *http://ccat.sas.upenn.edu/ jod/sanmarino.html*.

———. "The Virtual Library: An Idea Whose Time Has Passed." Archived at *http://ccat.sas.upenn.edu/jod/virtual.html*.

Oikarinen, Jarkko. "IRC History." Archived at *http://www.the-project.org/history.html*.

Ong, Walter. "Print, Space, and Closure." *Communication in History: Technology,*

Culture, Society, ed. David Crowley and Paul Heyer. White Plains, NY: Longman, 1995.

Pirsig, Robert M. *Zen and the Art of Motorcycle Maintenance*. New York: Bantam, 1981.

Polt, Richard. "Typology: A Phenomenology of Early Typewriters." Archived at *http://xavier.xu.edu/~polt/typology.html*.

"The Queen's Speech at the Banqueting House Luncheon Thursday 20th November 1997." *Buckingham Palace Press Releases*. Archived at *http://www.coi.gov.uk/ coi/depts/GQB/coi4810d.ok*.

Rheingold, Howard. "Democracy Is about Communication" (1996). Archived at *http://www.well.com/user/hlr/texts/democra-cy.html*.

———. "Grassroots Groupminds." In *The Virtual Community: Homesteading on the Electronic Frontier*. Reading, MA: Addison-Wesley, 1993. Archived at *http://www.well.com/user/hlr/vcbook/ vcbook4.html*.

Roberts, Lawrence G. "Connection Oriented." Archived at *http://www.data.com/ 25years/lawerence_g_roberts.html*.

Rose, Lance. "Net Perceptions." *Silicon Alley Reporter* 11 (February 1998): 43.

"Rumor vs. Fact: The Internet's Role in TWA Crash Probe." *CNN Interactive*, December 8, 1997. Archived at *http://www.cnn.com/ TECH/9712/08/twa.800.internet/index.html*.

Saba, Farhad. "Introduction to Distance Education." Archived at *http://www.dis-tance-educator.com/intro.htm*.

Sadowsky, George. "The Appropriate Role of Information Technology in Instruction." *Connect*, 20 January 1998. Archived at *http://www.nyu.edu/acf/pubs/connect/spring9 8/FromDirSp98.html*.

———. Interview with authors, New York City, 19 February 1998.

Salus, Peter H. *A Quarter Century of UNIX*. Reading, MA: Addison-Wesley, 1994.

Segal, Ben. "A Short History of Internet Protocols at CERN" (April 1995). Archived at *http://wwwcn.cern.ch/pdp/ns/ben/ TCPHIST.html*.

Shurkin, Joel. *Engines of the Mind*. New York: W. W. Norton, 1996.

Skilling, H. Gordon. *Samizdat and an Independent Society in Central and Eastern Europe*. Oxford: Macmillan, 1989.

"Spinning the Web" (17 October 1997). Archived at *http://www.data.com/25years/tim_bern-ers-lee.html*.

Stein, Hartwig. "An Approximation to Virtual University." Archived at *http://homepages.mty.itesm.mx/ ~hstein/Approx.htm*.

———. "Redesign of a Distance Education Course at the Monterrey Institute of Technology and Advanced Studies (I.T.E.S.M.) / Mexico" (September 1997). Archived at *http://www.caso.com/iu/ articles/stein01.html*.

Steinberg, S. H. *Five Hundred Years of Printing*. Harmondsworth, Eng.: Penguin, 1955.

Sterling, Bruce. "A Short History of the Internet." *Magazine of Fantasy and Science Fiction*, February 1993. Archived at *http://www.forthnet.gr/forthnet/isoc/short.his tory.of.Internet*.

Stork, David G. "The Best Informed Dream." In *HAL's Legacy: 2001's Computer as Dream and Reality*, ed. David G. Stork. Cambridge, MA: MIT Press, 1997.

———. "Computers, Science and Extraterrestials." In *HAL's Legacy: 2001's Computer as Dream and Reality*, ed. David G. Stork. Cambridge, MA: MIT Press, 1997.

———. "The End of an Era, the Beginning of Another? HAL, Deep Blue and Kasparov." Archived at *http://www.chess.ibm.com/ learn/html/e.8.1d.html*.

"Strategies for Learning at a Distance," *Distance Education at a Glance Guides* (October 1995). Archived at *http://www.uidaho.edu/ evo/dist9.html*.

Strauss, Robert. "When Computers Were Born; Technology: They Began Humbly Enough—The War Department Needed to Be Able to Calculate Numbers Quickly. Who Knew the Impact of the Revolution?" Archived at the Ada Project Web site at *http://www.cs.yale.edu/homes/tap/past-women-cs.html*.

"Ted Nelson Cites Him as a Major Influence: Douglas Engelbart." Archived at *http://jeffer-son.village.virginia.edu/elab/hfl0035.html*.

Thompson, Logan. "Roman Roads" *History Today*, February 1997.

Turi, László. E-mail to Joseph Hargitai, 17 February 1998.

"The Turing Machine." Archived at *http://math-serv.math.sfu.ca./History_of_Math/Europe/2 0thCenturyAD/Turingmachine.html*.

Turullols, Sebastian. "New Media: Nazi Takeover of German Radio" *Stanford University Program in BerlinNazi/Weimar Cultural Reconstructions*. Archived at *http://www-osp.stanford.edu/drama258/SebWeb/nazira-dio.html*.

"Using Telnet." Archived at at *http://www.ee.mcgill.ca/~yoontr/mega.html*.

Vafai, Jonathan J. E-mail to Joseph Hargitai, 17 February 1998.

Vallee, Jacques. *The Network Revolution:*

Confessions of a Computer Scientist. Berkeley, CA: And/or Press, 1982.

Weiner, Norbert. *Cybernetics, or Control and Communication in the Animal and the Machine.* Cambridge, MA: MIT Press, 1961.

Weissman, Jesse. "A Brief History of Clocks: From Thales to Ptolemy." Archived at *http://www.perseus.tufts.edu/GreekScience/Students/Jesse/CLOCK1A.html.*

Weit, Gaston, Vadime Elisseef, Phillipe Wolff and Jean Nandou. *The Great Medieval Civilizations.* History of Mankind Cultural and Scientific Development Series, vol. 3. New York: Harper and Row, 1975.

Wice, Nathaniel. "Videogames." Archived at *http://www.pathfinder.com/altculture/aentries_ew/v/videogames.html.*

Wolcott, Linda. "On the Definition of Distance Education, or 'If I Get a Videotape in the Mail from Chicago, Is It Distance Education.'" *Distance Education Report,* March 1998, 6.

Wold, Gary. "The (Second Phase of the) Revolution Has Begun." Archived at *http://www.hotwired.net/wired/2.10/features/mosaic.html.*

Wright, Fred. "The History and Characteristics of Zines." Archived at *http://thetransom.com/chip/zines/resource/wright1.html.*

Young, Jeffrey R. "UCLA's Requirement of a Web Page for Every Class Spurs Debate" *Chronicle of Higher Education,* 8 August 1997. Archived at *http://chronicle.com/colloquy/97/Webclass/47a02101.htm.*

YUFA. "The Real Issue Is the Classroom against the Boardroom" (1 April 1997). Archived at *http://www.yorku.ca/org/yufa/strike/student3.htm.*

———. "Summary of Outstanding Issues" (5 April 1997). Archived at *http://www.yorku.ca/org/yufa/strike/summary3.htm.*

Index

For specific HTML tags, see the HTML quick reference section in the Appendix, 233–236

<!— —> tags, 194, 223

<A> hyperlink tags, 114–116
accounts, obtaining student and class, 196, 198
ACTION attribute in forms, 184, 188, 236
Adelman, Michelle, 89–91
Adobe PhotoShop, 89, 151, 154, 159–160, 164
Adobe Premiere, 171–173
Advanced Research Projects Agency (ARPA), 45–51, 78. *See also* ARPANET
AIFF sound format, 165, 166
ALIGN attribute, 112
alignment: of columns in frames, 139; of images, 112; style properties for, 110; of table cell contents, 118, 135–137; of table rows, 118, 135–137; of tables, 117–118, 130–137; text, 109–110
ALINK or active link attribute in <BODY> tag, 128
ALT attribute in <IMG> tag, 112
alt.hypertext, 67. *See also* Tim Berners-Lee
anchors, 115–116. *See also* <A> tags; ALINK attribute
Andreessen, Marc, 67–68. *See also* World Wide Web, pioneers of
animation (GIF), 158, 164
anonymous FTP, 56
anti-aliasing, 163
appearance of text, 110, 234. *See also* fonts

Apple Video Player, 170–171
Archie, 62
ARPANET, 40, 41, 45–51, 56, 57, 58, 78, 237n. 2
Atkinson, Bill (HyperCard), 178
AU sound format, 165, 166
audio, 164–168. *See also* multimedia

Babbage, Charles, 29–30, 36; Analytical Engine, 30; Difference Engine, 29; and Ada Lovelace, 29–30
Babel, tower of, 14–16; Umberto Eco on, 15; "The Tower of Babel Project," 15–16
BACKGROUND attribute in <BODY> tags, 155, 234
backgrounds: color, 127–128, 225–226; images as, 155, 224–225. *See also* BGCOLOR attribute
Baran, Paul, 46–48. *See also* Internet, pioneers of
Berners-Lee, Tim, 65–67, 70, 104. *See also* World Wide Web, pioneers of
BGCOLOR attribute in <BODY> tag, 128; in <TABLE> tags, 136
bibliographic citation formats for Internet sites, 103
block quotes using <BLOCKQUOTE> tags, 110
Boolean logic, 72, 75
BORDER attribute: in <IMG> tag, 112; in <TABLE> tag, 117, 136–137

 line break tag, 106, 109, 234
browser-safe palette, 159–169
browsers, 67–68
bulleted lists in HTML. *See* lists
bulletin board script, 102, 196, 208